TOMMY
LAWTON

TOMMY
LAWTON

Head and Shoulders
Above the Rest

JACK ROLLIN

First published by Pitch Publishing, 2020

Pitch Publishing
A2 Yeoman Gate
Yeoman Way
Worthing
Sussex
BN13 3QZ
www.pitchpublishing.co.uk
info@pitchpublishing.co.uk

ISBN 978 1 78531 801 6

Typesetting and origination by Pitch Publishing
Printed and bound in Great Britain by TJ Books Limited

Contents

To my daughter Glenda and
grandson Harry

Foreword

TOMMY LAWTON was a magnet for spectators throughout his football career. Easter Monday, 29 March 1948 was no exception at the Greyhound Stadium in Southend-on-Sea, when he played for Notts County in a Third Division (South) fixture against Southend United.

Such was the interest at the prospect of seeing him play that local games were given early kick-offs to allow other footballers the opportunity of watching him in action. It was a few miles for me on a bicycle with no time to change out of my football gear. So with boots wrapped round the handlebars and a jacket thrown over my shoulders, it sufficed to ensure a place at the start among the 17,613 crowd.

One incident in the match erased whatever else I can recall from the proceedings, but it typified the sportsmanship of one of the finest centre-forwards ever seen in English football. I was 15 years old at the time. The incident developed with County on the attack two minutes from the interval. Lawton had already made the equaliser after half an hour. Under pressure, United's centre-half Frank Sheard, attempting a pass back to Ted Hankey, only succeeded in lobbing the ball over his goalkeeper's head into the net, with both players colliding in a tangled heap. Tommy, first on scene, sportingly rushed to their assistance, sidelining any natural delight in what proved to be the winning goal. Despite disappointment at their team going behind, the home crowd generously applauded this spontaneous gesture.

Of course the attraction of Lawton extended beyond his ability alone, as he was at the time the most expensive footballer in the world, having been transferred from First Division Chelsea to third-tier Notts County for £20,000 in the previous November. One might argue the incident at Southend was merely a showboating exercise to enhance his stature, costing him nothing, though you had to be there to appreciate the instant reaction to the situation. Yes, it was an impressionable teenager's reminiscence, but it was not the first time I had seen Tommy Lawton play.

That was at Wembley in an international for England against Scotland during the war when he scored a hat-trick. In *The World's All Sports Who's Who for 1950*, Tommy Lawton's best performance, in its opinion, was recorded as that exact match on 4 October 1944 against Scotland in front of 90,000. It stated: 'He scored a hat-trick and made the other three goals.' England won 6-2. But I recall it was the classic game of two halves. Scotland scored early, and Stanley Matthews could not get past George Cummings. It was left to Lawton to shake and stir some life into England in the second half. Aged 12, along with my father, a school friend and his dad, I was hooked by his performance. The Southend game was a memorable decoration. I was to learn later, that whatever else went on in Tommy's life, this exemplary attitude on the field remained unblemished.

CHAPTER ONE

Born to be a Centre-Forward

TOMMY LAWTON was born on 6 October 1919 at Farnworth into a modest working-class environment, the son of a railway signalman, his mother a weaver. But his parents split shortly afterwards, his father indicating that it was the end of the line for him. So, the lad's upbringing and encouragement as a footballer were immeasurably helped by his grandfather, Jim Riley, who had also played the game at a reasonable level.

The school playground with a tennis ball usually discovers those more likely to possess an aptitude that sets them apart from the rest. Then it often depends on the enthusiasm and encouragement received to dovetail with this promising talent. Invariably there is an interested sports master. With T. Lawton at Tonge Moor Council School in Bolton it was Mr 'Bunny' Lee who spotted a weakness in the boy's left foot, encouraging him after school hours to kick with a canvas shoe on his right and a football boot on the left.

The opening of the new Castle Hill School in 1928 brought a scholastic change but fortunately the headmaster there, Mr Fred Milner, was equally enthusiastic. Tommy was no educational dunce and he succeeded in gaining a place at Folds Road Central

School in Bolton where, unbelievably, their Mr 'Pop' Lever was of a similar soccer mind, as was Mr William Horrocks, later headmaster. After playing in a trial game, Lawton was selected for the Bolton Town Schools XI. Tommy's scoring instincts kicked in with an amazing 570 goals in only three seasons at Folds Road and for the Hays Athletic team – the figure rounded up nicely for posterity. Still, the progress achieved was outstanding by any measurement, with the firm establishment of Tommy Lawton as a natural goalscorer.

Tommy recalled in his book, *My Twenty Years of Soccer*: 'At Folds Road we used to chalk a set of goal posts on the wall and practise shooting-in or heading-in. We used only tennis balls at that time and looking back I feel that such practice helped me considerably to become such a deadly "shot" with my head when I graduated to first-class football.' He added: 'Naturally my main ambition was to join Bolton Wanderers.'

While at Folds Road, in a school match, some spectators took exception to the big lad using his weight in shoulder charging but Tommy was assured by the experienced referee Bert Fogg that his tactics were fair. During this time, Lawton also played for Lancashire Schools and had several international trials, scoring three in one match at Brighton.

Tommy remembered hearing the locals talk in glowing terms of those great Bolton cup wins of the 1920s. His grandfather and Mr Lever, acting as his advisers, approached the club to enquire what jobs would be on offer while Tommy was on amateur forms with Wanderers. But one at ten shillings and another half a crown cheaper were both turned down. Liverpool was next on the list but they did not follow up after their initial interest. Further afield, Bury failed to follow up their promise of watching Tommy, then it was Sheffield Wednesday's turn. Their manager

Billy Walker offered digs and ten shillings pocket money on top of finding work but this prospect was vetoed by Mrs Lawton who wisely thought 50 miles away was a step too far.

On 5 January 1935 Tommy made his debut for Rossendale United in the Lancashire Combination against Leyland Motors. He had already scored 88 goals that season in the Bolton Amateur League. Rossendale won 9-0, Tommy scored four times and three of them actually counted! Their manager was Mick Tolman, who noted the potential of a player likely to command a healthy transfer fee one day. The *Liverpool Echo* of 19 January commented: 'Look out for Tom Lawton the Bolton ex-schoolboy international [an accolade too far] centre-forward creating a furore in league football.' All this, of course, before he had scarcely touched such heights, illustrating the know-how these Lancashire folk possessed.

Tommy worked for a while at Walker's Tannery making golf clubs, later using that product to some further leisure effect. This was before the Burnley experience. In February 1935 Tommy signed amateur forms for Burnley Football Club of the Second Division, working with the ground staff and in the club offices. His record as an accomplished goalscorer had preceded him. His debut for the 'A' team was on 23 February at Victory Park, Barnoldswick against Lancaster and, as reported in the *Burnley Express*, he scored twice in a 3-2 win with second-half goals described by the reporter as 'an opportunist drive and a brilliant header'. His career was to embrace these twin accomplishments many times over. The Lawton trademark had been firmly stamped. The Burnley 'A' team was: Wilson; Bennion, Kiddy, Wilkinson, Pickering, Metcalfe, Perrin, Graham, Lawton, Laidman and Macartney.

On 9 March 1935, the *Liverpool Echo* reported: 'Burnley are very pleased with their capture of Tom Lawton, the Bolton

Dixie Dean-like schoolboy centre-forward.' The *Lancashire Evening Post* subsequently commented on the fact that two former County School team forwards who had both scored 100 goals in the season, Fred Taylor (Briercliffe) and Lawton (Bolton), were together at Burnley.

But Tom had another reputation, as a junior cricketer in Bolton. In fact, before the new football season, he played for Burnley's 'A' team and carried his bat for 42. He topped their batting averages in the Lancashire League. However, the first football trial match at Turf Moor – such an appropriate name for a football ground – took place on 24 August 1935, mostly youngsters plus a handful of professionals, including a couple of new signings. Tom Lawton, as he was invariably referred to in the *Burnley Express*, featured in the Clarets team. The reporter commented: 'The forwards were splendidly led by Lawton who fed his wing men with accuracy and good judgment.' He scored their second goal.

On the following Tuesday, the likely Central League team featured against the 'A' side, effectively the third XI, with Lawton leading its forward line. Against the professionals he showed promise. For the third trial he was brought on in the second half for the probable first team at the expense of England international George Brown, shipped into the stiffs. At the time there was no hint of a more permanent situation affecting the two players. Despite suffering from flat feet and needing arch supports in his boots, Lawton's footwork was speedy, swift and sure.

Events moved on apace. It was on 7 September that 15-year-old Tom played for Burnley's reserves at Huddersfield in a Central League match. Burnley's team was: Scott; Hartley, Hubbick, Oliver, Johnson, Hindmarsh, J. Lawton, Rayner, T.

Lawton, Kilcar and Weale. Jack Lawton was unrelated, though also came from the Bolton area, and had played for Manchester North End. However, displaying good control and shooting capability, Tom Lawton also possessed the confidence to dribble through the opposing defence on one occasion. Two days later he scored for the reserves in a 2-1 win over Preston North End. Then came the move that stunned Burnley supporters – when George Brown was transferred to Leeds United for £3,000 following an offer the club could not refuse, with takings at first-team matches often less than a third of this figure.

However, for the moment Tom Lawton switched back and forth with the 'A' team and, notably, on 19 October he was on hand for their first win of the season, beating Darwen reserves 5-3, Lawton recording a splendid four-timer. Three weeks later he snatched a hat-trick against Lancaster and was also included in Burnley's Northern Midweek League side that included both professionals and amateurs, which furthered his education.

Near the transfer deadline in March, Burnley signed Bob Brocklebank, a forward from Aston Villa, and he made his debut at Southampton. Then, on 28 March 1936 it was announced that 16-year-old Tom Lawton was to make his Football League debut at centre-forward against Doncaster Rovers at Turf Moor.

Tommy had already played in a dozen or more Central League games and had hit 18 goals for the 'A' team for whom he had appeared the previous week and scored twice against Morecambe reserves. The twin newcomers roused interest to the extent that a gate of 12,350 was attracted. But it was a poor game and ended 1-1. Lawton was then 16 years 170 days and, as expected, was well marked by the 23-year-old Doncaster centre-half Syd Bycroft, signed from Newark. He was a shade taller than Tommy plus a stone heavier and was making his first appearance at centre-half, though he had led the senior attack once before. He had previously been with Bradford and Hull City. But Tom showed sufficient promise to be given another chance. Burnley's team for his debut match was: Adams; Richmond, Hubbick, Hindmarsh, Johnson, Robinson, Hancock, Brocklebank, Lawton, Hornby and Fletcher.

W. M. Johnston's *The Football League 1935–36* referred to Lawton as follows: 'A youthful prodigy showed exceptional promise for the future.' Burnley clearly thought along similar lines and they kept him in a week later at Swansea on 4 April. Lawton scored twice at Vetch Field in Burnley's 3-1 win. His first came within three minutes of the restart after the break when a mix-up in the Swansea defence allowed him to lob into an empty net. Less than half an hour later he accepted a pass from Brocklebank for his second and throughout had better support.

Some 15 years later in his *All-Star Football Book*, Tommy referred to scoring in each half. 'Could I forget those two goals? Of course I could.' He had even forgotten the half-time break for starters. But on the day he had been brought back to earth when a colleague said: 'Tha've a long way to go and a lot to learn.'

However, on Good Friday 1936 Burnley entertained Manchester United and hoped for further points in their battle to stave off relegation. Though Lawton was generally well held by George Vose in the United defence, it was discovered after the match that he had sustained a groin injury. The match ended 2-2, against the team that would go on to win the league. However, as a result of his injury, on Easter Saturday the teenager missed the Norwich City match at Turf Moor, which produced another precious point in a 1-1 draw. Tommy also missed the return with Manchester United and the 4-0 defeat that ensued on Easter Monday.

Tommy was restored to the side at Bury on 18 April and responded with two goals in a 4-0 win at Gigg Lane that buried thoughts of demotion. His first after 35 minutes was a beautifully judged header following a cross from his namesake Jack Lawton, the second in the 80th minute when he rounded a defender and shot in off the crossbar.

Following a goalless draw with Tottenham Hotspur, Lawton scored his fifth goal for Burnley and his first at Turf Moor against Leicester City from a ground shot into the far corner. He also earned commendation for his splendid distribution. Burnley lost their last league game of the season 2-0 at Fulham but finished a comfortable 15th in the league table. During the latter stages of the season, Tommy had played seven league games, scored five goals and acquitted himself satisfactorily. He was still just 16 years of age.

At the start of the new season Tommy scored two goals in the 3-0 win over Nottingham Forest at Turf Moor. He also scored in the 4-1 defeat at Chesterfield but twisted his knee when Burnley lost 2-0 at Fulham, so missed the Aston Villa game on 12 September. His place was taken, ironically, by a new signing from Bacup – a schoolmaster at that – in John Gastall who scored on his debut. Though Burnley lost 2-1, Gastall kept his place and scored three goals in the next two winning games. After two matches looking for a goal, Lawton returned, with Gastall shifting to the right wing in the 1-1 draw at Southampton.

That was three days before Tommy's 17th birthday and amid speculation that he was about to turn professional at Turf Moor. He had already been selected to play on the following Saturday at home to Tottenham Hotspur. On the afternoon of his birthday he had an interview with club officials accompanied by his grandfather Jim Riley, who was employed at Turf Moor on the ground staff and was acting as his guardian. No announcement was made, which merely served to alarm supporters that the youngster's future might be as a professional but not at Turf Moor.

The revelation of what happened might well have ended Tommy Lawton's career as a professional footballer before he had even kicked a ball for money. Grandfather Riley had demanded a £500 signing-on fee! Threatened by the Football League with suspension for the player, common sense prevailed, though how Mr Riley remained in any meaningful employment at Burnley Football Club became a mystery, yet doubtless anything to keep the club's prize possession was paramount.

However, on the Friday Tommy signed as a professional for Burnley. A report in *Topical Times* explained that the necessary forms were completed at chairman Tom Clegg's mill offices. The following day Lawton scored all three goals in the 3-1 win over Tottenham Hotspur. His first was after only 30 seconds and was so quick that only on the mobbing by eight other Burnley players did the reality dawn on the spectators. His second was a 16th-minute header from a cross by Jimmy Stein. Finally, the hat-trick came from a brilliant effort in the second half after he had missed a couple of reasonable chances. Gastall had provided the trio of openings and Lawton had shown clever anticipation in accepting them.

Newspapers, never lacking the obvious adjective, were already calling him 'Boy' Lawton, shades of Cliff Bastin, etc. Shortly afterwards *Topical Times* pre-empted the Marvel comic of 1939 by calling Lawton 'the boy wonder'. Burnley's team on that day was: Hetherington; Richmond, Hubbick, Robinson, Woodruff, Clacher, Gastall, Brocklebank, Lawton, Miller and Stein.

Tommy later remarked: 'When as a lad at Burnley I was lucky to play between inside-forwards Bob Brocklebank and Billy "Golden" Miller. Both knew the exact type of pass on which a centre-forward thrives and my development was hastened by their support.' At 17 Lawton was the youngest to score a league treble.

Burnley scored only once in their next four matches before Lawton managed three goals in two wins – 2-0 at West Ham and 3-0 against Norwich at Turf Moor. At Upton Park the *Topical Times* headlined: 'Tom Lawton Sets the Thames on Fire', and apart from his two goals his general play was impressive. After being beaten 3-0 at Newcastle, a 2-2 draw at home to Bradford produced another Lawton goal. After another draw, 1-1 at Barnsley, Burnley won three on the trot, though Tommy's one goal against Sheffield United was to be his last in the claret and blue.

Following the 2-0 reverse at Doncaster Rovers on 28 December, after having beaten them 3-0 on Christmas Day, the *Burnley Express* said Lawton was unfit and he was not selected to play on 2 January 1937 at Chesterfield.

According to the opening gambit in his 1946 book, *Football Is My Business*, events leading to his departure from Turf Moor were unusual to say the least. On a daily basis it was young Tommy's first task after a spot of training to sort the morning post in the club offices before the arrival of the secretary, Alf Boland. He also had to answer the telephone.

The following call took place some three months after he had signed professional forms. Tommy answered a call and a voice said: 'This is George Allison, manager of Arsenal. Can I speak to the secretary, please?' Tommy responded, explaining Boland's absence: 'This is the assistant-secretary speaking,' he said. There was more chat then the Allison bombshell: 'I want to make an offer for the transfer of Lawton.'

That morning Wolverhampton Wanderers, Everton, Newcastle United and Manchester City also called. One club among these famous five was ultimately successful; however, in *My Twenty Years of Soccer*, Lawton revealed that there had been eight clubs chasing his signature. Anyway, on 31 December 1936, Wilf Cuff and Tom Percy, representing the Everton directorate, together with the club's secretary, Theo Kelly, invaded the Burnley boardroom. Burnley manager Tom Clegg, who had watched Tommy in a schoolboy international trial and had predicted an international career, asked Tommy whether he would agree to sign for Everton. Following a conference with his grandfather Jim Riley, Tommy agreed. As to the exact figure involved, the initial reports put it at £3,000, later £7,000, until it settled to a general acceptance of £6,500. Amazingly, the arrangement included Grandfather being included in the transfer to take a similar job on the Goodison Park ground staff to the one he had managed to retain at Turf Moor.

CHAPTER TWO

Tommy – the Boy Wonder!

EVERTON PAID £6,500 for Tommy Lawton on 31 December 1936. According to *World Soccer from A to Z* he travelled to Goodison by tram after putting pen to paper and was told by the conductor: 'You'll never be as good as Dean.' Anyway, on Tommy's first day at the club, Joe Mercer took him to Clayton Square for the customary Everton players' lunch. The dietetic devotees would have distanced themselves from the fare on offer: two eggs, chips, two slices of bread and butter then a cup of tea. At only one shilling and a penny, at least the value was not too difficult to digest.

'Tommy was not worried by modesty,' said Mercer in *The Great Ones*. When told he was 'a big 'un', Tommy replied: 'Yes, and I'm a good 'un.' Mercer went on to say: 'His confidence in himself was justified and there was no danger of developing a swollen head at Everton.'

It was strange that the 17-year-old Lawton would find more friendly faces than expected on his first game in the blue of Everton when he soon made his debut for the Toffees second string in a Central League game – against Burnley! Everton reserves won 2-0, he made a good impression and, after going close by hitting a post, he scored their second goal.

Tommy was selected for his first-team debut at Huddersfield on 3 February but went down with influenza. Bill (Dixie) Dean's damaged ankle was still causing problems so Bunny Bell, for whom Everton were said to be willing to listen to offers, was recalled to lead the attack and scored in the 3-0 win.

Everton's Dean, the legendary goalscoring machine, hated his nickname. At the time, he was still only 30 and averaging a healthy two goals every three games. The centre-forward's injury allowed Tommy, a dozen years his junior, finally to make his first-team debut away at Wolverhampton Wanderers on 13 February in the Everton team of: Sagar; Cook, Jones, Britton, White, Mercer, Gillick, Cunliffe, Lawton, Bell and Coulter.

Lawton had received many well-wishing letters from friends prior to the match. The *Liverpool Echo* reporter 'Bee' recalled Tommy 'flying through the Molineux mud, never-ending in his endeavour'. But the impetus was almost entirely with Wolves, who tore into Everton with a vengeance. Goals came in spurts at Everton's expense. But 15 minutes from the end they were awarded a penalty and Lawton was invited to take it. He shot well and true. The final score was Wolves 7 Everton 2. The Wolverhampton *Sporting Star* reported: 'Lawton did not have a bad match for he was rarely given the support so necessary to secure leadership.'

He did not play in the FA Cup against Tottenham Hotspur at Goodison a week later, which ended in a 1-1 draw, but two days later he was inside-left to Dean with Jimmy Cunliffe at inside-right for the replay at White Hart Lane. Within just two minutes Lawton put Everton in front with a blistering effort from 25 yards, critics recalling many a comparable Dean effort. According to Joe Mercer, it was the moment Dean realised his days at Goodison were numbered. However, as to the cup-tie replay, subsequent events appeared to be swinging inexorably in Everton's direction. With five minutes remaining they led 3-1. Then came what appeared to be a penalty when Spurs' Arthur Rowe was adjudged to have impeded Dean. Dr Barton, the referee, awarded a penalty but a linesman was flagging. After discussion it appears the ball had gone over the touchline before the cross that led to the incident. Mercer owned up later as the culprit!

So it was a throw-in for Spurs and not the chance of 4-1 to Everton. Then with just four minutes to go, Johnny Morrison reduced the deficit to 3-2, and Tommy Meads followed that up by cracking in a 35-yarder to make it 3-3 with one minute remaining. That proved sufficient time for Morrison to head Spurs' winner for 4-3. 'Stud Marks', compiled by Louis T. Kelly in the *Liverpool Echo* referred to it as: 'The finest match Everton have never won.'

Five days later Everton lost 2-0 at Birmingham and form was now becoming a concern. On 3 March Leeds United, another team in the toils, were visitors to Merseyside. Given their current form, it was unsurprising perhaps that Everton were destined to win only one more league match during the rest of the season, but this victory was an incredible 7-1 routing of Leeds. According to the *Liverpool Echo* it was 'won in a mud-trot'. Leeds endured without Bert Sproston for some four-fifths of the match through injury, which contributed to the wide disparity of the scoreline. Lawton was praised: 'In his first home senior game he showed how well he can take a ball, place it, or drive in before anyone has realised he is about to shoot.' He managed three goals in ten further outings, several times shifting to inside-right next to Dean with whom he got on well, on and off the field.

There were odd-goal defeats to Middlesbrough and West Bromwich Albion, a 1-1 draw with Manchester City, then Merseyside eyebrows were raised when Cunliffe was switched to centre-forward, with Tommy at inside-right against Manchester United in the 2-1 defeat. Lawton did not play at Portsmouth but in the return with United at Goodison he scored the best goal of the five recorded in the 3-2 defeat, with a sharp shot. Lawton played just twice more that season in odd-goal losses at Stoke and Preston.

Although there was no question mark over Lawton and Dean hitting it off as a partnership, Everton had struggled after having won three times as many games as they had lost by early October when they had beaten Wolves 1-0. There was no criticism of Lawton, described by the *Liverpool Echo* as 'already approaching the excellent mark in the matter of craft and penetrative powers'. It was not difficult to identify the reason for Everton's final position of 17th in the table: although they lost only twice at home, they only won twice away all season.

In the close season, there was a summer tour to Denmark and three matches in May against Danish selections. The Danes had insisted Dean was included in the party. The first match was won 4-3 and Lawton was the only change for the second game, in which he scored with a header from a Torry Gillick cross in the 4-1 success, with Alex Stevenson supplying a hat-trick. The third match was drawn 0-0. However, the Copenhagen venue would much later haunt Tommy Lawton by a subsequent event.

During pre-season there were photo opportunities for *Topical Times* on the golf links, with Tommy being loaded with clubs by Joe Mercer and Liverpool's Jack Balmer. Then came the cricket games, including the annual one featuring the Merseyside rivals taking the field as 'Liverton' against Orrell. Lawton hit 52 in an easy win for the combined team. There was also a day's outing at Bowaters sports ground with bowls and tennis on the agenda. There was an additional announcement that football training would include new ideas to spice up the quick walking, running and sprinting, dumb-bells, rowing machine exercises and other gym work. Scientific and entertaining football had long been the Everton culture, and the need to win matches now became even more important.

Among the new players there were Peter Dougal from Arsenal at inside-left and left-half Jack Davies, a Welsh schoolboy international from Chester. For the trial match on 14 August Lawton was in the Whites team, Dean leading the Blues, so had the idea of pairing the two been scrapped? Criticism of Dean centred on the fact that more and more goals relied on his headwork, and bigger centre-halves were getting wiser. Yet he then hit three goals with his feet! However, early on Lawton stubbed his toe, limped a little, then finally retired in the second half.

On the opening day of the 1937/38 season, Tommy was in the reserves at Sheffield Wednesday, with Dean leading the attack for the first team against Arsenal at Goodison Park. But the centre-forward taking the honours there proved to be Ted Drake with a hat-trick in a 4-1 win for the Gunners. Dean, the only Everton player to emerge with any credit, was their scorer. It was actually the fifth successive season he had been the first Everton player to open their account!

The following Monday, Lawton was in action for the reserves again and in a 4-3 win scored twice. He fitted in well with inside-forwards Bell and Dougal who snatched a goal apiece, too. On the Wednesday, the unchanged seniors were at Manchester City. It was a much improved defensive display, but only Geldard showed to advantage in the attack. Dean, lying back more, was ineffective in the 2-0 defeat. Meanwhile, two directors had taken in the Irish League v Scottish League in Belfast.

After deciding to reunite Dean and Lawton, the experience of the return of their partnership was not the answer against Blackpool on 4 September where one goal was enough to beat Everton. Dean and Jack Jones were both injured at Blackpool but returned after repairs during the game. While the *Star Green 'Un* said the two best players on the field were the home team's Jimmy Blair and Lawton, the *Lancashire Evening Post* reported that Tommy was 'not a constructive inside-forward'. Full marks for spotting that one! Tommy Lawton was a centre-forward.

The return match with City followed on the Wednesday. Dean was omitted, Stevenson came in at inside-right and Lawton led the forward line. Transformation followed. The *Liverpool Echo* said: 'Pity we cannot print it in letters of gold.' Everton 4 Manchester City 1 – rejuvenated! Lawton opened the scoring on 29 minutes, his inside partners Stevenson, with two goals, and Dougal scored the others. The report went on to say: 'A player who can use the body swerve so well, shoot with both feet and get off the mark so quickly is wasted at inside-forward and Lawton proved it.' Moreover, it was Everton's first win in the league since 3 March.

Brentford were seen off 3-0 on Saturday, 11 September, then Everton were away to Derby County the following Wednesday, the Rams still seeking a first win of the season. Within five minutes Everton trailed and it seemed to knock them out of their stride. Only Albert Geldard was causing concern to the Derby defence and in the 67th minute the home side seemed well on the way when they scored their second goal. Five minutes later a half turn and shot by Lawton went straight at Ken Scattergood, but the goalkeeper allowed it to slip away and trickle over the line for what was one of Tommy's luckier strikes. However, with Cliff Britton nursing an injury, it was not the happiest of evenings for Everton at the Baseball Ground.

For Lawton, Saturday brought a return to his home town and league leaders Bolton Wanderers, the team for whom he originally wanted to play. The directors were clearly satisfied with the team overall despite the loss at Derby, the only change being Mercer switching to accommodate Britton's replacement, Gordon Watson, for the trip to Burnden Park. Lawton headed Everton into the lead from a corner by Dougal, who was celebrating being given a season's contract after a successful trial. Everton played with an exaggerated 'W' formation, using a three-pronged attack, the other member of the trio, Stevenson, scoring the second goal in the 2-1 victory.

At Goodison against Huddersfield on 25 September, Everton squandered a 1-0 half-time lead and were edged out 2-1. Doug Trentham had been their scorer and general opinion was that this was their poorest performance since the opening day of the season, with the defence unusually hesitant and the forwards disjointed. However, no changes were made for the upcoming local affair at Anfield against Liverpool.

Four of the Everton players had never played in a Merseyside derby. Two of them scored – Trentham after 15 minutes, Lawton from a penalty some dozen minutes later after Geldard had twice been fouled in a matter of seconds. Liverpool scored late on but too late to take a point. Then a week later, Everton were again unchanged at Wolves, but the home team took a crucial lead a minute before the break through Tom Galley. Alas, Everton retreated into their shell in the second half, Stan Cullis in the

Wolves defence only having Lawton to worry him, and on 74 minutes it was 2-0, which was the final score. Interestingly, there was mention that only one Everton director was present at the match.

With Leeds United due at Goodison Park on 16 October, changes were made. Britton was back after injury but a little rusty, Mercer switching to left-half, and Torry Gillick was brought in on the left wing for the first time this season. It was he who was caught by Bert Sproston's outstretched leg for a penalty, which Lawton buried after only 14 minutes. Robust United were fortunate to escape other such punishment, but they gained a point when they scored shortly after the break. Everton's forward problems persisted and only Lawton offered any real threat. The *Yorkshire Post* referred to him as 'a bonny young footballer'.

Up next was a match at Blundell Park against fellow strugglers Grimsby Town on 23 October. This match coincided with the first international of the season at Windsor Park, Belfast with England on view, which necessitated changes in the Everton line-up. Geldard was on England duty, Cook and Stevenson for Northern Ireland, but at least the recent murmurs in the crowd of 'we want Dean' were answered, with him back at centre-forward. Stevenson's berth was handed to Lawton, who was doubtless grateful after the clattering he had been given in recent matches. Trentham was back on the left wing, Gillick taking the right wing in Geldard's absence, with Jackson at right-back for Cook.

Making his debut for Grimsby was Jackie Coulter, late of Everton, and he was to have the satisfaction of scoring the winning goal. With the enforced changes disrupting Everton noticeably, the Mariners gained early advantage and took a 26th-minute lead. But four minutes after half-time, Dean, who had only three shots during the game, fed Gillick for an equaliser. Lawton grafted tirelessly but Everton were well beaten, Coulter giving Grimsby the 2-1 victory.

Preston North End were the visitors to Goodison on 30 October, with more tinkering to an Everton team looking in need of desperate measures. Dean's brief reappearance was ended and Lawton was back to leading the line, with Cunliffe at inside-right. Bell, after noted reserve team-scoring feats was at inside-left, with both Cook and Geldard returning from international duty and Gillick switching to the left wing.

What followed was an eight-goal feast of scoring, sadly not in the Toffees' favour. Despite leading three times, Everton lost 5-3. Jack Jones gave away two penalties and two of the three Everton goals should have been saved anyway, so the scoreline was perhaps closer than they deserved. Lawton scored twice, bruised from some obvious elbowing, and Bell scored Everton's other goal. The *Daily Dispatch* commented: 'Preston the best team seen at Goodison Park for years.' The Everton crowd complained with cries of 'we want some players', mixed with more claims for the appearance of Dean. After their 'unlucky' 13th league game, the Toffees had taken just one point from their last four matches and sat third from the bottom of the First Division. What next for Everton?

Well, more changes for the match at Middlesbrough. Centre-half Charlie Gee was dropped for Tommy (TG) Jones, who had shone in the Central League, Stevenson replaced Bell, with Trentham as his partner instead of Gillick, and Sagar gave way to Morton. But Everton were seeking a left-winger. The match showed improvement for Everton when in the 23rd minute Mercer lobbed the ball forward for Lawton to head them into the lead. Then came another for Tommy as the Boro defenders, appealing for offside, left him in possession and, although he hesitated, shouts from Stevenson to 'go through, Tommy' led to him firing low under the goalkeeper's body. Middlesbrough were restricted to one goal ten minutes from time, as Everton recorded a 2-1 win, which could be summed up as a better performance by the team.

Everton were unchanged for the visit of Chelsea, and Cunliffe and Trentham were on target in the first half before Stevenson hit the angle of post and bar with a cracker. Lawton then added two more goals: a header and a swift sweep from close in. The match ended 4-1 to Everton, though there was criticism that the now familiar exaggerated 'W' formation was putting too much pressure on the wingers.

After showing some improved form, Everton were brought back to reality at The Hawthorns on 20 November, with West Bromwich Albion racing into a two-goal lead within eight minutes through Boyes and Mahon, the former apparently being watched by Everton – though clearly not by the defenders on the day! Thrown out of their stride, the sole rejoinder was an 84th-minute penalty from Lawton. Albion then added a third goal so late in the match there was no time for a restart.

On 27 November Stanley Matthews and Stoke City visited Goodison. This was not a happy hunting ground for the visitors, whose last success there had been during the 1905/06 season. The luck was clearly still against them when, three minutes into the second half, Lawton's shot appeared to be going wide but took a deflection off Cunliffe and went in. Stevenson scored a second with a daisy-cutter that the goalkeeper should have saved but Lawton's second in the 3-0 victory was a classic. The *Liverpool Echo* reported: 'He beat Challinor with ease and grace, lured Wilkinson out of goal then cleverly hooked the ball into the net.' It received an ovation from the crowd.

Lawton had now scored nine goals in his last five games and was already being touted for an England cap, while TG Jones had equally shone and was ready for centre-half duty for Wales. Reporting on the Stoke match, the *Sunday Express* commented that Lawton had been the 'inspiration of the Everton side which reached great heights in the second half'.

Moving into December, Everton were at The Valley, facing a Charlton team seeking a first win in seven weeks, and found stoic opposition. Everton fell behind to a goal on 30 minutes but Cunliffe levelled nine minutes later and the scoreline remained the same until the last ten minutes when, amid sleet showers, Charlton scored twice to win 3-1. However, reporting on the match, the *Green 'Un* did mention that Lawton possessed 'pleasing craft'.

Tommy then went off injured in the 10-1 romp against the Army at the Command Ground in Aldershot – a place young Lawton would see much of later – and missed the next league match with Birmingham on 11 December. Dean came back for his fifth senior game of the season, the only alteration from the Charlton match. The Midlands team struck early, in only the second minute, to nudge Everton out of their stride and it was not until the 71st minute that Geldard managed a leveller. During this same month, undersoil heating was installed at Everton's practice pitch!

For the match at Portsmouth, Lawton returned and the Dougal–Trentham left-wing partnership was reinstated. Pompey went one up on ten minutes, then made it two after 21 minutes, on a sunny day but with frost in the air. Eight minutes later a speculative floater from Trentham was mishandled by the goalkeeper and the ball trickled over the line. However, apart from one other shot more or less on target, this was the sum of the Everton parts in attack. Lawton was held – literally sometimes – by Tommy Rowe and was unable to be effective. On 55 minutes it was 3-1 to Portsmouth and another crisis situation loomed after a poor Everton performance, with them third from bottom of the league.

For the Christmas Day match at Leicester, Sagar returned in goal, Bell replaced Dougal, and Cunliffe moved to inside-left. Dense fog made the match a farce. Appointed referee McBride was a no-show, so senior linesman Tatem decided that the responsibility for calling the game off was too much for him and it went ahead. Trentham headed Everton in front but then a harmless back pass from Britton found its way past Sagar for Leicester's equaliser. Late in the game Leicester added two further goals, which meant that Everton had taken just one point from their last four matches and the crisis was deepening.

The return fixture two days later saw Gillick in for Geldard but the opening phases of the match were all Leicester. Then Sagar dislocated his shoulder and Bell had to take over in goal, but this mishap incredibly inspired ten-man Everton, who from then on dominated proceedings. Lawton scored in the 57th minute, Trentham added a brilliant effort six minutes later, then Lawton smashed home his second with ten minutes left. Bell had a fairly easy time of it between the posts. It was a much-needed improvement, so what would the New Year bring?

On 1 January at Highbury, high-flying Arsenal had to bring in three reserves to face Everton but one of them, Reg Lewis at centre-forward, scored with his first kick of the ball after 12 minutes. George Hunt then added a second for the Gunners 20 minutes later. With Sagar injured, Harry Morton was in goal for Everton, Stevenson was back and Bell left out. The Everton forwards could not get going, and Norman Sidey, deputising at centre-half for Arsenal, kept Lawton quiet. In fact, Tommy failed to get in a single shot all match. Cunliffe pulled a goal back in the 63rd minute and was Everton's best player, then Gillick hit the bar, so Everton were unlucky not to get a draw.

League concerns were shelved on 8 January with an FA Cup tie to be played at Chelsea. Gillick was at outside-left, with Geldard on the right wing. The match brought further signs of improvement, with the Stamford Bridge team restricted to just a couple of shots. Their first, near half-time, was hoofed off the line by Britton, then play switched immediately to the other end with both Lawton and Stevenson going for the same cross until the latter told Tommy to 'leave it' and all 5ft 6in of Stevenson nodded in the only goal of the tie.

Back to league duty a week later, Blackpool visited Goodison. Geldard was ill, so Gillick was in his place and Watson had to fill the left-wing slot. As 'Stork' reported in the *Liverpool Echo* it was the half-back line of Britton, TG Jones and Mercer that again impressed. The visitors were handicapped by two injuries and unable to contain Gillick and Everton goals came from Cunliffe, Lawton and even Watson in a 3-1 win. Would the revival continue? Alas, no.

The fourth round of the FA Cup brought holders Sunderland to Goodison. Everton lost the toss and the match despite battering away at Johnny Mapson's goal most of the time. Bob Gurney scored the only goal for Sunderland just after the half-hour mark. Lawton went closest to levelling but the Sunderland goalkeeper stood firm and luck was with him when Lawton failed to hit the mark.

Then came a midweek venture to London to play top-of-the-table Brentford on 26 January. While the football flowing from Everton was such that the *Liverpool Echo* summed it with the well-worn phrase of 'will win more than lose' playing that way, the final score was Brentford 3 Everton 0. The first goal two minutes before the break had changed the outcome of the match. On this same day the club had been watching Norman Greenhalgh, the New Brighton left-back.

Everton faced another title-chasing team three days later when Bolton Wanderers visited Goodison. Geldard returned to the side, Trentham was omitted for Gillick, and Greenhalgh, signed hours beforehand, was included instead of Jack Jones. The damage was done to Wanderers in the first 20 minutes, although the *Liverpool Echo* considered they were 'streaky goals'. For the first goal on six minutes, Geldard fired from distance against a post, Gillick scoring from the rebound. In the 17th minute Lawton's shot was only pushed out by the shaky Swift – Fred, brother of Manchester City's Frank – and Stevenson slotted home. Two minutes later another Swift fumble from a Stevenson shot presented Geldard with Everton's third goal. Bolton, looking ordinary, did get a goal back in the second half but when Cunliffe was tripped, Lawton, still seeming to struggle after his recent injury, converted the 72nd-minute penalty. But apparently Everton had not matched their first-half performance at Griffin Park against Brentford!

At Huddersfield Town on 5 February, Jack Jones returned to left-back. Within four minutes Town were ahead from a curious Lewis Brook effort after a Joe Hulme corner had come off TG Jones's foot and gone through Mercer's legs. It took until the 23rd minute for Everton's superiority to show some benefit when Cunliffe ignored some offside claims to level the scoreline.

Gillick added a second shortly afterwards. In the second half Lawton finally mastered Alf Young but fired his shot straight at Bob Hesford, which brought a confession of 'I should have scored' from Tommy afterwards. Despite that miss, Stevenson wrapped up the 3-1 win in the 82nd minute.

It had been a long wait for the second Merseyside derby of the season and topsy-turvy Everton were true to recent performances, or lack of consistency at least. The Anfield club had to pay the Blues £1,000 compensation for playing the match midweek, but that was the extent of Everton's benefit. Behind after just 30 seconds through Jack Balmer, Everton did manage a sweet leveller when Lawton floated Britton's lob into the net in Dean-like style after eight minutes. But that was basically it. The young Liverpool forwards, average age 20, shredded the Everton defence and deservedly won 3-1. Form – if such a word can be used – had gone out of the window again and question marks persisted about the left-wing problem.

Since injury, then missing the Birmingham game, Tommy Lawton had scored five goals in 11 matches, compared with ten goals in the previous eight, statistics perhaps not conducive to expecting above average shooting accuracy by the time Everton faced Wolverhampton Wanderers on 19 February. The wind was unhelpful to both teams and defences remained on top. Near the interval TG Jones suffered a knee injury and retired. He returned but only to take the troublesome left-wing berth! Cunliffe took Jones's place, but with Lawton working tirelessly to get the better of Stan Cullis, the wonky front line was unable to penetrate and, in the 84th minute, Wolves scored the only goal of the match.

Fresh from a week's sojourn at Harrogate Spa, the visit to Leeds initially only served to spur United. The previous day,

Everton's long-awaited new left-winger was signed: England international Wally Boyes from West Bromwich Albion, all 5ft 4in of him. TG Jones's ankle was still not right so Gee deputised for the first time since 30 October. It was a day for him to forget. On four minutes, United leader Gordon Hodgson opened the scoring, then made it two after 11 minutes. At least this shook Everton enough to provoke a response. Lawton fed Boyes and reduced the arrears from the return pass with 23 minutes gone. Then just three minutes later Everton were level through Cunliffe. But that man Hodgson restored Leeds' advantage and he also had another headed effort denied, as the referee considered another Leeds player, lying in the goalmouth, to be offside.

Everton levelled again on 65 minutes when Cunliffe scored his second to make it 3-3 before the best goal of the game came with five minutes left. Lawton hooked the ball over his and Tom Holley's head to sink it for a 4-3 lead. Britton cleared off the line but Hodgson scored his fourth to make it 4-4 by heading in a free kick in the 88th minute. Boyes, who had one leg shorter than the other and cost £7,000, had made a fine debut before being injured in the last half hour. The *Liverpool Echo* reporter reckoned there had been 'eight perfect goals'. Another interesting statistic was that Lawton was now joint top scorer in the First Division with 21 goals.

For the following week's match against Grimsby at Goodison TG Jones was back at centre-half facing the wily Hughie Gallacher, while ex-Toffees winger Coulter was another familiar face in the Grimsby line-up. Sunshine greeted the lively ball and Everton scored on 27 minutes – Lawton responding quickly after Cunliffe had missed a chance. Six minutes later Stevenson extended the lead from 12 yards. Grimsby's response came in the 54th minute through Coulter but Lawton reinstated Everton's two-goal lead after 78 minutes despite making heavy work of it. Killing the ball had given him less time but his unerring accuracy had secured Everton's third goal. Gallacher hit a second Grimsby goal and at the final whistle shook Jones's hand.

Then came the daunting prospect of facing Preston at Deepdale, in view of the pounding that North End had given Everton back in October at Goodison. But events of the previous day overshadowed the match. Bill (Dixie) Dean, who had been left out of the reserves for a couple of weeks, was transferred to Notts County for £3,000, the sum Everton had paid Tranmere Rovers for him in 1925. The Everton players sent a telegram of good wishes to their former colleague. That same day Joe (Ten-goal) Payne was transferred to Chelsea from Luton for the same sum.

As for Deepdale, it was one of the best displays of the season by both teams. Everton began well but Preston eventually overcame them in the second half, their clever switching of forwards tipping the advantage. Cunliffe had opened the scoring for Everton after nine minutes and there was controversy over Preston's equaliser five minutes later. Bob Beattie's shot was going in when Dougal, clearly offside, leapt in to make sure. In fact, the referee originally signalled a free kick but the goal stood. Shortly afterwards Lawton nearly shredded the rigging with a shot but was given offside. Bud Maxwell scored Preston's winner in the 57th minute. Following this match, the *Lancashire Evening Post* came to the conclusion that only nine First Division clubs were safe from relegation – and Everton was not one of them.

Middlesbrough found themselves a goal down after four minutes to a Boyes effort at Goodison on 19 March but it was no signal for an avalanche, as chances went begging for Everton. After Lawton miskicked, Bell, in for Stevenson on the day, failed before a gaping goal. Everton were made to pay for their missed chances when Middlesbrough equalised on 16 minutes, although they were fortunate with their second. Tom Cochrane's shot hit Benny Yorston's leg and was diverted past Sagar. It took Everton until five minutes from the end to salvage a point when Bell atoned for his earlier failure to score, the match ending 2-2.

Back at Stamford Bridge two months after their FA Cup victory there was to be no repetition of Everton's success. Having watched the Grand National the previous day, the players travelled on the Saturday morning. There was further talk of Lawton as a possible cap for England. Everton's use of the long ball did not help him or the team and Bob Griffiths at centre-half for the Pensioners kept a strict rein on Tommy. Chelsea, marginally better at least, kept it wide. Jock Thomson, the Toffees non-playing captain, at least made his first appearance and was just about their best player. Payne made it easy for Wilf Chitty to score for Chelsea after 17 minutes, then broke his own duck in their colours for a 2-0 victory. Everton had just one win in seven and their place in the First Division was looking insecure. Even Dean had not prevented the team being relegated in 1930 – could Lawton stave off a similar ending?

On 2 April at home to West Bromwich Albion it was a drizzly day that produced a deluge of scoring. Eleven times the ball was in the net, including two from penalties, although there were three goals disallowed. Mercer was in for Britton, Cunliffe for Bell. On seven minutes Stevenson hit the bar but Geldard buried the rebound, before the Throstles had one disallowed for handball, despite claims that it hit a shoulder. Stevenson managed Everton's second from 30 yards after 32 minutes, then Cunliffe made it 3-0 five minutes later. Jack Mahon snatched one back for Albion on 39 minutes before Lawton made it 4-1 from the penalty spot after a handball with two minutes remaining of the first half. Then Albion's luck was out again when Harry Jones was fouled in the area but carried on to find the net, only for the referee to recall him for a free kick! Lawton added his second on 57 minutes, though laughably offside at the time. Thomson conceded a penalty on 80 minutes for West Bromwich to score through Cecil Shaw, then two minutes later Jones bundled the ball and Sagar into the net to make it a flattering 5-3 defeat for them.

It was a much quieter affair at Stoke in the next match and by then it had been reported that, had Micky Fenton the Middlesbrough centre-forward failed a fitness test the previous week, Lawton would have won his first England cap. On 30 minutes, a Cunliffe shot hit a defender and spiralled up for Tommy to sink but five minutes later Everton were unlucky to concede the equaliser. Syd Peppitt scored it while TG Jones was being impeded by Tommy Sale but a useful point had been taken for the unchanged Everton.

The three-match Easter programme might prove to be the key to whether Everton survived in the First Division. Entertaining Sunderland on Good Friday produced six goals shared. Everton were initially on top but Sunderland fought back and certainly deserved their point. Cunliffe scored twice, on 14 and 17 minutes, the second with a suspicion of offside, but Raich Carter and Eddie Burbanks made it 2-2 by half-time. On 72 minutes Thomson struck splendidly from the edge of the area, only for Burbanks to grab his second and Sunderland's third with six minutes remaining.

Britton was back at right-half instead of Mercer as Charlton Athletic provided the Saturday fare at Goodison and looked a strong defensive side. However, after 23 minutes they suffered an injury to George Tadman who went off. Although he resumed for a while at outside-left, he missed the entire second half. This had an obvious effect on Charlton's performance. A minute before the break Geldard opened the scoring for Everton and the industrious Lawton converted a 63rd-minute penalty. Five minutes later Geldard scored his second and Everton's third. Depleted Charlton were awarded a penalty when Thomson fisted the ball out but Bert Turner's penalty hit the crossbar and Sagar cleared up the pieces.

Easter Monday at Sunderland was never going to be easy for Everton after their experience on Good Friday. Oddly enough they conceded twice at Roker Park in the first half during their best period of the match. Little, if anything, went their way. Lawton had a hard time against Alex Lockie, and Cunliffe suffered a knock. They also fell foul of the referee, who had words with four players, though 'Stork' reporting for the *Liverpool Echo* questioned his actions. Mr E. D. Smith had also queried 29 throw-ins, to underline his pedant approach. The scribe also mentioned a Lockie handball incident and John Feenan clearing off the line with the goalkeeper beaten. But, following this 2-0 defeat, the net result over the holiday period was three points from three games and a continuing concern.

Sitting 16th in the table but only two points off bottom place, Everton had three matches remaining to save the situation, including a four-pointer against fellow sufferers Birmingham in the next match. Unchanged from the defeat at Sunderland, at least Everton tore into the fray from the start and the *Sports Argus* remark of being 'on top' was well offered.

Despite Harry Hibbs's heroics in the Birmingham goal a score seemed inevitable, and Stevenson had it after 25 minutes. Before half-time Boyes added a second from Cunliffe's pass. Cunliffe then reacted to a Stevenson shot that had been charged down to make it 3-0 after 53 minutes. It was certainly a welcome win.

Portsmouth, facing even more dire straits than the Solent, were next up at Goodison on FA Cup Final day. Everton hit two goals within 20 minutes through Stevenson, which roused Pompey, but just when their act was beginning to take shape, Boyes, suspiciously offside according to the *Portsmouth Evening News* report, made it three on 37 minutes. Cliff Parker scored with his head to get one back four minutes later and Jimmy Beattie brought Pompey within one goal of Everton with another successful headed effort on 56 minutes. Everton had paid for defensive slackness; however, Lawton had a simple tap-in for Everton's fourth goal on 66 minutes and Stevenson secured his hat-trick near the end from a Boyes set-up for 5-2. Everton looked safe at last!

Derby County were the visitors to Goodison for the final league match on 7 May. It was a quiet affair, with neither team chasing nor avoiding anything. Two goals were scored within a minute of each other and honours were even. Dally Duncan opened the scoring for the Rams on 47 minutes, Geldard equalising a minute later. It was Duncan's 100th league goal. Lawton was not on the scoresheet but finished top scorer in the First Division with 28 goals at the age of just 18.

The season was not quite over as the Blackpool Hospital Cup was on offer on the following Monday. It ended 2-2, Everton then losing the toss to Blackpool who won the trophy. Cunliffe and Lawton, who was preparing to whack the willow in the summer, scored for Everton. At the end of the season the club retained 30 players and placed six on the transfer list, with Dougal its only real surprise.

However, the club had accepted an invitation to participate in the Empire Exhibition Trophy in Scotland at the end of May, going into June. In the quarter-finals they met Rangers and beat them 2-0! Lawton opened the scoring in the 38th minute with a shot from ten yards. Cunliffe scored in the fated 14th minute of the second half after three players had collided in the goalmouth, leaving Cunliffe with an open goal. The Rangers goalkeeper Jerry Dawson had to go off, but Everton then relaxed against the ten men.

In the semi-final against Aberdeen, Everton led after only ten seconds. Lawton played the ball to Cunliffe, who passed it out to Gillick. He aimed for the corner and Willie Cooper, rushing back to clear the ball, hit it against a post before it trundled in. The Dons fought back with goals on seven and 29 minutes to put them ahead but in the second half Boyes, and Lawton with a header from Mercer's cross, carried the day for Everton at 3-2.

The final against Scottish League champions Celtic went to extra time and only then did the Celts manage the only goal of the match. Everton's performance in the tournament had been outstanding and augured well for the new season. However, missing from the squad was Albert Geldard, transferred to Bolton Wanderers for £4,500.

During Tommy's time at Everton, the trainer was Harry Cooke and the masseur Harry Cook! The latter was blind, having lost his sight in the First World War at Gallipoli as a result of a grenade attack. However, he qualified as a masseur and was able to distinguish the players on his treatment table from their physical differences. In the case of Lawton, he had the biggest feet for his height and weight! At this time, Tommy also featured in many series of the various cigarette cards that were popular at the time and in one he was No. 28 – exactly the same number of league goals he had scored in 1937/38.

CHAPTER THREE

Championship Winner and Top Scorer at 19

AUGUST 1938 saw the trial matches. In the first, the Blues beat the Rest 3-1, Lawton scoring two goals. The *Liverpool Echo* reminded readers of one aspect of Tommy Lawton's game: 'The first-time hook shot on the half-turn – few get such power behind the drive.' There was also the first Jubilee Fund match against neighbours Liverpool before the more serious stuff. Stevenson opened the scoring for Everton on 28 minutes and seven minutes later they were awarded a penalty from which Lawton shot wide! He later received a cut eye from an elbow, went off, returned and, within three minutes, atoned for his previous error by hitting an 'unstoppable gem'. Everton won 2-1 and it was much easier than the scoreline suggested.

Everton were at free-spending Blackpool for the first league affair of 1938/39, where they had never previously managed a First Division point. Stan Bentham, rediscovered after no senior outings the previous season, was handed Jimmy Cunliffe's inside-right berth. Mercer and Thomson were the wing-halves, otherwise the team was as expected. Everton were under the cosh early doors, but it changed on 13 minutes when Stevenson, receiving from Lawton and amid claims for offside, opened the scoring. Six minutes later it was two when Gillick passed to Tommy, who headed it down, moved forward and drove fiercely. Alex Roxburgh got a hand to it but the upward spiral took it into the goal. Everton had started the season with a 2-0 victory.

On the following Wednesday, the same 11 started at home to Grimsby Town. After scoring three goals in 25 minutes, Everton rested on their laurels again, perhaps a worrying trend or simply supreme confidence. Gillick's snap shot started the scoring, then two goals described as 'wonder shots' by young Tommy were acknowledged thus by 'Stork' in the *Liverpool Echo*: 'Dean has never scored two better.' This was surely the highest praise for an Evertonian. There was a nice gesture by referee Dr A. W. Barton entering both dressing rooms after the game to congratulate the teams on their sportsmanship. After two matches, only Leeds had also managed two wins and Everton led the table on goal average, a reversal of the previous season when they were bottom at the same stage.

Brentford were at Goodison on the Saturday and heavy rain had cleared before the kick-off. Lawton was quickly into the action with a shot and then a header but the first goal had to wait until 41 minutes, when he scored with a clean, lightning left-foot strike. Brentford were active and on 71 minutes a free kick by Bobby Reid levelled the scores, the presence of Gerry McAloon hampering Sagar and suspicions of handling in the incident. It was the first goal Everton had conceded in 251 minutes of play but ten minutes later Lawton took Gillick's pass and the pace of his shot was too much for Crozier to handle effectively. Everton now had a maximum six points from three games.

Just two days later at Villa Park Everton had the same 11 on duty. Injury-hit Villa began confidently enough but after 20 minutes had elapsed Boyes crossed from the wing, Stevenson shot and scored to give Everton the lead. On 39 minutes, after a four-man move, the roving Lawton swerved neatly round Jimmy Allen and added a second. Everton were then held up until 70 minutes had passed when the Boyes–Stevenson combination led to number three. Even Villa fans were murmuring 'what beautiful football'. After this 3-0 victory it was off to Bushey Park to prepare for a tilt at the champions Arsenal on their home ground.

The players had been able to watch Arsenal being beaten at Brentford in the week and Everton started with supreme confidence, taking the lead on 14 minutes after a roaming Lawton flicked the ball on for Stevenson to score. Seven minutes before the interval Tommy ran across the face of the goal, then half-turned to add number two. The *Daily Herald* quoted some of the older wiseacres in attendance that 'this is the football we've been waiting for, the real stuff'. It was at least half-time before Everton decided enough was enough and settled back.

Arsenal had their chances to cut the lead, Eddie Carr missing wider than wide and Jack Crayston twice hitting the post, Dave Nelson doing the same once. Eventually Bryn Jones paid off a bit more of his £14,000 fee with a root-skimmer, though Sagar was unsighted in that 65th minute. Even so, the *Daily Herald* remarked that Arsenal, the champions, were 'outclassed'. The 2-1 victory meant that Everton had the only 100 per cent record in the First Division.

At the weekend Tommy Lawton was chosen to lead the Football League attack against the Irish League. Meanwhile, an exiled Everton fan in London quoted one of the capital's newspapers that referred to Everton's display against Arsenal as 'the best football since the war with Stevenson the controlling genius making Lawton an England centre-forward'.

In the next match, Portsmouth scored at Goodison after only seven minutes through Billy Bagley. It took another ten minutes before parity was achieved when Bentham's outstretched foot found the ball and the corner of the net. Lawton, for once escaping the arms of Tommy Rowe, was allowed too much freedom and scored with his first headed goal of the season from Gillick's pull back, making it 2-1 by half-time. Pompey were on the ropes in the second half. On 62 minutes Gillick shot through goalkeeper Walker's legs, then ten minutes later Lew Morgan, under pressure, put through his own goal from a Stevenson effort. Finally, with five minutes remaining, Boyes arrowed in number five after a long pass from Mercer.

Tommy's first representative selection took him to Windsor Park, Belfast, playing for the Football League against the Irish League. The Football League team was: Woodley; Sproston, Hapgood, Willingham, Cullis, Welsh, Matthews, Robinson, Lawton, Goulden and Morton. It was the 40th meeting between the two leagues. After a couple of minutes Stanley Matthews floated a centre tantalisingly in front of the goalposts, with both Lawton and West Ham United's left-winger Jackie Morton ready to pounce. Morton got a touch with his head but it appeared the ball was already over the line. The Irish League levelled but, on 35 minutes, Lawton scored on his debut, the ball deflecting off a defender. After pulling back to 2-2 the Irish team faded fast. Don Welsh scored a third then Tommy rattled in two more in two minutes just after the hour and also scored the Football League's seventh in the eventual 8-2 win. A four-timer on his first appearance was not a bad return for the still 18-year-old Lawton. International honours were now a formality and around this time the *Lancashire Evening Post* remarked: 'Height, thickness of build with it'.

Back in the First Division and chasing a record seven wins in succession, it all fell apart for Everton at Huddersfield Town on the following Saturday. Not that they gave in easily, but two goals in arrears within three minutes was not the best start to the second half. Tom Hinchcliffe had both, the first on 50 minutes getting the luck of a rebound off Cook to score with a low shot, and the same player hooking a lob on the volley three minutes later. Everton threw it all at Huddersfield, even TG Jones becoming a sixth forward. Huddersfield owed much to their centre-half, Alf Young, who kept the lively Lawton quiet. However, one too many passes in the opposing penalty area contributed to Everton's downfall as they conceded a third goal with five minutes left, to Jimmy Isaac.

Defeat at last and how would Everton respond with the first Merseyside derby a week hence? No changes were made to the team but two controversial incidents were revealed at Goodison. H. C. Williams, a linesman who had previously been a referee, was back controlling his first match in the First Division. Perhaps he tried too hard, who knows. Anyway, his pedantic attitude led to 20 free kicks in the first half, mostly for innocuous clashes – 14 against Everton, six against Liverpool. Then, just before half-time, after a collision between Herman Van Den Berg and Sagar, Williams blew his whistle. The Liverpool forward said later that he thought it was against him. Either the goalkeeper was protecting himself from bodily contact or he pushed the Liverpool forward. Whichever it was, a penalty was awarded, which Jackie Balmer converted. Everton had already scored twice by this time but so incensed was Norman Greenhalgh, the nearest player to the incident, that after his protest and play resuming he swept away Nieuwenhuys and earned a booking. At half-time there was booing from the crowd and paper tossed in the referee's direction, to the extent that the official asked a police inspector to have words with a section of spectators.

Earlier, Everton had taken the lead on 14 minutes after a corner to the far post by Boyes and Bentham cutting in to head home. Then on 39 minutes it was 2-0 as a Stevenson shot was knocked out for Boyes to finish off. Tom Bush did keep Lawton in check, but Everton had the better of the later exchanges and had won 2-1.

International calls caused Everton's first team alterations of the season for their next league match at Wolves. With Willie Cook and Stevenson playing for Ireland, and Gillick opposing them for Scotland, George 'Stonewall' Jackson came in at right-back, Cunliffe at inside-left for Stevenson, plus Arthur Barber at 19 made his league debut on the right wing. Wolves were delayed and had to de-train at Edge Hill, the fleet of taxis not arriving at Goodison until three o'clock. Having changed en route, the start was delayed by only five minutes.

The upset did not seem to affect the visitors and they stretched Everton at times. For once Stan Cullis was nowhere near Lawton, who went close with a shot. Then two minutes later the Everton leader, who had promised the Wolves centre-half that he would score against him, did so. Bentham nodded down to Tommy who drove wide of the goalkeeper on 28 minutes. Cullis was finding Lawton a handful and was reduced to charging him off the ball when able to do so, as Everton suffered the inconsistency of contrasting officials – one week too severe, the next too lenient.

Shooting from either side was at a premium and the only other incident of note was at the close when both Bentham, with blood streaming from his face, and Cullis were stretchered off after a collision. Both players suffered concussion and Cullis was sent to a nursing home to recover; however, both players were fit in time for their respective teams' next matches. So, after nine matches Everton and Derby County led the rest by four points, with the Toffees top on goal average.

However, there was another hiccup for Everton at Bolton Wanderers on 15 October, but it was a fine advertisement for First Division football. Skipper Thomson had to cry off with a heavy cold and George Milligan, late of Oldham Athletic, was drafted in at left-half. There were ominous early signs for Everton when they went behind after ten minutes, with Roberts putting Bolton ahead, but within a further ten minutes the visitors were level. Stevenson picked up the ball when there was a defensive mix-up to score. Jackie Roberts scored his second from a dozen yards to put Bolton back in front, before Lawton found the net from six yards after good work by Gillick ten minutes before the break.

In the second half, Bolton were not to be resisted, as Tom Woodward made it 3-2 after 75 minutes, then as Everton pressed for another equaliser, Jones was caught out helping the attack. George Hunt's shot was only partially stopped by Sagar and Roberts finished it off for his hat-trick in Wanderers' 4-2 win. Fortunately for Everton, Derby also lost, so the Toffees remained top of the table, but Bolton were closing in.

There were more international calls on 22 October with the *Liverpool Echo* predicting 'Lawton in for a row of caps'. Tommy was on duty against Wales along with Boyes, while TG Jones was in opposition for Wales. The England team was: Woodley; Sproston, Hapgood, Willingham, Young, Copping, Matthews, Robinson, Lawton, Goulden and Boyes. Clifford

Webb in the *Daily Herald* referred to 'Young Master Lawton'. On the following Monday, his column noted the 4-2 spanking given to England by Wales in Cardiff. Tommy did score from a penalty for an unfair handball decision but had another goal ruled out for offside – an equally wrong decision. Four days later, England faced the Rest of Europe at Highbury! Only two alterations were made to the team, Alf Young giving way to Stan Cullis at centre-half and Willie Hall taking Jackie Robinson's inside-right berth.

At Highbury, the FA's 75th anniversary match against Europe's best was a fairly low-key affair. Matthews set up Hall for a goal on 20 minutes and the second was Everton-fashioned, Boyes's effort deflected for Lawton to score on the half-hour. Near the interval there was some typical Lawton sportsmanship when the Rest's Italian goalkeeper Aldo Olivieri went full length in making a save and Tommy held back to prevent any chance of injuring the keeper. Len Goulden added a third goal for England. The *Liverpool Echo*'s comment on Lawton was that he had received 'buffeting but few passes'.

Lawton resumed his Everton place on Saturday, 29 October but it was a bad day at the city – not for Leicester, the home team lying 16th full value for their 3-0 win. Everton's defeat also cost them top spot, now in Derby's hands. Leicester's first goal on 25 minutes came from Eric Stubbs's cross to an unmarked Arthur Maw just outside the area. In the second half Everton escaped a penalty when Greenhalgh handled but, with the forwards distinctly out of touch, it was Leicester who added to their tally through George Dewis after 78 minutes when Cook slipped, then two minutes later they got their third through Griffiths.

More representative duty for Lawton beckoned on the following Wednesday for the Football League against the

Scottish League at Molineux. Boyes opened the Football League's account and Derby County's Ronnie Dix scored a second on 23 minutes. Dix notched his second just after the break, then Greenhalgh conceded a penalty for Tommy Walker to give the Scots a goal in their 3-1 defeat. The nearest Lawton came to a goal was when he hit an upright.

There were Saturday fireworks when Middlesbrough visited Goodison Park a few days later, with the *Liverpool Echo* reciting: 'Please to remember the 5th of November, and Lawton's power of shot.' The line-up against Middlesbrough was back to the expected one and there was a welcome return to the delightful football of Everton. Lawton opened the scoring with a 16th-minute header, drove in his second five minutes later after a couple of misses, then had one disallowed for offside when a linesman flagged. In fact, the ball had grazed Bob Baxter's head to put him onside. Lawton then made Stevenson's goal on 80 minutes before completing his hat-trick after Gillick was tripped. His penalty rocket singed the fingers of the Boro goalkeeper. The nearest Middlesbrough came to scoring was when Jackie Milne hit a post. It was Everton's seventh successive home win, but title rivals Derby had won eight of their last ten fixtures.

Two games a week was the norm for Tommy Lawton by now and next it was England duty for the visit of Norway to Newcastle. At a sunny St James' Park it was a bright opening for England on 13 minutes with left-winger Reg Smith of Millwall scoring on his international debut. His inside partner and also debutant, Dix, added a second five minutes later. In the 25th minute Lawton won a heading duel and scored, though the Norwegian goalkeeper got a hand to it. Smith scored his second before half-time thanks to Lawton's belting left-foot drive that crashed against the bar before rebounding to Smith. England then eased up in the second half, content with four.

It was away days for Everton on 12 November and another loss, this time at bottom club Birmingham. There was plenty of good approach work from Everton at St Andrew's but no bite. There was both dismal weather and a wretched show by Everton's attack, though the defence was not to blame for the defeat. TG Jones was out with ankle ligament problems courtesy of the international match, so Gee was at centre-half. Birmingham's side included two half-backs having to play up front in the second half, too. Charlie Phillips with a header near half-time was the scorer of the only goal of the match. However, Lawton, on double shifts for five weeks, was still the leading First Division marksman.

On Wednesday, 16 November Ireland were at Old Trafford to play England, which was Lawton's fourth consecutive England cap. The match became a personal triumph for Willie Hall, the Tottenham Hotspur inside-forward. Even so, it was Lawton who opened the Irish defence with a fierce effort from the edge of the area, the pace of the drive defeating Twomey's fingers. Then Hall struck: his first from Matthews's pass, the others laid on by Lawton – respectively on 34, 36 and 38 minutes. Into the second half, Hall went nap on 54 minutes, then hit a sixth on 63 minutes. Matthews, who had provided an outstanding contribution, grabbed the seventh goal after a solo effort from the halfway line.

Everton's next match was at Goodison against Manchester United and at least their home form continued to produce results. In fact, if it had not been for Everton's over-elaboration, they would have had four goals by half-time. However, all they had to show was the one goal after Stevenson hit the bar and

Lawton buried the rebound on eight minutes. In the second half Boyes almost added a second goal but, in a scramble, Lawton found the net with 53 minutes gone. Late on Gillick added a third goal for Everton.

Away to Stoke City on 26 November only the failure of the City attack prevented another defeat for Everton, clearly having worrying problems on road trips. Greenhalgh did well to keep Stanley Matthews from causing serious damage but the rest of the Stoke front line suffered from over-anxiety in the goal precinct. The nearest they came was when they hit a post, but at least Everton avoided another reverse in a goalless draw. Derby still led the table, now by three points, but had played one more match than Everton, and their goals for columns were almost identical, the Rams having scored one more.

Chasing another Goodison victory with Chelsea as visitors, there was a first-minute shock when Joe Payne netted, only to be pulled back for an infringement. Then Dickie Spence missed an open goal. Everton's lightweight attacking strategy was slowed by the heavy surface and there was no scoring by half-time. Then on 57 minutes Lawton opened the account, only for George Mills to level six minutes later. However, the tide was turning Everton's way at last and Lawton scored his second, followed by Gillick and Stevenson to make it 4-1. It was Everton's ninth successive home win and according to reports Lawton had been 'irresistible'.

Given the paucity of Everton's away-day successes, prospects at Deepdale against Preston North End on 10 December looked meagre. However, a fine opening 15 minutes at a crucial time set the scene for improvement and, with the defence holding firm, prospects appeared brighter. Lawton came nearest to a first-half goal, his rocket shaving a layer or two off the crossbar whitewash. However, it was not until six minutes from time that they managed to score the only goal of the match. Bentham took a throw, Gillick without hesitation crossed the ball into the area and there was Lawton's head to make it 1-0 and a home defeat for proud Preston, their first of the season.

Charlton arrived for Everton's tenth home fixture and the clawing heavy pitch was another test for the close-passing style of the Toffees. By using the flanks Everton were sensible but goals were unlikely to follow, and in the middle of the park they were bogged down. Even so, three easy chances went begging and it was ex-Evertonian Monty Wilkinson who scored a shock first goal for Charlton after 38 minutes. Gillick equalised on 51 minutes but then it was all Charlton. George Tadman after 57 minutes, 'Sailor' Brown three minutes later, and Tadman's second with a minute remaining, left Everton's home record shattered by a 4-1 defeat. For the last 20 minutes the injured Stevenson had limped on the wing. The only consolation of the day was that Derby lost by the same scoreline at home to Middlesbrough.

Everton were quickly back on track when Blackpool visited the following week. Within six minutes, Lawton, facing his own goal, fed the oncoming Gillick, who put Everton ahead. Tommy also laid one on for Cunliffe, in for the injured Stevenson, before the break. When Bentham was cut down, Lawton declined to take the penalty as he was suffering a leg strain, so Willie Cook – captain for the day with Thomson out and Watson in – took the kick. Jock Wallace saved his first attempt but the full-back made amends with the rebound. Cunliffe scored his second goal in the 4-0 whitewash of the Tangerines.

Then came the crucial twosome over Christmas against title rivals Derby County – certainly a pointer towards any prospect of honours. At Goodison on Boxing Day the *Daily Herald* reported it as a 'tremendous struggle'. Lawton was out with a strained muscle and a pulsating game finished 2-2, including another Cook spot kick.

It was off to the Baseball Ground the next day, and Lawton returned to the team. A Derby goal arrived after half an hour when Dave McCulloch successfully headed in from Crooks. Ten minutes later Jack Howe was adjudged to have pushed Bentham and Cook scored his third consecutive penalty to level the scores. But three minutes into the second half Dally Duncan put Derby ahead from an almost impossible angle from a Crooks centre with what proved to be the winning goal. Everton had critically dropped three points to their rivals over the two matches and were now three points behind the league leaders with a game in hand.

The following Saturday, New Year's Eve, Everton made the trip to bottom of the table Brentford and named an unchanged XI. Inside 20 minutes Everton were on the ropes. Les Townsend, son of a local fireman, was already stoking the embers for another away-day defeat for the Toffees from an opportunist effort. Everton were still trying to play their usual passing game but Brentford's dash was more effective and Townsend crowned a special day with his, and his team's, second goal. The *Sunday Mirror* said Everton had been 'disappointing'.

They had now lost three times in the season to the bottom club. Is this a record? Whatever, the dawn of 1939 was not looking too bright for Everton's championship challenge. Obviously, a change of style on wintry surfaces was now a priority. Looking ahead, though, there was respite from their league woes – how about an FA Cup third-round tie at Derby County to see in the New Year!

After training at Harrogate, where snow forced the Everton players to hire a tennis court for practice, a sudden thaw changed the Baseball Ground to mud and pools of water. Defences were on top but, while the Rams persisted in short passing, Everton spread their wings for a change. Derby claimed a goal when McCulloch's header appeared to have gone over the line as Sagar fell on the ball, but referee Jewell demurred. Then after 52 minutes the deadlock was broken when Bentham centred over Jack Nicholas's head and Boyes nodded Everton into the lead, despite appeals for offside. With Bentham tracking back to bolster the defence, Everton held on for the narrow win.

It was then back to league fare with champions Arsenal at Goodison and another fine performance from both teams enthralling the crowd. For nearly an hour there was no breakthrough, Arsenal using quicker methods to Everton's precise build-up. Then, on 56 minutes, Bentham took the ball off Bryn Jones – who previously appeared to have escaped 'hands' – Lawton sold Bernard Joy a dummy and, as Crayston came across to tackle, Tommy let fly with a shot that almost took the legs off goalkeeper Alex Wilson. Everton were in front and had a second strike after 85 minutes through Boyes from Stevenson's pass after the pair had interchanged. It was premature perhaps, but certainly it was an improvement to report for Evertonian fans.

The cup again held the attention on 21 January with Third Division (North) Doncaster Rovers visiting Goodison. For half an hour it was a competitive game then three goals in ten minutes set Everton towards an easy conquest. Boyes began the rout on 35 minutes, added his second eight minutes later and Lawton scored his first with a minute to go before half-time. In the second half, Lawton added another two to complete his first Everton hat-trick. Stevenson also scored, after 77 minutes,

Gillick on 81 minutes, then Tommy's now four-timer came with three minutes to go. For Lawton, he had finally ended the jinx that Rovers centre-half Syd Bycroft had over him in two previous meetings! Eight goals for Everton and the famous Goodison trumpeter had gradually switched from 'Lights Out' to the 'Last Post'.

Given the hard time that struggling Huddersfield had given Everton in September, putting the record straight was surely the order of the day at Goodison in the next league fixture. But they gave the Blues another difficult game and a minute after half-time took the lead through Pat Beasley with a first-time shot. Four minutes later a controversial incident brought an equaliser. Young had been 'embracing' Lawton most of the game; this time it happened in the penalty area and the resulting spot kick was despatched by Cook and the referee had words with Young. A minute later Gillick crossed and Tommy scooped in a low header for the lead. Three goals in 11 minutes had changed the outlook of the match. After 67 minutes Lawton headed down for Stevenson to net but, by no means out of it, Huddersfield scored a second through Billy Price who had another effort ruled out for handball, as Everton claimed a hard-fought 3-2 victory.

The rearranged Portsmouth match took place on the following Wednesday and Pompey's wastefulness saved Everton – a conservative count putting it at four sitters going begging in the first half. Ground conditions were fine, so Everton had no excuse. Portsmouth also claimed a penalty but it was ball hitting hand in Cook's case. It was then Everton who broke the deadlock on 53 minutes when Mercer and Boyes combined to find Lawton whose left-foot drive found the target for the only goal of the game.

Clearly a different outlook was required for the Merseyside derby at Anfield and hopes of a double over their city neighbours, last achieved in 1931/32. There was a much smarter approach by Everton, and on 14 minutes Bentham headed in Gillick's corner to give them the lead. Being a derby affair this did not prevent Liverpool pressurising the Everton defence but the strength of the opposing halves was a key factor. After 73 minutes Gillick found Lawton, who shook off two defenders for Everton's second goal. Stevenson hit a post, then after 82 minutes his effort had Dirk Kemp fumbling in the Liverpool goal, leaving Tommy with a simple tap-in for a 3-0 victory. There was much shaking of hands afterwards and Everton were now back on top of the league on goal average, as Derby had drawn at Blackpool.

The fifth round of the FA Cup brought spring weather to the Midlands and a visit to Birmingham for a second time this season. Everton had lost 1-0 there in the league in November when the Brummies were propping up the table, a position they still occupied. Again Everton found them resilient and the tie became an interesting struggle in a fine cup-tie atmosphere. A minute before the interval Cook's clearance was picked up by Owen Madden, who put Birmingham in front. However, it was only briefly, as within half a minute Lawton fed Stevenson who levelled with a low left-foot shot.

On 64 minutes Frank Clack fisted out a corner that fell to Boyes, whose left-foot effort hit Lawton's legs on the way in – Tommy later refusing to take credit. Dennis Jennings missed an easy one to put Birmingham level and Stevenson went close to his second goal. But on 83 minutes Madden made it 2-2 before Clack saved a Lawton effort, turning it round the upright. Tommy also suffered a battering and had bruised ribs to show for it. It was honours even and a replay awaited on the following Wednesday.

Quickly out of the traps in the replay, Everton accepted a second-minute lead. A centre from Boyes presented Gillick with a chance and his rising drive found the net. But again Tommy did not get much joy from Gerry Halsall's marking and the early goal did not inspire Everton. In fact, Birmingham had the better of matters from then on, Fred Harris finishing a four-man move with a slick half-volley to make it 1-1 after ten minutes. Birmingham kept up the pressure in the second half but, sadly for the visitors, then came an unfortunate 87th-minute blow. Don Dearson, believing his goalkeeper was nowhere, turned Boyes's header round the post with his hand, though there were other defenders who could have helped out. Cook converted from the spot. On the final whistle Orpington-based referee Daly took aside Halsall and Lawton and congratulated them on their fine sportsmanship throughout.

There was no respite for Everton as a few days later came a trip to Lawton's home town of Bolton for what should have been his 100th league appearance. But suffering from his previous battering he was unfit, Bell taking his centre-forward position. There was another quick goal for Everton on six minutes when Mercer's cross rebounded off Atkinson for Gillick to finish off. Their lead held for another 11 minutes before ex-Evertonian Albert Geldard made it 1-1. Ten minutes before half-time Harry Hubbick, in trying to clear Mercer's cross, only succeeded in putting through his own goal. Bell had a couple of opportunities that went begging and Bolton's attacking was largely contained by Everton's defence as the match ended 2-1 to the Toffees.

Third-placed Wolves were on the prowl on the following Wednesday and Lawton was back for his ton-up but playing at inside-right, with Bell retained. Morton was in goal for the injured Sagar, otherwise the team was as before, though the portents of success for Everton were not encouraging after Wolverhampton suffered 18 hours of rain, leaving the Molineux pitch inches deep in mud and water. The Blues did not play badly, they just played the wrong game, and even the right one would likely not have beaten Wolves, who received the accolade from the *Liverpool Evening Express* of performing as the 'acme of perfection'. The final score was 7-0, a scoreline slightly exaggerated, as Gillick and Mercer were struggling with injuries in the second half.

Dennis Westcott scored on two minutes before the floodgates were opened by Dickie Dorsett, who completed his hat-trick with goals in the 24th, 37th and 48th minutes. McIntosh made it five after 55 minutes, then Dorsett scored his fourth and Wolves' sixth, leaving Westcott to complete his double with five minutes remaining. TG Jones, unusually for him, had a poor game in the heart of Everton's defence. He had been suffering from ear problems. Generally speaking, while the Blues were still trying to tip-tap their way, Wolves were flinging the ball all over the ground. The experiment of Lawton at inside-forward did not work and in the second half he swapped with Bell, but it was much too late. This was Everton's match in hand over Derby, but Wolves were now in second place in the table, just two points behind Everton.

Blues secretary Theo Kelly went to the Wolves dressing room after the game and congratulated the players on their performance. The *Sunday Mirror* reckoned the young Wolves team's average age of just over 21 years was worth £100,000 on the transfer market and Major Frank Buckley's boys were now favourites for a league and cup double – provided they could repeat this type of performance in the latter competition when they met Everton again in the sixth round at Molineux!

There was no time to dwell on events. Licking their wounds after the Wolves mauling and minus four players out at Leeds, with Cook (ankle), Thomson (back), Gillick (shoulder) plus Stevenson (leg) missing, Everton replaced them respectively by Jackson, Watson, debutant Eric Barber and Cunliffe. Leeds might have been slumping but Everton were clearly shaken by their experience at Molineux and rarely troubled Reg Savage in the United goal. George Ainsley even gave Leeds the lead on 28 minutes with a rising drive in off a post. Despite a much sounder showing, Jones slipped once but Eric Stephenson failed with just a tame effort. As for an attacking response, Barber trod on the ball while in a promising position, while Lawton suffered ankle and facial injuries and had a nosebleed. At long last, in the 71st minute, struggling Lawton managed to create an opening for Bentham to equalise. With ten minutes left Boyes dribbled and sent in a centre that Cunliffe finished off with a cracker of an effort. Harry Sutherland hit a post for Leeds but Everton held on for the win before moving to Harrogate for the cup-tie warm-up.

Pre-cup tie, anonymous scurrilous letters to Lawton, as well as Alec Scott and Stan Cullis of Wolves, thought to be IRA-inspired, were ignored. Apart from Thomson, the other casualties returned. As to the football, this was totally removed from the recent league meeting of the two teams. Wolves' passing was wayward and they were being caught in possession. Everton, more precise, certainly had the better of the first half but crucially missed a couple of chances, Lawton giving Boyes the best of the two before tragedy hit the Blues just before half-time. Westcott, on a solo run, produced a splendid goal that went in off the post. It enlivened Wolves to a better second-half display after Lawton's early effort was ruled out, clearly offside. Tommy had a quiet day. Westcott scored his second goal on the hour, leaving the Molineux men chasing a double, for which they remained favourites.

At least Everton could now concentrate on the league but had only a few days in which to sort matters with Leicester City due at Goodison on Wednesday, 8 March. With the visitors scrapping to avoid the drop, Everton did at least force the issue. Within 15 minutes they led, when Bentham shaped to feed Gillick and turned to give Stevenson the shot. Five minutes later Boyes lobbed over the goalkeeper's head for a second goal that was touched in by a defender.

In the second half, on 48 minutes, full-back Greenhalgh scored. He began inside his own half, appeared to lose the ball twice but, with Lawton acting as a decoy, he forged on before scoring his first league goal, only to be swamped by delighted colleagues. Lawton, though still not at his ebullient best, scored a goal at the death, almost put in the net for him by Mercer.

Trekking to the north-east on the Saturday, Everton collapsed in the first half to Middlesbrough, with goals in the second minute from Cliff Chadwick, four minutes later from Benny Yorston, then one for Jackie Milne on 32 minutes. Then came three goals in three minutes. Stevenson appeared to have touched in the first but admitted his swing at Lawton's shot had not connected. Tommy then scored another goal before Micky Fenton regained Boro's advantage as they led 4-2 at half-time. But the Everton fightback in the second half was exciting. Four minutes after the restart an irresistible Lawton headed in Gillick's corner for his hat-trick. Then late on Lawton had another counter, his first Blues four-timer and Everton might well have won had not a linesman flagged that Stevenson's goal, agreed by the referee, be called back for Boyes being offside. But eight goals shared after being adrift at the break was a bonus.

'May the fourth be with you' – from a different age of course but at least true in Birmingham's case with number-four clash with Everton, including two cup ties. Stoic opponents, as previously, and, but for poor finishing, Birmingham could have had two goals in the first 15 minutes as Everton still had obvious problems kick-starting matches. Wilson Jones fired straight at Sagar and John Brown hit the bar. Sagar did well to keep his charge intact. It took half an hour for the Evertonians to shake a meaningful leg in a bewildering bout of scoring. Fred Harris opened for Birmingham after 27 minutes, Lawton headed an equaliser and Watson fed Gillick for a 2-1 Everton lead all in a couple of minutes. There had still been time between Everton's two for a Cyril Trigg own goal to be ruled out because of a previous foul on Bentham!

It stayed that way until the 71st minute when Bentham gave Everton a 3-1 lead. Eight minutes later Lawton's second and Everton's fourth was a gift as Frank Clack only pushed out a Bentham drive, leaving an open goal. Wilson Jones pulled one back for Birmingham three minutes later to make the final score 4-2 to Everton.

Eleven days elapsed before the next encounter at Manchester United for which the Everton team was unchanged. A brighter opening phase developed for Everton and Gillick might have improved it further but merely went close with two opportunities. Yet with the Everton defence holding firm and Sagar in command, the stalemate was broken in the 41st minute. Mercer and Gillick were involved after a throw-in, the latter switching neatly to Lawton who converted a typical left-foot drive. On 69 minutes there was a second Everton goal when Gillick finished off a clever move by Boyes. This had been a more mature performance by Everton, clearly benefiting from the longer period between fixtures. It was possibly also a defining moment in the chase for the title as it was a dark day for Wolves, who had lost the Black Country derby at Stoke 5-3. Surprisingly perhaps, Wolves and Everton had scored the same number of goals, though the Midland team had the superior defensive record. However, Everton now had a five-point advantage.

Everton announced that their summer tours to Germany and the Netherlands had been cancelled; a German party of footballers had previously called off their trip to watch that Stoke–Wolves match on a 'lame' excuse! But Jack Jones and Cliff Britton were selected for the FA tour of South Africa and Lawton was pencilled in for England's controversial European venture.

On the first day of April, Stoke City's second-string goalkeeper Doug Westland proved to be no fool in keeping Everton from scoring more than once at Goodison. Admittedly the Blues' target practice was not all it should have been and several gilt-edged opportunities were also wasted. In fact, Stoke even stole the lead on 65 minutes, Tommy Sale scoring with a splendid effort. The nearest Everton had managed to a goal was when Lawton shaved the bar with an angled hooked effort. Tommy did rescue a point with a quarter of an hour remaining though, and with a heavy Easter schedule ahead, it was no time to lose sight of the championship race.

Roker Park was no easy venue, so it was a timely Good Friday bonus with a Lawton goal in two minutes courtesy of a defensive error by Sunderland. Len Duns levelled in 15 minutes after TG Jones had headed away but parity existed only for another two minutes before Gillick, on his second attempt, made it 2-1 for Everton, though all three successful strikes had scarcely had the classic tag. Both sides continued to miss opportunities and back in defence, Everton's rearguard stood up well to the Sunderland attack. Bentham suffered a head injury, necessitating stitches.

Then came another away day in London – at Stamford Bridge on the Saturday against Chelsea – with the recent wing capture Jimmy Caskie, at 5ft 3in, another Scottish import, given his Everton debut in place of Boyes. Despite limping a little from a knock, Lawton, who had recently looked to have recaptured his fire, went on to make both Everton goals in the 2-0 victory. On 70 minutes he laid one on for the grafting Stevenson and a minute later provided another for Gillick. Bentham shone in the attack, but TG Jones went off ten minutes from time with an ankle injury. However, a fine, clean game had given Everton two more invaluable points, while Wolves had lost at Preston to leave the Toffees eight points clear at the top of the table.

Easter Monday welcomed Sunderland to Goodison, where the surface was virtually bare of grass except for the extreme edges. Jones was missing injured so Thomson was at centre-half. Bentham was first on the target for Everton with a header from a Caskie corner on 12 minutes and there was another for him when Lawton produced his usual slick back pass on 36 minutes. Arthur Housam reduced Sunderland's deficit a minute before the break from Duns' corner kick.

In the second half, Everton took off. Lawton gave Stevenson the chance for 3-1 within five minutes of the restart, before Bentham departed with a cut left eye to be stitched. Already crowd favourite, Caskie, scored on 69 minutes and Lawton, with a lightning despatch of a gift from the defence, added Everton's fifth two minutes later. Bentham came back and hit the sixth goal ten minutes from time for a splendid hat-trick before, in the last minute, Duns made it 6-2. Unless a complete collapse occurred in the last four matches, the championship was destined for Goodison Park.

Everton had already equalled the club's First Division record of 56 points, though they had once taken 61 points in winning a Second Division title. Eleven Everton players had achieved either representative international or received summer tour selection honours in the season: Cook, Jack Jones, Greenhalgh, Britton, Watson, Tommy (TG) Jones, Mercer, Gillick, Lawton, Stevenson and Boyes. Of course, goalkeeper Ted Sagar had already been capped by England on four occasions.

Moreover, two more points and that would be enough for the First Division championship. The venue was Goodison, the visitors Preston North End, and expectancy was high among a packed attendance of 31,987. Of course, international commitments meant that Everton were without Mercer and Lawton, on England duty against Scotland at Hampden Park.

Alas there were no fireworks, the attack never functioning adequately, and the match petered out into a goalless draw. Wolves had beaten Charlton Athletic 3-1, so with three matches remaining, with Wolves six points behind but with a superior goal average to the Blues, it still looked like an Everton title that could only be lost. The Blues' next opponents – Charlton!

But, as mentioned, it was Scotland on the agenda for Tommy and Joe that day at Hampden Park. *Sports Argus* set the scene with 'driving, persistent rain and a treacherous turf'. Despite these conditions the match provided fine football. England wore numbers, the Scots maintained their opposition to them. Lawton kicked off but it was slick, speedy Scotland on top in the first half. On 22 minutes the England defence was in a tangle and Wolves' Billy Morris, under pressure from Tommy Walker, attempted a suicidal pass back to the advancing Vic Woodley, but Preston's debutant Jimmy Dougal reacted quicker than Cullis and Mercer, virtually walking the ball in.

It was Scotland's first half but England shook the rain off after the resumption. However, it took until the 65th minute to dampen the Hampden roar. Pat Beasley, on his international bow, scored with a rising shot after a short pass from Lawton. The tide of fortune was now with England and both Matthews and Lawton went close to another goal. But it took until the 88th minute for the winner – a perfect Matthews centre and, according to the unbiased *Edinburgh Evening News*, a 'brilliant header from Lawton'. It was England's first win at Hampden since 1927 and there was a triple tie between England, Scotland and Wales for the Home International championship.

Mercer and Lawton were back in action for Everton on 22 April against Charlton, but it was sleepy time down south at The Valley. From the kick-off Watson was robbed by 'Sailor' Brown, who passed to Cyril Blott. His cross was headed in by Harold Hobbis for a Charlton goal in under half a minute. Four minutes before the break Robinson added a second Addicks goal – where now Everton? Gillick pulled one back on 62 minutes but Charlton became the only team to complete the double over them this season. The Everton players then had to wait in the dressing room before the news filtered through that, as Wolves had only drawn with Bolton, the championship was theirs! Yes, a funny old game! The club's chairman Will Cuff was to become president of the Football League, too.

There was to be no respite as Everton then played another friendly against the Army, winning 5-3, though there was no Lawton. This coincided with the announcement of the Military

Training Act affecting men aged 20 and 21. They were to be called up for Army training for six months, then either join the Territorials or Reservists. Only TG Jones was likely to be affected in this age group and Lawton was still only 19. Everton already had one player in the Territorials, William Keenan, and it was thought they might form their own battalion.

On 29 April, the new First Division title holders entertained Aston Villa and the Goodison Park crowd of 23,667 with a more championship-like performance. Bentham scored on ten minutes, Gillick with a diving header after 23 minutes, then there was a Cook penalty after Bentham's header had been handled by Bob Iverson on the line, which eased Everton to a 3-0 win. Lawton suffered an ankle injury late in the match.

On the following Wednesday, Everton played a friendly in Ireland against Linfield, with Boyes back after injury, Caskie on the right wing and a recovered Lawton able to level the score at 1-1 in the 71st minute. Having already cancelled a proposed tour to Germany and the Netherlands, another, to Switzerland and to the Dutch, was now scheduled for late May.

The final league game was at Grimsby Town, and again an early goal was a blow from which Everton did not recover. Pat Glover was the scorer on four minutes. In the second half he scored a second 15 minutes from the end and Jimmy Boyd added a third as Everton were well beaten. Dr A. W. Barton, the Repton referee, handled his last match before retiring.

During the season, Everton had used 22 players in league and FA Cup matches. Ten of them appeared in 36 or more league games – only left-back Norman Greenhalgh was ever present – while only at left-half was there any real change when Gordon Watson replaced the injured Jock Thomson for the last dozen or so fixtures. Injuries accounted for almost all of the other alterations. Tommy Lawton was leading First Division marksman with 34 goals from 38 league games, arguably, at 19 years old, the youngest to finish as the top scorer in the top flight.

Despite criticism of Everton's style of close passing, which they adhered to almost throughout the season, and the seven-goal mauling by the Wolves, they kept their nerve even when results went seriously against them. Lawton was outstanding for one so comparatively young, but there were many other excellent players in a real team performance during the season. The distinguished journalist L. V. Manning wrote: 'Every man was enjoying a game of football and not making a job of work of it.'

However, Lawton and Mercer were on duty for England in the controversial tour of Italy, Yugoslavia and Romania. Fears were quickly dispersed as the general public in the three countries greeted the visitors in a most welcoming fashion. In Milan against Italy Lawton put England ahead from a Matthews corner in the 19th minute when his reactive header caught Aldo Olivieri unawares. Amedeo Biavati levelled two minutes after the start of the second half and was involved in the controversial goal that gave the Italians a 2-1 lead on 63 minutes. He passed to Carlo Piola, who had his back to goal and clearly handled it before hooking it past Vic Woodley. Despite England's protests the German referee, Dr Bauwens, after consulting his linesman, allowed the goal. It almost produced a diplomatic incident after the match – with the Italian hierarchy on England's side! However, 13 minutes from the end, Hall equalised for 2-2.

Five days later – in Belgrade for Yugoslavia in oppressively sweltering heat – an early injury to Eddie Hapgood disrupted the England defence. Even so they had chances to score and the young Yugoslav goalkeeper, Lubomir Lovritsch, a law student in his first full international, needed to be aware. Once, he bravely flung himself at Lawton's feet to prevent a certain strike. But Svetislav Glišović put the hosts in front on 16 minutes, then Frank Broome made it 1-1 on the half-hour. Nikola Perlić scored what proved to be the winner on 58 minutes, as opponents Yugoslavia presented themselves as physically tough and resilient throughout.

In Bucharest it was dull, cold and a nasty Romanian wind was blowing. The visiting team had been shuffled due to Hapgood's injury absence and several other players were given a game. Len Goulden gave England an eighth-minute lead and Don Welsh scored a second within minutes, heading in from a cross by Broome. Lawton was presented with an easy one but whacked it over the bar. Generally, with his reputation preceding him throughout the trio of matches, Lawton was well taken care of, but after a gruelling season at all levels his stock remained high.

CHAPTER FOUR

War and Called Up to Become PT Instructor

THE MUNICH fiasco of September 1938 having floated Prime Minister Neville Chamberlain's flimsy paper trail into history, the Germans had taken the Sudetenland and six months later marched into Czechoslovakia. In a further escalation, Poland was the latest facing invasion. Yet, despite the worsening political scene in Europe, football plans still went ahead as normal. Everton's trial match saw the Whites beat the first-team Blues 4-3 but Tommy Lawton scored twice, described as two 'gems', for the losing team, one of them a charming gliding header. But Everton lost the Jubilee Fund game 2-1 to Liverpool, though again it was Lawton who obliged with the Blues counter.

Brentford opened 1939/40 at Goodison Park and Everton had no new faces in their line-up. The *Sunday Mirror* reported that the quickest goal on record was avoided when Tommy topped his effort rather than striking it correctly – in two seconds – a newspaper sensation rather than fact but the point was understood. Lawton did get on the scoresheet amid claims for offside and it was just as well as Brentford went home with a 1-1 draw. Then on the Monday at Villa Park, Everton looked more like a championship-winning team, winning 2-1, Lawton heading in the best goal of the three on view on 16 minutes.

On the following Friday, Hitler entered Poland. England and France demanded a withdrawal with a deadline of Sunday at 11 o'clock by which to agree. Children in London and the south were to be evacuated to safer areas on the Saturday, and several kick-off times were altered to accommodate these movements.

Unchanged Everton played at Blackburn and drew 2-2, Lawton bagging both goals. He had scored four of Everton's five goals so far in the First Division, Bentham scoring the other one. With no response from Germany, war was declared the following day and all entertainments instantly stopped. The Football League programme was scrapped, players' contracts cancelled but clubs kept their registrations. Depending on whatever happened on the war front at home, some form of football might be possible later on.

With restrictions on the size of crowds, friendly matches began within a couple of weeks and eventually regional league competitions were started with players paid 30 shillings a week if they had a game. Guest players would be allowed providing the club holding their registration agreed. Everton lost a friendly 2-1 at Blackpool on 16 September, Lawton scoring, but he was unable to play the following week at Bury. He then had a 33rd-minute low drive finding the net in the 3-3 draw with Preston North End. In a 4-1 win against Liverpool on 7 October, the day after Lawton's 20th birthday, he scored with two scorching efforts. Tommy might be on fire in attack but tragically by then Warsaw was in flames and neither England nor France had done anything to assist the Poles. Two minutes from the end of the friendly with Burnley, Lawton kept up his scoring run in every game as his former club were beaten 4-0.

Meanwhile, the FA had recruited players for the armed services as PT instructors. From Everton, Joe Mercer was one of the first for the Army, followed by the skipper Willie Cook. Mercer was in Group 1 at Aldershot, while Group 2 had Cook and Cliff Britton.

In the regional football groupings Everton were placed in the 12-strong Western League that included Liverpool, Tranmere and the two Manchester clubs. Stoke City were the first visitors to Goodison Park, on 21 October, the players being paid to play again at the Football League-stipulated rate of 30 shillings (£1.50) a week to 11 players and one reserve. Everton chucked away a four-goal lead and had to share eight goals as Tommy Sale hit a hat-trick for Stoke. Lawton scored his only goal two minutes after the interval.

New Brighton proved to be no pushovers in Everton's next match, with only a Gillick goal on 41 minutes overcoming them. Lawton blazed one over the bar and found amateur centre-half and Liverpool Corporation worker Steve Hughes a tough opponent. Hughes managed to achieve the feat of preventing the England international from scoring for the first time in the season.

In a midweek affair for the Red Cross Fund, Lawton and Mercer were respectively on duty on either side for the Football League v All-British XI at Goodison. The maximum attendance allowed was 15,000 and six goals were equally shared. Tommy was held well by his Everton colleague TG Jones. Then in Saturday's Western League match against Manchester City, Lawton was back on the scoring trail with a goal and another disallowed in Everton's 3-1 win.

It was international time on 18 November, and Lawton and Mercer were in the England team against Wales in Wrexham. The match ended 3-2 to England with all five goals coming in a second-half spell of 12 minutes. Tommy's effort was from a left-foot drive that was headed into his own net by Everton colleague Tommy Jones.

At the weekend it was also announced that Tommy would be moving away to Leicester on war work at a firm situated between Coventry and Leicester. There was an agreement between the club and Leicester City for him to be a guest player. Tom Bromilow, the City manager, was the brother-in-law of Everton secretary Theo Kelly and had been Lawton's boss at Burnley! Tommy's work consisted of filling containers with Army No.9s and other pills for the troops. There had been hopes that he could still get to Merseyside on matchdays, but his work did not finish until noon on Saturdays. Much later, in the 27 April 1940 edition of *Picture Post*, there was a photograph of Tommy Lawton signing on at the labour exchange. This photograph was clearly taken months previously as there was a caption referring to him playing for the Army in France! But there was a war on.

On 25 November 1939 Lawton made his first guest appearance for Leicester City in the Midland League. It was a scoring debut but Birmingham won 3-1 at Filbert Street. A few minutes from the end in fading light Tommy managed to force the ball in with Brummie's keeper Harry Hibbs left completely in the dark! The following week Tommy was on international duty for England against Scotland at Newcastle and on target after ten minutes with one of the goals in the 2-1 win. Matthews dropped the ball invitingly near the posts and, though Tommy was closely policed by Baxter, he reacted quickly to forehead the ball that caught Dawson in goal napping. He might have had another but hit it straight at the Scottish goalkeeper. Again the maximum crowd allowed of 15,000 was achieved.

On the morning of 9 December Lawton had to register for military service after receiving his calling-up orders, but he managed to reach Walsall in the afternoon for his second Leicester outing. Tommy hit a right-foot shot in the tenth minute that reached home, scored a second from an Eastham pass just before half-time and completed his hat-trick on 57 minutes, all this from his only three chances according to reports.

A week later Leicester entertained Luton Town and Lawton obliged with a goal on 36 minutes, trapping the ball just inside the penalty area and finding the target in a 3-3 draw. It was his fifth strike in three matches. In the run-up to Christmas, Lawton's work then took him to a post in the Liverpool area.

Tommy was back with a bang in an Everton shirt at neighbouring Prenton Park against Tranmere Rovers on 23 December and there was a pre-Christmas bonanza of goals, 9-2 in Everton's favour. Lawton was back, hitting the third and fourth with great drives on target, plus the sixth and ninth for a four-timer. Goalkeeper Ted Sagar was allowed to take a penalty, too, but had it saved and had to scramble back to the other end in haste!

Christmas Day saw a friendly with Liverpool at Anfield and Tommy scored one goal in the 3-2 win but missed the return as he was on call for the Football League against the All-British XI in Wolverhampton. It was a first-class exhibition at Molineux with 13,647 viewing and, according to the *Yorkshire Post*, Tommy scored a splendid header in the 75th minute as the six goals were shared. Late changes in both teams escaped many reports. For example, Stan Cullis failed to make the kick-off; Dick Rhodes, once of Wolves but then Rochdale, deputised for 15 minutes, before Cullis turned up and came on as a substitute amid cheers.

On 30 December it was another friendly, with Blackpool visiting Goodison. There were chances galore, mostly missed, but the Tangerines achieved away-day success, 3-2, although Lawton scored one of the Everton goals. In another friendly, on New Year's Day, Everton visited Southport, the match finishing 2-2, and Tommy was on the mark with a sweet header from a corner kick.

At last, it was back to competitive fare on 6 January 1940 with Manchester United at Everton. United goalkeeper John Breedon saved one penalty from Alex Stevenson but Lawton's blast from another spot kick might have needed several others to prevent it. Everton won 3-2. Events off the field were about to speed up as well, but first there was the Liverpool Senior Cup match with Tranmere Rovers and the sense that another high-scoring affair was likely. Indeed, there were eight goals divided equally and a replay was necessary. Lawton opened the scoring in the first minute with a low drive into the corner of the net, had two disallowed, the second when he appeared to handle, and another attempt that was scooped suspiciously off the line.

That weekend of 13 January the engagement was announced between Tommy Lawton and Miss Rosaleen May Kavanagh of Brindle Cottage, Walton, Liverpool, whose photograph was published on the front page of the *Liverpool Evening Express* on 15 January. She had worked in a chemist's shop near Goodison and they met when Tommy was on his way to training. But Tommy's call to other arms was likely soon, too. Previously it had been reported elsewhere that he might be joining the RAF to be trained as a physical training instructor.

Meantime, it was another Western League fixture, this time against Wrexham on 20 January, and the nearest to any kind of a goal was when Lawton fired just wide of an upright in a goalless draw at the Racecourse Ground. He was also pencilled in for yet another League v All-British affair at Bradford on 2 March, but on 29 January it was announced that Lawton had started an Army PT instructor's course 'somewhere in the south' – which was actually Aldershot, home of the British Army. Two days later he was late leaving Lime Street for points south.

The Army had already decided he would become part of the touring team to go to France entertaining Allied troops – even though he had barely climbed into khaki. With conscription long in place for the French, the opposing team were taken from the Maginot Line! It was said the Army team, paid 22 shillings (£1.10p), represented £100,000 of football talent. On 20 January there had been an Army v England XI at Selhurst Park, the soldiers losing by the odd goal in seven. The BBC had broadcast the match with writer Ivan Sharpe as commentator.

Since weather forecasting was forbidden anywhere in the media lest it gave aid and comfort plus information to the enemy, 3 February provided just one football match in the land at Plymouth. It was not for the want of goals, as Argyle beat Bristol City 10-3.

On 7 February, the Army FA announced that Lawton would play centre-forward against the French team in four days' time but there were newspaper reports that Tommy might turn out for Charlton Athletic against Chelsea that weekend! This apparently emanated from one of the Addicks players, George Green, who was on the same course at Aldershot, having written to the Charlton manager Jimmy Seed suggesting Tommy might be a useful addition to their front line!

But the Army repulsed the idea and Tommy crossed the Channel, one of five in the party who were poor sailors. Sergeant-Instructor Joe Mercer commented: 'Tommy arrived wearing an ill-fitting Private's uniform.' The party stayed at the British Leave Club – clearly trying to get away even in those days! However, they were feted by the local population. This was still very much part of the Phoney War scenario.

Many British troops were among the 35,000 crowd at the Parc des Princes on Sunday, 11 February singing the 'Beer Barrel Polka' and surprisingly the Army team had to swallow the fact that they only drew 1-1 with the French. All 11 French players had been in the international team that had beaten Portugal 3-2 on the same ground on 28 January. Skipper Stan Cullis remarked: 'They were one of the best international teams we have played since 1937.' Maurice Edelston, the Reading amateur, scored after 30 seconds, Henri Hiltl levelling seven minutes later. It was then on to Reims for another tilt, where Cullis sustained a head injury but Eric Stephenson's goal on 15 minutes gave the Army victory. The short tour was wound up in Lille on Sunday, 18 February. Lawton was left out of the side this time but scorers Stephenson and Joe Mercer provided a 2-1 success.

Back to PTI course matters, Lawton was proving to be one of the most popular on the course, and Frank Swift was said to be the life and soul of the entire group. However, on 24 February that Charlton guest outing gave him the chance to play against Brentford, his presence boosting the gate, although he was off target in the Addicks' 3-2 win. A week later, playing at Portsmouth, it was another win, 3-1, but again there were no Lawton goals; however, he was getting back to something like match fitness.

The next phase for Tommy was the need to return to the goal standard, Army duties permitting of course. On 6 March, the opportunity arose just a short distance from Queens Avenue, the HQ of the Army Physical Training Corps in Aldershot, at the Recreation Ground home of the Third Division (South) team. They had a rearranged League South 'B' fixture with Chelsea. Shots manager Bill McCracken was also on the prowl for top-class players to complete his team and naturally Tommy Lawton fitted the bill perfectly. Frank Swift went with him and there was one other international, Tom Brolly, the Millwall and Northern Ireland wing-half. There were four of Aldershot's own players and a delayed kick-off.

In Aldershot's subsequent programme notes, the writer commented on the Shots' 5-1 win as follows: 'You never in your life saw such cleverly manoeuvred goals and yet they all looked so simple. Chelsea could also have had three or four.'

Lawton was part of a four-man move that gave Aldershot an interval lead through Queens Park Rangers' Johnny Pattison. After just three minutes of the second half, Jimmy Hagan (Sheffield United) was brought down and Tommy's spot kick was so fierce that it went in off the Scotland international goalkeeper Johnny Jackson's right leg. Lawton then made the third and fourth goals for Pattison and George Raynor, respectively. Peter Buchanan replied for Chelsea but Lawton headed in with 12 minutes remaining for a fifth goal, as the light then began to fade. The following week at Southampton, with no Swift in goal, Lawton was made captain and scored, memorably, twice with some force but the hat-trick chance went awry. Although his penalty attempt was of such ferocity that it struck the Saints goalkeeper Eugene Bernard on the shoulder and knocked him into the back of the net, the ball lifted over the bar! In between these two games Lawton had been a reserve for the Army against the Football League at Liverpool.

On Good Friday, 22 March, Sergeant-Instructor Tommy Lawton passed out as a PTI and was posted to Birkenhead. The *Topical Times* interviewed him: 'The course was harder than anything I've ever done in training. Yet I now weigh 13st 11lb and never felt better,' Tommy said. The same day he turned out again for Everton, after a lengthy absence, in a friendly at Goodison against Wolves. Everton won 4-2 but there were no Lawton goals, although every effort had been made by his colleagues to get him on the scoresheet. The following day he played again for Everton, in a 2-1 defeat at Crewe. However, the *Liverpool Echo* reporter commented: 'He has completely lost his shooting power.' Later, Lawton replied by saying that at Aldershot he 'had been hitting them from 30 yards and they were going in like bullets'. Judging by two of those penalty kicks, the strength was there, if the direction was slightly out of kilter.

The return friendly at Molineux on Easter Monday was drawn 2-2 but Lawton again was not a marksman. Liverpool were due at Goodison on 30 March; could this be the breakthrough for a desperate Lawton to renew his affinity for Everton goals?

There were two goals within a minute but both were Liverpool ones, from Billy Liddell and Berry Nieuwenhuys in the 28th and 29th minutes. This put Everton on the defensive again at Goodison. Lawton did manage a goal on 82 minutes with a right-foot shot in a crowded goal area from a pass from Cec Wyles, but Liverpool won 3-1. The *Liverpool Daily Post* reiterated its previous comments: 'Lawton is right out of touch with his game.' He had another goal disallowed in the match when he bundled both ball and goalkeeper Arthur Riley into the net.

On 3 April, another home game, this time against Stockport County, produced a runaway 7-0 success for Everton with two goals from Lawton, one from a penalty. But, three days later, there was another disappointment, losing 2-1 at Port Vale, although the standard of play from both sides was good. Tommy missed a sitter in this one, too. Games were still coming at a steady rate – even a friendly over-45s match at Ellesmere Port Town's ground, one team skippered by Joe Mercer made up from local trades people, the other from Bowaters with Lawton as captain. Both Joe and Tommy were playing at centre-half!

The next day Lawton was in an Army XI against Chester and scored once in a 3-0 victory and had another disallowed. However, interestingly enough, in a newspaper interview around this time, he did reveal a reason for his present form – due to his work as a physical training instructor. 'While I get plenty of exercise and fresh air, it isn't the kind of exercise that improves your speed off the mark. I have felt for some time that I was getting slower from the off,' he said. 'The same goes in sizing up situations – and other PTIs have agreed with me.'

On 13 April, the Lancashire Senior Cup semi-final at Goodison was watched by a crowd of 13,563, and it renewed the local challenge against Liverpool. Everton were clearly on top of this one, winning 4-1. Lawton headed a goal and received a fist in his face from South African goalkeeper Dirk Kemp in the process. He also neatly made Bentham's second goal.

The Football League was about to launch its War Cup to revive interest in the game as the regional competitions had failed to grip the public's imagination, although, as *Mass Observation* reported, for a variety of understandable wartime reasons attendance at matches was down 65 per cent on pre-war figures. Everton faced a tricky tie with home and away legs against Preston North End. But before that there was another Western League tilt with Tranmere, always good for a goalscoring affair.

In this one Rovers still had the edge on the hour. Albert Malam headed them ahead on 32 minutes but Stevenson levelled five minutes before the break. Bentham gave Everton the lead on 55 minutes before a back-pass own goal from Maurice Lindley made it 2-2. Manchester United's Charlie Mitten, on guest duty, pushed Rovers in front on the hour. Then a dramatic fightback by Everton produced goals for Lawton (penalty), Mercer and Boyes for 5-3 at the final whistle. Only 1,142 attended in a match in which Everton's third-team winger Billy Sumner was given an outing.

The first leg of the War League Cup on 20 April at Goodison against Preston North End proved to be a classic. Preston certainly opened with the greater confidence. After 16 minutes Jimmy Dougal gave them the lead and it was not until a minute from the interval that Everton's considerable improvement produced a goal, Jones heading in Barber's corner. Previously, Harry Holdcroft had just prevented a Lawton header finding home. Some neat work between Stevenson and Barber produced Everton's second on 49 minutes for the Irish international and Boyes much later buried his own rebound for a 3-1 first-leg lead.

Lawton was not selected for the British Army team against Scotland on 24 April but three days later came the second instalment of the War Cup against Preston. It proved to be another absorbing encounter. Bobby Beattie should have put Preston ahead on 25 minutes but only shot at Sagar. Dougal hit a post then scored twice in two minutes just after the half-hour to give Preston a 2-0 half-time lead. On 49 minutes there was another Beattie miskick and the ball was cleared up to Lawton, who forced Bob Batey into a rare error and then beat Jack Fairbrother. Tommy later suffered a knee injury in a collision with the goalkeeper. At the death, Bentham levelled the scores at 2-2 to allow Everton to progress 5-3 on aggregate.

Rochdale were up next in the War Cup, with the first leg at Goodison. It was a bit of a scrappy affair at first but Lawton was quickly into it, beating three opponents before firing just wide. It was TG Jones who opened Everton's scoring with a fine header five minutes before the interval. Bentham had previously hit the bar and a Lawton penalty claim was turned down; however, there were signs that the old Tommy was on the case. Within eight minutes of the second half starting he had scored twice, although, in fairness, it was when Joe Duff had gone off for repairs, leaving Rochdale vulnerable. But as the *Rochdale Observer* remarked: 'Lawton only needed half a lapse let alone a chance.' Duff resumed and Lawton completed his 'real' hat-trick. Ten minutes from time Doug Redwood netted for Rochdale only for Stevenson to make it four for Everton, who then added a fifth for a comfortable first-leg lead.

For the second leg at Willbutts Lane, Rochdale, Everton had to make changes. Jones was out injured so Maurice Lindley moved to centre-half, with Wyles to his right and Sumner on the right wing. The latter scored a splendid opener, taking Lawton's pass and rounding Bill Byrom to finish expertly after eight minutes. Everton then took their foot off the pedal and Arthur Richardson made them pay after 16 minutes. In the second half they almost lost their gears completely. On 49 minutes Davie Colquhoun lobbed Sagar, then, midway through the half, Duff twice gained revenge by turning centres into goals to move to within just one goal of parity on aggregate. Wyles spoiled it all for Rochdale from a Lawton pass to make it 4-2 to the Spotland boys who added another to win 5-2 on the day but Everton progressed 7-6 on aggregate. The *Rochdale Observer* headlined: 'Rochdale almost shock the Soccer world.'

There were just two days to recover before the Liverpool Senior Cup Final against Liverpool. However, this proved to be no problem as Everton were four up in just over half an hour through Bentham in the first minute, a Matt Busby own goal on eight minutes, Caskie after 19 minutes and Jones with 36 minutes on the clock. Busby hit one at the right end six minutes into the second half, then Nieuwenhuys reduced the deficit for Liverpool to make it 4-2 after 58 minutes, before Lawton got in on the act after 67 minutes and Stevenson with two minutes left. There was still time for 'Nivvy' to hit another Liverpool goal in their 6-3 defeat. It was Everton's 26th Liverpool Cup trophy, this time playing to a crowd of just 5,834.

Three days later and Lawton was in Joe Mercer's Everton plus guest stars team for a Red Cross Charity match at Ellesmere Port Town's ground against Tom Corley's XI who won 2-1. This came a mere two days before the knockout War Cup tie against Stoke City, which was settled by just one goal, a Lawton blockbuster of a penalty hit after Stevenson had been shoved in the back.

Now came a rearranged Western League game at home to Wrexham on 22 May. Only 589 turned up to see the visitors score two in three minutes at the start of the second half, and the meagre Everton response was a successful and typical Lawton-type glided header in the 88th minute, which was insufficient for the day.

Thus, there was little inspiration when facing Fulham at Craven Cottage in the War Cup three days later. Two goals in the first 90 seconds, by Viv Woodward and then Ronnie Rooke, put Everton on the back foot and they were almost in the dressing room when Jimmy McCormick made it 3-0 after 20 minutes. Lawton clawed one back five minutes later but any prospect of a recovery was ruined a minute after the break. Woodward scored his second Fulham goal with a shot that hit Greenhalgh's leg on the way in. Gillick managed another Everton goal, Tommy hit a post, but Johnny Arnold made it four for Fulham. Charlie Gee, in at centre-half for the injured Jones, had a torrid time trying to hold Rooke and then gave away a penalty. Woodward scored but the referee nullified it as McCormick had encroached into the area. Sagar saved the re-take but Everton went down 5-2. *The People* said Everton had been hit by 'blitzkrieg' – well, someone had to mention it first.

Four days later it was another rearranged league game, this time at Stockport County. Everton took two points from this one, with teenager Sid Simmons and Bentham the scorers in a 2-1 win. Simmons had previously hit two in a Lawton-less win over Crewe in November. Then Everton's final Western League fixture came on 1 June at Old Trafford against Manchester United. It was a personal triumph for Alex Stevenson. Four minutes from the end of what looked like being only their second goalless draw of the season, he scored two in a minute, had another saved at the second attempt by Ed Goodall, a guest from Bolton, but still managed to score his hat-trick on the final whistle! Sagar had saved a seventh-minute penalty from Alex Herd (Manchester City guest). In the final standings Everton finished third in the table behind champions Stoke City, but also behind runners-up Liverpool!

It all left the Lancashire Senior Cup to be disputed with Bury, who won the toss for the match to be played at Gigg Lane.

Tom Burdett gave the Shakers the lead after seven minutes and they also hit the woodwork twice. Then Lawton from a penalty on 15 minutes and Bentham with a superb header on 32 minutes gave Everton an interval lead. George Davies scored Bury's second but Lawton, with a hard low effort into the corner, made it 3-2 and Stevenson scored one with a header, which broke badly on the hard surface and found its way in for 4-2. The attendance was 3,522. Lindley joined the RAF after the match.

Everton had succeeded in completing the season without having to use any guest players. Of course, with the continuing call-up for the armed forces, this situation was unlikely to remain. Lawton had played in 20 Western League and War Cup matches, scoring 18 goals. While he struck out in his two Charlton outings, Tommy had four counters in two Aldershot appearances and was into double figures in the two Senior Cups plus Everton friendly games. For the first time since his schooldays he had averaged well above a goal a game.

While the threat of invasion remained, early Dunkirk survivors were cheered at the War Cup Final at Wembley. Then with the miracle achieved on the coast signalling the end of the Phoney War and Winston Churchill off the bench to play a full part, it was left to the RAF in the Battle of Britain to prevent us losing the war.

CHAPTER FIVE

Football and the Battle of Britain

IN 1940/41 there was a shock for Blues fans at the start of the second wartime season when Tommy Lawton appeared in a red shirt! Though it wasn't an Anfield design – it belonged to Tranmere Rovers in their trial match. He was in the second stringers opposing the likely first team wearing Blue. However, he had Joe Mercer for company and both were given permission by the Everton club for this temporary loan. Even so, it was a surprise that these two Evertonians were merely a couple among only five professional footballers appearing in that team, as Tranmere were to rely chiefly on amateurs in the season.

The 'guest' pair finished on the losing side 3-2 but Lawton had the satisfaction of scoring both goals for the Reds, though one was definitely a dodgy affair unlikely to have been allowed in a more competitive encounter.

With the Football League abandoning the unpopular regional groupings, they produced something that proved even less palatable. The country was split into two – North Regional and South Regional – with a small additional competition in the south. Points were replaced by goal average as it was unlikely that all teams would be able to play an equal number of games due to travel problems. It was not expected of clubs to venture too far out of their regions, though Everton did. Lancashire Cup matches were also included in the final table!

On 31 August, the new-look campaign started for Everton at Manchester City, the visiting team playing in white. It was clearly to be a red, white and blue season for Tommy Lawton! He went close on two occasions, with foot and head keeping Frank Swift busy in the City goal. Everton had a promising newcomer at outside-left, Alf Penlington, and Tommy nodded one of the youngster's centres just wide of the target and the match ended goalless.

A week later, it was the return match at Goodison Park. Lawton put Stevenson through only for him to hit the woodwork, then Lawton and Penlington had shots blocked. In the 35th minute Stevenson's effort was stopped but quickly locked on to by Lawton, whose terrific effort beat Swift for what proved to be the only goal of the game. Everton had nine of their championship-winning team on view, plus the young wingers Sumner and Penlington.

There was then a midweek charity diversion for the Army Comforts Fund when the Western Command met a Czech Army XI at Anfield. It was a feast of scoring with the strong services outfit winning 12-6! Tommy Lawton bagged four for himself.

With Preston North End's Deepdale being used for security purposes, Everton played them at the Leyland Sports Ground in the next regional league match. With Stevenson on target after eight minutes, then Gordon Bailey 20 minutes later after Lawton had forced Holdcroft into action, Everton relaxed two goals ahead. Jimmy Dougal snatched one back for Preston before half-time and they saved the game with a second-half equaliser from Cliff Mansley.

The following Monday the Czech Army were on duty once more, this time at Tranmere Rovers – proceeds for the Spitfire Fund. Lawton again had permission to assist, helping his younger colleagues to a 5-2 win, scoring once himself. But on 21 September Chester's visit to Goodison was a real wake-up call. The *Chester Observer* considered that the Cestrians' first-half performance was nothing short of 'copybook football'. They also succeeded in finding the net on more than one occasion.

Chester raced three ahead within 29 minutes, but after a Lawton attempt being followed up by Stevenson heading in, Everton reduced the deficit before half-time. After the break it was the 'Lawton 45 minutes'. Within five minutes he fired in a real stinger. Then, in combination with the debutant amateur winger C R (Charlie) Lewis – said to be 17 but really 19 – he levelled the scores and completed his hat-trick with a header. The trio of goals was accomplished in just 16 minutes. The *Liverpool Echo* said the dashing and deadly Tommy had been 'unstoppable'. Another prospect from the A team, Norman Hankin, had played right-half, Mercer having gone to centre-half with Jones absent. Everton won 4-3.

Leeds United were the next visitors to Goodison, on 28 September, and by now there had been widespread air raids, not only in the south of the country. In the fifth minute Stevenson was put through cleverly by Lawton for the first strike. Everton's lead lasted only five minutes before Malcolm Baird equalised. Everton applied the pressure from then on, though, scoring through Mercer with a spectacular effort, a brace from Bentham and a peach of one from Lawton as they coasted to 5-1. After the match it was announced that Tommy was to return 'to the south' for a PTI refresher course. So it was back to Aldershot.

On 5 October, Tommy took the trip with Aldershot to Southampton, with Swift also in tow once more. It was one goal each at half-time but 3-2 to Aldershot at the final whistle. The first two Aldershot goals were scored by Joe Proud and Bill Chalmers, Tommy hitting their third. Don Roper and Les Laney were the two Saints marksmen. A week later and *The People* newspaper splashed: 'Lawton gives full value for money!' It was Aldershot 5 Bristol City 1 at the Recreation Ground and Tommy had scored a treble. Hagan and an own goal by Cliff Morgan completed their scoring, with Lance Carr replying for City.

Back on the south coast at Portsmouth on 19 October, Aldershot led on 20 minutes when Chalmers crossed, Bill Rochford slipped in defence and Proud opened the scoring. Charlton's Don Welsh, on guest duty for the Shots, made it 2-0 on 29 minutes and winger Proud hit his second three minutes later. Lawton then set up for Welsh but the chance went astray so the score remained 3-0 at half-time. Pompey responded with a second-half goal through Andy Black (Manchester City).

On 26 October Lawton was back for Everton at home to a virile Bury team that included a few Bolton Wanderers guest players. Mercer played at outside-right but missed an early easy chance and went to inside-forward in the second half. Everton were two ahead within 15 minutes through Bentham and Lawton before Carter got one back for Bury. However, with 15 minutes remaining Stevenson scored Everton's third goal to seal a 3-1 victory. Ted Sagar reported for Army duties after the game.

The return at Gigg Lane was played on a heavy pitch and, with Sagar absent, Percy Lovett took over between the posts.

Gordon Watson was at outside-left and Harry Finnis, a 29-year-old local lad, was introduced at left-half. The Shakers again lived up to their nickname and scored twice in the first half through George Davies and Tom Burdett, the latter with an unusual one! Lovett, who had played well on his debut, cleared the ball, which hit the Bury forward on the head and knocked him over, with the ball careering into the goal! Simmons replied for Everton midway through the second half but Bury hung on for a 2-1 win.

Manchester United were at Goodison Park on 9 November and were first on the attack but it was repulsed and, from Stevenson's centre at the other end, Mercer finished adroitly for a two-minute Everton lead. Both teams produced clever football and strong attempts on goal. Lovett in the Blues goal was alert and busy but not as under pressure as John Breedon between the United posts. He faced a Lawton in real determined mood. The *Liverpool Echo* reported: 'Tommy Lawton only had four real chances and cracked in four of the real old-time Lawton goals.' Remember, this is comment on a player still aged only 20. Tommy's first came from 29 yards, the second from just outside the area, the third just after the goalkeeper had punched the ball away and the fourth from Stevenson's neat back-heel.

The handful of Everton goals might have flattered them as Lovett had to be constantly aware. He had twice beaten down shots before having no chance of stopping Jack Smith from netting, then Jock Dodds strode through all opposition for the second United counter. However, Everton came away with a 5-2 victory.

In sharp contrast, a week later in the return it was both teams' defences that dominated proceedings. Again they both adopted an attacking strategy, Everton playing it close and

Manchester United having more of an open approach. The nearest to an actual score came in the second half when, with Breedon out of position, Lawton drove fiercely towards the goal only for the keeper to fling himself across his untended goal, the ball hitting his body and going out of play! So it was goalless at Old Trafford and a display of expert defence worthy of more than the 2,000 attending.

Seven days further on the calendar, 23 November, brought another amazing turnaround of a result. At Prenton Park, home of Tranmere Rovers, Everton won 9-0! The previous week Rovers had conceded ten goals at New Brighton. Tranmere's young amateur goalkeeper Walter Teasdale was constantly in action, although Everton, who eased off, might easily have added more to their score in the second half. Lawton scored a first-half hat-trick, netting in the second, 12th and 27th minutes. Stevenson's own treble came firstly on six minutes, then the last couple in the 75th and 80th minutes. Simmons netted twice after a quarter of an hour and on 58 minutes, with John Arthur from the right wing hitting the other goal on 22 minutes. Boyes, who had obtained leave the week before for his first Everton game of the season at Old Trafford, was the only non-scoring forward.

The following week, a service call across the border into Scotland meant that Tommy was playing for the Army in England against the similar lads in Scotland. With the calibre of players on view, it was almost a mini-international. The visitors won 4-1 but Lawton did not score. There were further demands on many servicemen for football the following Saturday when the Army played the flyboys at two locations – Manchester and Nottingham – with Lawton in at Maine Road where the RAF won 4-2. Tommy hit one in for the khaki lads.

Tommy was back for Everton on 14 December to put Tranmere through the grinder once more at Prenton Park. Tranmere put up a better performance and had had the better of the play before Lawton opened the scoring. From then on the usual pattern emerged, though some of the goals allowed were dubious. Certainly one of Bentham's three was offside and Boyes's effort was pretty much borderline. Lawton scored a second, Simmons and Cook making eight, although plucky Tranmere had a couple of their own thanks to John Griffiths.

Lawton was next playing for the Army on 21 December against Blackpool and losing 4-2 but he scored once. He was certainly getting a variety of games and on Christmas Day was on double duty – for Everton in the morning in the 3-1 defeat at Anfield against Liverpool – Bentham scoring for the Blues – and in the afternoon as a guest for Tranmere Rovers, scoring both goals in the 2-2 draw with Crewe Alexandra!

A further complication for followers of wartime football trying to fathom the goal average system instead of points was that for Merseyside folk the Lancashire Senior Cup fixtures also counted in the overall table. Everton and Liverpool were to meet home and away on the first two Saturdays in January. On 4 January at Anfield both teams were showing many changes. Everton had the edge initially, young John Lyon at inside-left scoring memorably on his debut with a volley, then Lawton wheeling himself into position for an effort making it two before half-time. Liverpool included Teasdale – the Tranmere amateur goalkeeper who had been at the end of several shellackings for Rovers. He did well, though might have done better with Lawton's effort. Bob Paisley responded for Liverpool and they plugged away to the end for an equaliser, with Billy Liddell prominent, but Everton hung on for 2-1.

At Goodison in the second leg, Liverpool were really in with a shout for the first quarter of an hour, taking the lead through Shafto to level things up on aggregate. After that, though, it was all Everton – mostly George Jackson, the usual right-back, who was deputising for Tommy Lawton at centre-forward and scored all four goals in the 4-1 victory! He was destined never to score a goal in the Football League! But he also missed two sitters and two more when he could have reasonably scored. However, it remained a feat for which he should be applauded and it was 6-2 on aggregate and a tie against Lawton's old club Burnley to follow in two weeks.

On 15 January, on Army leave, Tommy Lawton married Rosaleen May Kavanagh at Walton Parish Church and they set off for their honeymoon in Scotland. It was not to be without football! The club arranged for a temporary transfer of Tommy to Morton and on the following Saturday he played against Hamilton Academical, scoring the first goal with a hook shot in 26 minutes of what turned out to be a 3-3 draw. The attendance of over 5,000 was double the usual gate. Tommy made good friends with Jack Calder, the player he displaced, too!

In the Lancashire Cup, renewing acquaintance with Turf Moor and Burnley, Lawton appeared with his right arm in a plaster bandage but scarcely visible under his long-sleeved shirt. He had broken a small bone in his wrist. There were team problems for Everton too. Sagar had not arrived and as kick-off time approached neither had Bentham. Frantic efforts to locate a reserve goalkeeper, due at Rossendale, proved futile. Twelfth man Simmons got changed and Burnley's A team forward Les Courtier was ready to guest for Everton when Bentham finally arrived. The previous round's four-goal hero Jackson took over in goal! You could scarcely invent this. Bob Brocklebank opened the scoring for Burnley but Lyon made it 1-1 by half-time. Lawton then obliged with a header and a tap-in from a Boyes pass but Brocklebank scored his second goal for Burnley to give the Blues a slender 3-2 first-leg advantage.

League matters returned with Barnsley making the trip from Yorkshire to Goodison Park on 1 February. Everton had another disruption to selection on the day when Watson was unable to play, which resulted in a shuffle, Bentham moving to half-back with Catterick and Lyon at inside-forward. On 14 minutes Catterick was involved in Lawton's goal, with Tommy timing his deflected header to perfection in true Dean-like execution. Mercer then conceded a penalty but Bob Shotton blasted yards wide. Lawton scored his second, again with Catterick involved, then came the best goal of the match – a free kick from Tommy Jones three yards outside the penalty area. Eric Bray pulled one back for the Tykes after Sagar had saved from Gavin Smith but 3-1 to Everton it was.

Lawton had been chosen to play for England in the first international of the season against Scotland at St James' Park, Newcastle in aid of the Red Cross. Tommy was involved in the opening goal after seven minutes when he headed down for Ralph Birkett to score. The advantage lasted but ten minutes as Joe Bacuzzi headed through his own goal after Sam Bartram had partially saved from Gordon Smith. Lawton restored England's lead five minutes before the interval but there was still time for Doug Wallace, the surprise choice from Clyde in place of Alex Venters of Rangers at inside-forward, to make it 2-2 before half-time.

Though England dominated early in the second half, they missed a number of opportunities near goal. Jerry Dawson in the Scotland goal had been at his best and midway through the period Wallace won the game for Scotland at 3-2 with a splendid 20-yard drive, vying with his goalkeeper for man of the match. Lawton's duels with Jimmy Dykes, the Hearts centre-half, were fairly even. However, the *Sunderland Echo* reporter had been unimpressed with Everton's centre-forward, referring to him being 'too slow on the turn'. Of course, he had still been involved in both England goals! As for the *Daily Mail*'s Frank Carruthers – he reckoned Wilf Mannion to have been England's best player. The attendance of 28,000 produced receipts of £2,104.

Meantime, the second edition of the League's War Cup, which had injected life into the regional fare on offer, was up for Everton a week later on 15 February away at Old Trafford in the first leg. Both teams succeeded in fielding 11 of their own players, something of an achievement. Manchester United took the initiative and led in the 15th minute from the penalty spot, Bert Whalley converting. Sagar was kept busy in the Everton goal, but three minutes before half-time Lawton snapped up a clearance, outwitting Billy Porter to steer the ball in.

While the contrast in styles was interesting – United cutting out the frills, Everton precise as ever – five minutes after the resumption Lawton again had the better of his marker and scored another fine goal. It lasted exactly two minutes before Greenhalgh slipped and Jack Rowley pounced to level the first leg at 2-2.

At Goodison in the return, Everton's left-wing international partnership of Stevenson and Boyes was unavailable. Lyon, on the eve of his 17th birthday, and Wyles replaced them. Jack Jones had to play as Watson was also missing at left-half, and Catterick took Arthur's right-wing berth. Lawton looked to have opened the scoring but Breedon, the United keeper, reacted brilliantly to prevent it. Then Rowley, with a cross shot, put United ahead in the tie before half-time and there was little between the two sides in a full-on cup match. In the second half Everton levelled when Lawton headed down for Catterick to score. Just four minutes later Tommy picked up a move started by Mercer and returned the pass for the latter to finish memorably. A better attendance of 6,598 had witnessed what the *Liverpool Evening Express* described as a 'delectable game'. Referee George Twist was also commended for his handling of it.

However, several newspapers in Scotland mentioned the imminent switch of Tommy Lawton moving to Scotland on another Army posting. Morton were said to be keen on renewing acquaintance. It did not occur, though. Instead Tommy was in the War Cup side at Goodison against Southport, who turned up neatly in green and white. With Boyes unavailable, there was the welcome return of Trentham on the left wing, partnering Stevenson. Within five minutes Lawton was on the scoresheet with a low right-foot effort from a Mercer pass, then on 19 minutes he had another with a header. Three minutes later Catterick took advantage of a defensive error for a third Everton goal and shortly afterwards grazed the bar. Lawton netted again but was offside as Everton led 3-0 at the break. In the second half Bobby Jones, the Southport goalkeeper, stopped a free kick with his knees but Catterick made it a fourth strike and TG Jones headed Everton's fifth from a corner. Lawton also ignored an open goal for a hat-trick to allow Stevenson to benefit but he missed.

For the return leg with Southport on 8 March at Haig Avenue, Stevenson resumed and Lyon moved to the wing. Catterick missed a chance early on but Lawton had rattled in four goals of his own by the break! For the first on ten minutes he barely grazed Greenhalgh's free kick with his head but it was

The fan base at its admiring best meet their idol Tommy Lawton.

Arsenal's Tommy Lawton, extreme left, gets above the Chelsea defenders.

Tommy knows all about heading, so when in Russia carry on with it.

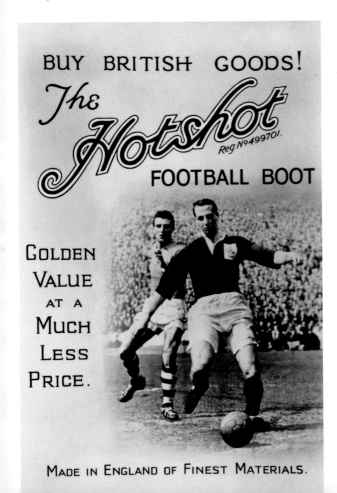

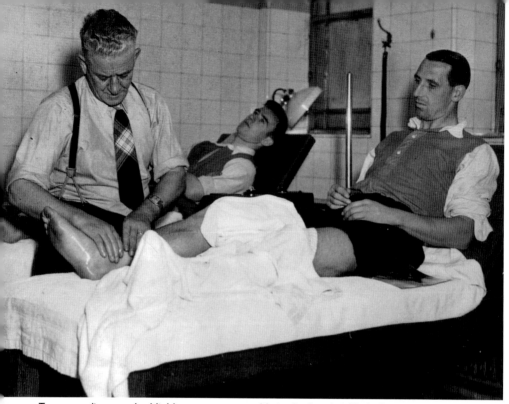

Tommy reclines on the Highbury treatment table in the hands of Bob Common.

Talking to the Notts troops, manager Tommy Lawton puts his message across.

That Tommy Lawton does pull a decent old pint at the Magna Charta.

Tommy passes a selective word or two with Pools Panel boss Lord Brabazon.

Managers meet: Ted Drake (Chelsea) and Tommy Lawton (Kettering Town). Both are former Arsenal players.

Tommy Lawton reminisces with the family album.

Tommy's testimonial at Everton. Left to right: Bobby Moore, himself, Joe Mercer and Bobby Charlton.

Notts County players line the route at the funeral of Tommy Lawton.

enough to flat-foot the Sandgrounders' goalkeeper. Number two on 17 minutes produced a net-finding drive of some quality from Lyon's pass, the youngster being given excellent assistance throughout by Alex Stevenson. Mercer was the provider for Tommy's third on 37 minutes and the fourth came from the penalty spot after Southport's goalkeeper Harry Stevenson held Lyon's leg, allowing Lawton to completed his four-timer.

Despite noticeably easing up in the second half, Everton had goals by Lawton and Mercer ruled out for offside, Lyon hit the bar and Lawton tried desperately to get Stevenson a goal but the Irishman was way off target. Bentham scored a fifth, which was their only goal in the second period, but it was a 10-0 aggregate win for the Blues. Lawton now awaited a posting back to Aldershot and TG Jones was about to join the RAF. Fortunately, Everton still had plenty of youngsters available.

Army duties now took precedence for a change and it was not until 5 April that Lawton managed another game, this for Aldershot against Brentford in the London Cup. This was a spin-off competition as the London area clubs were becoming unhappy about travel arrangements being handed them by the Football League, based in the north-west of England. The Shots lost 4-2 at Griffin Park and Tommy suffered concussion but staggered on. He was pronounced fit for the return at the Rec the next Saturday but it was a 2-2 draw and again no goals for Tommy.

However, it was not for the want of trying, and his duels over the two matches against the Brentford goalkeeper, Wales international George Poland (Liverpool), were high spots. At Griffin Park, Poland dived courageously at Tommy's feet to prevent one certain goal and went full length to divert a rasping drive from him on another occasion. At the Recreation Ground, with 3,750 attending, the Shots scored through Raynor at a second attempt, while he and Lawton lined up Jimmy Hagan for their other successful strike. The *Middlesex Chronicle* commented that 'Lawton was a constant menace'.

Then, with a spot of Army leave, Lawton returned to Merseyside and an Everton shirt for Blackpool's visit on Easter Monday. Jackson had been given yet another role, this time at left-half, while Mercer went to centre-half in Jones's absence. Lawton, quickly off from the start, had a good shot in the first minute and then fired home after 20 minutes when he dashed between two defenders to angle a fine effort into the net. He also made use of his head to give both Catterick and Lyon chances. Catterick later scored the other Everton goal but Blackpool managed a 2-2 draw.

Chosen again for the Football League XI against the All-British XI at Anfield, the fixture became arguably the finest exhibition of entertaining football to be seen during the war period. There were 16 goals scored, the League getting nine to their opponent's seven. Eleven goals came in the second half. Lively Lawton skimmed the crossbar after eluding Cullis and forced Poland into saving a header. Eric Stephenson, the Leeds United and England inside-forward, started the avalanche in the 13th minute, Berry Nieuwenhuys levelled with probably the best of the match from 18 yards three minutes later, then Dickie Dorsett put the League ahead on 24 minutes. Ten minutes before the break Cullis brought it to 2-2, then Lawton began his revenge against Poland with the first of a hat-trick on the day!

The second-half scoring sequence continued like this: (League first) – 3-3, 4-3, 5-3, 5-4, 5-5, 6-5, 7-5, 7-6, 8-6, 8-7 and 9-7. League goalkeeper Alf Hobson (Chester) had to go off injured, so Billy Liddell, who had been a spectator, was drafted in with Tom Galley having to go between the posts. Liddell scored the League's fifth goal. It was a pity only 12,000 attended but £500 was raised for charity.

Lawton was passed over by the England selectors for the games against Wales and Scotland, the thinking being that he might be unavailable because of Army duties, but it is unlikely that a request for him to be included would have been ignored by Tommy. However, in his place, Don Welsh, the versatile Charlton Athletic player, scored all four against Wales and two against the Scots!

Next for Lawton was wearing the red and blue of Aldershot against Tottenham Hotspur, visiting on 26 April, the day of the Scotland match. Andy Beattie, the Preston North End and Scotland full-back, turned out for the Shots. Sharing four goals with Spurs in the first half, including a goal from Tommy, the Whites achieved a second-half winner. The following week Fulham visited. Beattie appeared again as he had been unable to travel to turn out for Scotland at Hampden Park. Cliff Britton played right-half. Lawton scored and the Shots were leading 3-0 eight minutes before the end, before the Cottagers blew the roof off and drew 3-3!

But even more amazing matches were to come for Tommy Lawton and Aldershot. A third home match on the trot brought Queens Park Rangers to the garrison town, and they were seen off 5-1, although they had Alf Ridyard injured in the second half and, with several stitches inserted, he was advised not to continue. Britton scored a penalty, Hagan had two and Lawton was another on target. Tommy's was the first goal – one of his specials. He received a cross, pivoted on his left foot and hit a right-foot first-timer from 35 yards, which sailed home past Bill Mason.

Aldershot also went nap the following week, at least in scoring, but dropped off as far as sustaining a likely win. It was the Hampshire Combination Cup semi-final at Fratton Park against Portsmouth. Aldershot led 3-0 before Pompey managed one before the break. Lawton made it 4-1 early in the second half before a home rally took it to 4-4. Albert Dawes restored Aldershot's advantage to complete a hat-trick, only for a linesman's flag leading to a move that gave parity to Pompey once more. Extra time was played and Portsmouth ran riot, scoring five more goals for an incredible 10-5 win. Two of the goals were dubious – one for a free kick for some obscure offence, another blatantly offside.

On 24 May Tommy finally played another game for Everton, against Sheffield United at Goodison Park. Everton had struggled in recent weeks without Lawton, winning only one of a handful of games. Tommy did oblige with a rocket shot of a goal but the Blades cut a dash of their own and were worth the 3-3 draw.

Then it was payback time for Aldershot – Portsmouth, complete with six of the FA Cup-winning team of 1939 on parade at the Recreation Ground. Well represented, too, Aldershot had Stan Cullis playing his first game as a guest. Both Hagan and Lawton, linking up brilliantly with each other, hit hat-tricks, Britton put away another spot kick and, leading 4-0 at the interval, Aldershot went on to win 9-2! That would have wiped off the drenching they had received off the Solent! There was then one more fixture for Tommy with the Shots against Watford on 6 June at the Rec, and he responded with another treble in the 3-1 win.

CHAPTER SIX

Shots Benefit from the Tommy Touch

TOMMY LAWTON was no stranger to appearing in another club's pre-season trial match. He had done so at Tranmere Rovers with the permission of Everton, and on 23 August 1941 he added Aldershot to his CV. Shots players and guests from other clubs were stationed locally in the Army, so Tommy played for the Red and Blues against the Black and Whites – his immediate opposite at centre-half was his old adversary Stan Cullis of Wolves and England fame. Jimmy Hagan from Sheffield United was inside-right alongside Lawton.

It was an atrocious day of torrential rain and ruined the gate plus the proceeds for the Mayor's Air Raid Distress Fund, as only 200 drenched souls braved the elements for the occasion. The duel between Lawton and Cullis was the highlight. Tommy scored twice in the first half, Hagan once but Cecil Ray, the pre-war Shots centre-forward, managed a goal for the Black and Whites a minute into the second half. It was estimated that the 22 players had represented £50,000 worth of talent.

The London League had now formed as a breakaway organisation from the Football League, with its entire complement of 16 clubs stripped of their FL membership and regarded as rebels. Coincidentally, in the opening fixture they produced a fixture list for Aldershot to play at Fulham, where Cullis was a guest player opposing Lawton! The result of this renewed clash was double the ratio of goals, Aldershot winning 6-2. Tommy hit the first, Hagan the second. They both had two each by the end, with George Taylor (Bolton Wanderers) and Herbert Glasby (Military Police and an Aldershot amateur signing) also scoring for the Shots. Ronnie Rooke snatched the Fulham goals, including a lucky penalty.

A week on and Tottenham Hotspur at the Recreation Ground produced a contrast in styles, with Spurs' combination against better individual play from the home team. First, Jackie Gibbons neatly put away a good opportunity for Spurs. Then Harry Bamford (Brentford) crossed from the wing for the Shots and Ginger Palmer levelled. Cliff Britton, one of Tommy's Everton colleagues, found him with a pass and Lawton let loose from 30 yards. Percy Hooper in the Spurs goal was off his line but managed to knock the ball down, then fell full length and made a grab at the ball but the pace was such that it still went in. Lawton was sandwiched, elbowed and finally floored. Britton's penalty acumen did the rest. Gibbons scored his second of two cleverly conceived goals for Spurs, but they were beaten 3-2.

Britton, Hagan and Lawton were on duty for the Army's tour in Ireland, so Aldershot had to manage at Portsmouth without them. During the match, Andy Black, racing forward, careered into the goal, pulling down the net and woodwork to bring an end to the affair 13 minutes from time! Immediate repairs were impossible, so the London League decided the 2-2 result would stand.

Lawton did not play in the first match in Belfast against Ireland but Hagan scored a hat-trick in the 4-1 win. In the second game against British troops based there Tommy scored twice in the 6-1 win, up against Sagar in goal. His first goal came when he outran Tom Brolly for possession.

On 27 September Hagan and Lawton returned to Aldershot colours at home to Charlton Athletic led by Don Welsh. One goal settled it. On 30 minutes George Pescod, another military policeman once on Liverpool's books, found Lawton, whose pass to Hagan produced a sharp cross drive close in. Ten minutes from time Dawes found Chalmers, whose back pass to Lawton was put away nicely only for Tommy to be given offside. Near the end, Cyril Putt in the Shots goal pulled off a fine save to deny the Addicks a point.

The England game with Scotland robbed Aldershot of Hagan on 4 October – both he and Welsh were on target in the 2-0 win at Wembley. Other absentees for the Shots at West Ham were Putt, Trevor Walters (Chester), Glasby, Pescod and Halton, all playing for the Aldershot Area Army XI against Birmingham and winning 4-2 after turning up an hour late at St Andrew's. There was no Lawton either at Upton Park as the Shots lost 3-0. Tommy was getting a hat-trick for that Army XI!

Seven days later, with a fully representative Aldershot side for these times, Watford were beaten 8-1 at the Recreation Ground. Lawton had two early on, Britton put a penalty in and a fourth came when well-placed Lawton allowed Hagan to score. Lawton hit the fifth for his treble from a Halton centre, before the best goal of the game belonged to Watford! Frank Briggs (Wrexham guest) beat four players before shooting past Putt. Raynor added another for the Shots, shaping to centre then deciding to take a pot. Hagan and Halton with a drive on the run made it 8-1.

Yet another home fixture saw Clapton Orient as the visitors and only a sterling performance in goal by Stan Hall kept them in the game. Hagan took a knock but carried on, then on 20 minutes Aldershot scored when Lawton headed on for Halton to finish expertly. A slip in defence allowed Ted Crawford to level for the Os and he even missed an easier chance in the second half. Late on, Hall saved from Raynor and from a Tommy header, and Britton had a shot kicked off the line, as the score remained 1-1.

As well organised as the London League proved to be, a succession of home fixtures was not ideal. Millwall became the next team to visit Aldershot on 25 October. Hagan was on England duty in Birmingham against Wales and scoring in the 2-1 win. For Lawton, a spot of R&R saw him back on Merseyside and managing to take in a game for Everton against old foes Liverpool; however, he was on the losing side as the Reds won 3-2. Tommy only had one real chance but the goalkeeper made a fine save. He also declined the opportunity offered to take a penalty, so Willie Cook obliged. Lyon scored the other Everton goal.

For Aldershot, without him, it was a game of two halves. The Lions held a 2-0 interval lead but Reg Halton went on to complete a splendid hat-trick in a 5-2 Shots win. Certainly, Lawton and co. had put the modest Third Division (South) Aldershot on the football map in double-quick time, so much so that on 1 November, the trip to Tottenham Hotspur's White Hart Lane ground to play London evacuees Arsenal was afforded a second-half commentary by the BBC. Listeners would have heard how George Marks, the Arsenal goalkeeper, was preventing Aldershot from equalising. The Gunners had taken the lead when Leslie Jones robbed Britton, fed Denis

Compton on the wing, and his cross had been headed in by Norman Miller (Arbroath guest). On 14 minutes it was 2-0, Compton scoring from 20 yards. Doug Blair (Cardiff City guest) nicked one for Aldershot before the break but Compton made a third for Arsenal, put in by Reg Lewis. Meanwhile, Raynor was running Denis's brother Leslie Compton at left-back ragged and made it 3-2. Then Marks in the Arsenal goal was busy and Lawton hit the underside of the bar but the danger was cleared.

Queens Park Rangers were at Aldershot the following week and Lawton opened his account with a header that Bill Mason got a hand to but only enough to tip it on to the post and in. Tommy's second, three minutes after the interval, was of such ferocity that it went through Mason's hands and legs! On 78 minutes Laurie Kelly gave away a penalty and Johnny Pattison – Shots guest in 1939/40 – made it 2-1. With ten minutes remaining, Chalmers crossed the ball and Lawton beat Mason to it for his hat-trick. In the 83rd minute it became a Tommy four-timer with a belter from 25 yards. Blair, who had been outstanding for several games, was twice unlucky.

At neighbours Reading on 15 November the inside-forward trio of Hagan, Lawton and Blair scored for Aldershot in the 3-3 draw, described locally as the best game seen at Elm Park in the season. Hagan's cross shot on five minutes started things and five minutes later it was Lawton heading in Raynor's centre for 2-0. On 40 minutes Tony MacPhee got the better of a tussle with Walters and reduced the Biscuitmen's arrears. He then levelled on 68 minutes after successfully challenging and charging Putt for possession. Blair restored Aldershot's lead but Len Duns of Sunderland, who had previously assisted the Shots, put the ball across for Wilf Chitty to make it 3-3.

Lawton, on leave, next played and scored for the Mayor of Lewes' team against Brighton in a 5-0 win. Then he helped Everton against Manchester City at Maine Road. On four minutes his high-rising effort put them in front. Jack Boothway made it 1-1 half an hour later from a penalty, before another spot kick – this for Everton when Stevenson was brought down – saw Tommy oblige, as presumably Cook was not interested this time. Lyon scored a third for Everton, then on 63 minutes Lawton was through when impeded and scored from the penalty for his hat-trick, although Boothway then did the same for City, who were just edged out 4-3.

In Tommy's absence, Aldershot survived a hectic barrage from Brighton at the Recreation Ground before eventually winning 5-1. Then, on 29 November at Griffin Park, Hedley Sheppard was delayed by a road accident and Jones was late arriving. Brentford allowed one of their junior players, Webb, to complete the Shots team after a general shuffle around. Meanwhile, Putt, Lawton, Hagan and Halton were playing for the Army XI against the RAF at the Command Ground in Aldershot. At Brentford, Blair had had a shot handled and Britton, from the penalty kick, was Aldershot's sole reply as Brentford hit five. The Army side, with practically everyone who had played for Aldershot in the war thus far, lost 5-2 to the flyboys, although Hagan and Lawton both scored.

Then came Aldershot's first home defeat of the season – 2-1 to Crystal Palace, with only Putt of the Army gang back. At St Andrew's against Birmingham Lawton was providing yet another treble for himself in the Army XI's 6-3 win, Mercer also featuring on target.

For the Fulham match Aldershot had to draft in two from the previous season's 'A' team – Roy Miles and Les Monk – as neither George Taylor nor Albert Dawes were able to make it. But Lawton, Blair and Albert Geldard (Bolton, ex-Everton) gave the visiting defence a hard time. A cross by Blair and Geldard outwitted Harry Freeman to give the Shots a 1-0 lead. Then young Monk centred and Lawton scored their second with a clever header. Lawton was brought down five minutes later but it was Geldard who put away the penalty for 3-0. Tommy was left limping afterwards. Jones was involved in another promising attack and Geldard – once described by Lawton as the fastest over ten yards, 'he could catch pigeons' – secured a first-half hat-trick with Aldershot 4-0 ahead.

Lawton was injured again in the second half before retiring. On 75 minutes Jack Conley beat Sheppard and provided Dennis Rampling with a Fulham goal. Sheppard was unlucky again when he was hit on the hand by a shot off the post and Ronnie Rooke scored from the penalty. A Freeman clearance then found Rooke, who reduced the arrears further to 4-3 as Aldershot's ten were tiring but held on for the win.

The return fixture at White Hart Lane against Tottenham Hotspur was ruined as a spectacle by fog. Both sides were well represented, although Hagan was unavailable for Aldershot. It ended 1-1 with both goals coming from corner kicks. Halton and Lawton were involved before Raynor gave the Shots an interval lead but Roy White equalised in the second half after a corner had been cleared to him.

On his Christmas leave Lawton returned to Everton's line-up for a home game with Stockport County. His No.9 shirt was handed to Bob Kinnell, an 18-year-old Hearts player, for a promising scoring debut, while Lawton was at inside-right but still able to score three of his own. Stevenson and Cook – back taking penalties – made it a six-goal romp. Two days later at Sheffield Wednesday, Tommy, restored to centre-forward, struck twice early on and took another treble for himself in the whitewash at Hillsborough. His presence increased the attendance to 11,721. Tommy Jones was also back for Everton at centre-half for this one. How much longer could Lawton be left out of England selection?

In Lawton's absence, at least Aldershot had Hagan for both holiday games. Pompey were beaten 3-2 at the Rec on Christmas Day but two days later Chelsea took the points at Aldershot in a 3-2 win, with Shots' Wilf Dixon being allowed to play for the Londoners, who were short of a player!

Then the Aldershot coach driver lost his way trying to find Charlton Athletic's ground at The Valley. As a result, there was no half-time break and just 40 minutes were played each way. Perhaps it suited Aldershot, as it was 1-1 at half-time, then with three in a spell of ten minutes following the change round, they ran out 5-1 winners, Welsh scoring for the Addicks. Lawton and Jones grabbed two goals each, Hagan the fifth. Dixon was back on the right side but Blair (Blackpool guest) had been posted overseas but had thanked the club for allowing him games. There was then another 5-1 score on 10 January but this time it was the visiting Hammers who were too strong for the weakened Shots at the Rec. Lawton, Hagan and Taylor had been required for Army duties.

But there was excellent news for Tommy Lawton – back in the England team on 17 January against Scotland at Wembley, even though his inclusion was due to his Everton team-mate Joe Mercer being injured and Don Welsh vacating his No.9 shirt for a No.6 at left-half! The Scots, declining to wear numbered shirts as usual, had to borrow 11 old ones from Tommy Walker! The crowd was given as 64,000, despite 66,720 tickets being sold. The match was for the 'Aid to Russia Fund', with Mrs Churchill, three Cabinet members and King Peter of Yugoslavia in attendance. Hagan was off the mark with a goal in 50 seconds for England after dribbling past two Scottish defenders. Ten minutes after the interval Lawton side-footed a centre from Denis Compton in to deny his marker's intention to tackle, and midway through the half he headed in Matthews's pinpoint corner for his second goal. Near the end, Scots winger Caskie suffered concussion and was taken to hospital. *The Scotsman* reported: 'Lawton outshone all the other attackers.' It was 3-0 to England.

There was much talk in Aldershot of the team's contribution to this international as far as the goalscorers were concerned. Naturally, Lawton's pedigree was well established previously but Hagan had grown in stature thanks to his exposure in an Aldershot shirt. He was to play five times more for the club than his own Sheffield United during the season.

The Aldershot visit to Clapton Orient's Brisbane Road on 24 January saw the 'international brigade' back. Lawton suffered a slight head injury so the scoring was left to others. Halton scored twice, while Hagan, Jones and Britton, from a penalty, added to produce five goals without reply. However, Tommy was back on Merseyside the following week in an Everton shirt against Wolves. It was a match of three penalties, Everton edging it 2-1, with Cook getting both for the Blues. Lawton went close a couple of times, had one disallowed for offside, and finished headlong in the back of the net when one of his headers just failed to make the goal.

On the same day, a depleted Shots at Millwall awaited Bert Knott of Hull City, previously assisting Lincoln City, to help them out. He failed to make it and winger Jones was another absentee. The Lions kindly loaned Ron Gray – oddly enough a registered Lincoln player – but it was hard grafting and Millwall won 3-1.

It was such a rollercoaster of a season for the Shots and, on 7 February, came the long-awaited first visit of an Arsenal senior side, as pre-war only their reserves had played at the Aldershot Recreation Ground. With no Army calls to affect team selection, Aldershot faced the top-of-the-table Londoners with confidence. However, according to subsequent programme notes, it had been necessary for the defence to be 'bold and brave' to withstand a first-half onslaught, and Charlie Briggs was overworked in goal. Aldershot showed more adventure in the second half and, from a clearance, George Jones on the wing centred in front of goal where Raynor tapped the ball aside for Lawton to score from close range after 64 minutes. Despite having only a narrow target, it was sufficient for him to squeeze it in. It was enough to spike the Gunners before the crowd of 8,700.

On the following Wednesday then the Saturday, it was Army field duty for Lawton against the Belgian Army and an RAF XI respectively. There was a Tommy hat-trick against the Belgians in a 4-0 win, with Denis Compton the other scorer, though Tommy had a penalty saved by Huwaert, the visiting goalkeeper. But it was all square with the fliers – both matches staged at the Command Ground in Aldershot. That Saturday, 14 February, Aldershot won at Loftus Road against Queens Park Rangers without their stars and with more new faces in attack, Raynor scoring twice and another clean sheet being recorded.

The Aldershot programme notes appealed for supporters to give clothing coupons as the club had donated generously to the Army with kit in the early days of the war and what was left was wearing thin. On 21 February at the Rec, Reading put up a strong rearguard action in a 0-0 draw but Tommy was on Everton duty at Oldham and being beaten more easily than the 1-0 result suggested. Seven days later at Brighton there was another 5-1 scoreline for the Shots who were in commanding style, Hagan getting two in the first ten minutes and completing his trio after 53 minutes. Lawton scored the fourth and Palmer number five. Frank Swift was in goal for the Shots. That 'Mr Everywhere' Don Welsh hit the Seagulls' goal after 82 minutes!

In the next match on 7 March, Brentford scored three at Aldershot but the Shots doubled this to win 6-3. Meantime, was his journey really necessary? Lawton was turning out for Everton at Wolves and on the wrong end of an 11-1 hammering! Injuries to Wally Owen and then TG Jones did not help the situation. Owen returned in the second half but as a passenger, while Jones, with a facial injury, had to go to hospital when Wolves were 2-0 up. Manchester United's Jack Rowley with five goals took advantage as his team's match had been postponed, so he took the place of Reg Kirkham who failed to arrive in time! Lawton was isolated, having to play the Wolves defence on his own.

A week later Lawton was at Aldershot but at the Command Ground on parade for the Army against an FA XI, the match attracting around 10,000, predominantly in khaki. The Britton–Cullis–Mercer half-back line, arguably wartime's finest, provided the link between defence and attack in some style. Hagan scored twice, said by the *Sunday Mirror* to have been 'the inspiration', and Ralph Birkett the other goal in the 3-1 success. Meanwhile Aldershot inflicted a first home defeat for Crystal Palace, 2-1 at Selhurst Park, they being the last in the London League to lose their unbeaten home record.

Whether or not the trauma of that Wolves mauling had an effect on Tommy Lawton is not known, as he was not registering goals. In the next two London Cup games for Aldershot, they suffered 6-2 at Brentford and 2-0 at home to Queens Park Rangers. Les Maskell scored both goals for the Shots at Griffin Park. George Smith, Charlton's centre-half, played in both matches for Aldershot, and Hagan in the Rangers tie.

Then came a change of shirt and scenery, which at least brought Lawton some finishing relief. Playing for the Army in England against the Army in Scotland at Hillsborough on 4 April he registered a hat-trick in the 4-1 win, Maurice Edelston the Reading amateur international getting the other one. Hagan burrowed through the Scots defence in the fourth minute to provide Tommy with his first goal, then on the half hour Birkett miskicked close in but Lawton snapped up the gift for his second. Hagan gave Edelston his goal chance and Tommy completed his trio with a header. Peter MacKennan replied for the Scots before the crowd of 28,567. On 11 April Lawton was expected to play for Everton against Liverpool along with Caskie but neither made it. The same day the Shots succumbed 4-1 at Millwall.

Then it was international duty for Lawton, Hagan, Mercer, et al. at Hampden Park against Scotland on 18 April. The 'Aldershot duo' combined for England's first goal, Hagan making a clever move to put Lawton through after 21 minutes. Four minutes later Billy Liddell headed Scotland level from Willie Waddell, before Jock Dodds put the Scots ahead on 29 minutes, assisted by Liddell. In the second half Hagan made it 2-2 six minutes after the restart, only for Dodds to net again in the 57th minute. Alex Herd then missed an open goal before Dodds managed a fourth for Scotland to bag his hat-trick. Then in a flurry of scoring in the last five minutes Lawton scored for England, Bill Shankly scored with a chancy lob for the Scots, before Lawton completed his hat-trick as England lost 5-4. The *Sunday Mirror* rated it the best game at Hampden for a generation.

Lawton was to divide the rest of the season between Everton and representative fixtures. His return for Everton was in a disappointing return in the two-legged War Cup ties with West Bromwich Albion. At The Hawthorns on 25 April the Throstles were on top from the outset and on ten minutes took the lead through Charlie Evans. Tommy was starved of the ball throughout, and when Billy Elliott scored a second Albion goal after the break it became more of a struggle for Everton. Cliff Edwards made it 3-0 before Lawton replied five minutes before the end amid cries for offside with no foundation. But it left a mountain to climb for the second leg, of course. However, before that there was a Lancashire Senior Cup date at Southport.

Everton made six changes, clearly resting some players for the War Cup, including Lawton. The Blues already had a 3-1 lead from the first leg and, although losing 2-1 at Haig Avenue, went through to face Manchester City in the next round. Wally Owen, usually on the flanks, led the attack and scored Everton's goal.

On the Saturday it was West Bromwich Albion at Goodison, and the visitors were even more dominating than in the home leg as Everton found themselves totally outplayed. The old fault of conceding early was, to say the least, unhelpful. Within seven minutes the duo of Evans and Elliott had each found the net. Then when Boyes wrenched his knee and retired after 25 minutes there was little hope of any meaningful comeback. Lawton had to carry the attack on his own, the *Liverpool Daily*

Post putting it that he had to do the work of three players. He did make a goal for Bentham that was quickly nullified when Peter McKennan (Partick Thistle guest) scored Albion's third. Elliott and McKennan added further goals in the 5-1 routing.

Manchester City had to be faced in the Lancashire Senior Cup first leg with Lawton absent, playing for England against Wales in Cardiff. There were no goals for Tommy or England, and not even for Everton, who lost 2-0 at Maine Road. Marks, the England goalkeeper, was hurt after 20 minutes in the play leading to the Welsh goal but refused to be taken off yet had to go to hospital with internal injuries after the match. Wales deservedly won – Billy Lucas scoring the only goal. There was some confusion as to the scorer as the player had swapped jerseys with Frank Squires before the kick-off.

Everton, with a two-goal deficit against Manchester City from the first leg of the Lancashire Senior Cup, had Lawton back for the second leg on 16 May. The inclusion of Frank Soo, the Stoke City and England international, in the Everton attack at inside-left helped materially to an outstanding second-leg performance by the Blues. Their approach work was better than for weeks. Lawton and Alf Anderson provided a 2-0 interval lead to level the overall deficit but Boothway upset this with a City goal on 53 minutes. Then Soo, linking well with Stevenson, who was playing on the left wing, scored twice. In the last five minutes Lawton scored twice to complete his hat-trick for a 6-1 victory before an attendance of 9,863.

On 23 May at Goodison Park, Western Command beat an Everton team 7-3 and, near the end, were leading by seven clear goals. Waking up late, Everton scored three in five minutes. That was a good one to miss for Tommy Lawton. Amazingly, two days later there was another friendly, this time Everton entertaining Bolton Wanderers, and the scoreline was exactly the same, save for Everton being on the winning side this time. Stevenson scored three goals, while Soo hit a brace of his own. Teenager Nat Lofthouse scored twice for Wanderers.

Unfortunately, Soo was unable to make the Lancashire Senior Cup Final against neighbours Liverpool. Anderson was another non-starter. The Reds could only muster three of their own players, so guests had to fill the gaps. On eight minutes Jackie Wharton (Preston) scored for Liverpool, then Cyril Done, after a three-man pile-up, added a second. Although Lawton had the ball in the net for Everton, an earlier infringement ruled it out, then Johnny Carey (Manchester United) made it three for Liverpool. Done added his second and Lawton responded for Everton, who were beaten 4-1.

Not finished for the season, Tommy was involved in another charity game, featuring the FA XI and an RAF XI at Luton on 6 June, where Hugh Billington, the local boy made good, was in the former team and scoring twice in another pleasing and entertaining draw, 6-6. Tommy signed off for the season with two goals for himself, with Len Goulden and Cliff Bastin completing the scorers for the FA. Arsenal's Ted Drake hit a couple for the flyboys.

Aldershot finished fourth in the London League on goal average behind West Ham United, the highest position in the club's Football League history since 1932. They had used 73 different players in the season – just in competitive matches!

Lawton played more matches for Aldershot than any other team, services or civilian, during the season. In talking about this season at his adopted wartime base, both as a serving member of the Army as a PTI at Queens Avenue and a guest player for Aldershot, he remarked in his book, *Football Is My*

Business, as follows: 'We could get no higher than fourth in the London League and failed altogether to qualify for the London Cup. Perhaps it was the chopping and changing week after week when men were unable to get leave which upset our side.'

CHAPTER SEVEN

Six-Timer Tommy Tops the Hatters

TOMMY HAD won the long jump and 100 yards in the Aldershot District Military Athletic Championships! Meanwhile, Everton, preparing for the 1942/43 season, expected the nucleus of a first-team squad despite services' needs and war workers on shifts, although Tommy was not expected too often. However, he did make the first game against Manchester United at Goodison Park on 29 August. The opposition almost did not. Their train was delayed so the kick-off was 40 minutes late. Oddly enough, Everton's only two guest players, Ted Anderson and George Mutch (Preston North End), both scored. Lawton had a penalty saved by John Breedon in the United goal, so some kinks would have to be ironed out with him. Apparently coasting to victory in the last 20 minutes, Everton faded and goals by Stan Pearson and Everton's own loaned Harry Catterick secured a 2-2 draw.

A week later it was FA XI duty for Lawton against the Civil Defence at Brentford, not a particularly happy hunting ground for Tommy the previous season. Since Joe James, who managed to keep Tommy fairly quiet then, was in the FA team, one concern was eliminated. Anyway, Lawton scored twice and the FA won 4-1.

117

Then Tommy travelled across the Irish Sea to Northern Ireland for three matches for the Army, the first against Ireland, which was basically the Irish FA XI, at Windsor Park. The *Belfast News Letter* doubted 'a better big match' had been played there. Belfast Celtic's McCartney scored on 25 minutes, Davy Cochrane added a second on 49 minutes, but then Alex Herd reduced their lead by scoring a minute later. He then shot a penalty straight at Tom Breen. Carey made it 3-1 on 57 minutes, but Lawton managed a goal for the Army with 12 minutes left.

On the Monday, the opposition was the Army in Ulster, played at Cliftonville's ground. This was Lawton's match without a doubt, as he scored a hat-trick. His first goal came after he swept through the defence, he scored with a header from Jimmy Mullen's centre a minute before half-time and nodded in another on the hour. The Army beat the local Services team 5-3. However, there was no respite with the Irish League to be faced on the Wednesday in what was another closely fought contest, at Grosvenor Park. The match ended with the Army winning 3-2, with Jack Rowley for the Irish League notching the best goal of the five. Jack Vernon kept a close grip on Lawton throughout.

On 26 September Lawton was back in the Shots' red and blue against Watford, displacing McCulloch at centre-forward, the Scotland international moving to inside-left, partnering England cap Arthur Cunliffe. Hagan was at inside-right and the versatile Reg Halton at centre-half in the 4-0 win. Lawton scored two goals, Hagan and Cunliffe one each.

In double-quick time Tommy was back playing for Everton at his former club Burnley at Turf Moor. On 15 minutes, a slick move involving Mercer, Lawton and George Mutch led to Norman Higham scoring. Then 12 minutes later, play-anywhere-Jackson on the right wing added another Everton goal, followed by a 38th-minute Lawton header for 3-0. Cook from the penalty spot and one goal in response from Richard Waddington completed the scoring at 4-1 to Everton.

On 10 October at Wembley it was a different outcome for England and Scotland at the Empire Stadium, in sharp contrast to the two countries' last meeting at Hampden Park when nine goals had been scored, Scotland winning 5-4. For this match, Scotland paraded a new centre-half in Willie Corbett and their defence as a whole played outstandingly well throughout. Lawton, with limited service, found the going difficult. The match ended goalless but an attendance of 75,000 was a wartime record thus far. The match was also watched by King George of the Hellenes and King Haakon of Norway, plus Cabinet members on a three-line whip from Winston Churchill. Marks showed no ill-effects from his internal injury any more than Cullis from breaking his leg the previous season.

Aldershot was next for Tommy Lawton, in a match against West Ham United, and surprise, surprise, the Hammers' centre-half was the same Corbett in the guise of a Celtic guest! This time the Scot lacked the extra cover he enjoyed at Wembley and Lawton cleverly drew him out several times to put Hagan through for a first-half hat-trick. Lawton grabbed one himself and Hagan, determined to wipe the Wembley memory away, completed his four-timer. There was some small reward for the Hammers – via Sam of that ilk in the 5-1 scoreline. The 7,500 crowd watching Tommy play was a tenth of the previous week of course! After eight matches Aldershot were placed third in the Football League South, a point behind the leaders Arsenal.

Another international loomed for Lawton, this time at Molineux against Wales, with England's new faces including a trio of centre-forwards for a three-pronged attack. Tommy scored England's only goal when Ronnie Rooke of Fulham passed to him and he cleverly side-stepped before scoring with a fine right-foot drive from the edge of the penalty area with 11 minutes played. That was virtually all England could muster and it must have been a huge disappointment for Eddie Hapgood on his 42nd appearance for his country, equalling Bob Crompton's figure, and also acting as skipper for the 33rd time. The *Daily Herald* said Lawton looked 'more forlorn than ever'. Horace Cumner scored twice for Wales, who were 2-1 winners.

Meanwhile, Hagan had been Aldershot's scorer at Brentford in their 4-1 defeat but he had Britton, Cullis, McCulloch, Cunliffe and Lawton for company against Millwall at the Recreation Ground on 31 October. There were goals aplenty as the Shots led 3-2 at the turnaround and 7-4 at the final whistle. Lawton and McCulloch each bagged hat-tricks and Cunliffe was the other marksman. Then it was off to the coast for a trip to Brighton the following week, astonishingly with the same 11 players! With the embargo on visitors lifted, the attendance at 3,800 was much improved at the Goldstone, knowing too that a handful of international players were being paraded.

The Seagulls had four Liverpool guest players in their line-up and at half-time were holding their own. It was only late in the game that Aldershot managed to break through the Albion defence. With 15 minutes left Lawton scored, before Hagan made one for McCulloch and repeated the link-up for the Scotland international's second with a header for 3-0. McCulloch was now leading scorer in the Football League South.

Crystal Palace visited Aldershot on 14 November but there were changes in the red-and-blue shirts as there was an Army v Civil Defence representative match taking place at Millwall, which took Britton, Hagan and Cullis from the home side, plus the Dawes brothers, Fred and Albert, from the Palace team. Lawton scored with an early header from a Cunliffe centre to put the Shots ahead, but Palace had the chance of levelling when Albert Robson was tripped, only for Bill Barke to shoot the spot kick straight at Dennis Herod. From a Raynor cross, Tommy headed another goal for a 2-0 interval lead.

Palace were in no way out of it and within seven minutes of the restart had made it 2-2, through Fred Bastin and Trevor Smith. Phil Joslin (Torquay guest) was kept alert in the Palace goal, saving from Lawton and McCulloch, and Tommy had a header ruled out for offside. It was not until eight minutes from time that McCulloch, out on the left, crossed for Lawton to hit a ground shot in off the upright for a hard-fought 3-2 win. Meanwhile, tickets were already being sold for the Arsenal game the following week at the Rec.

The clash with another charity event, FA XI v RAF at Stoke, deprived Aldershot of Cullis but the Gunners suffered more with Marks, Hapgood, Joy and Kirchen on duty for the fliers. It did not deter from what became an incredible switch of fortune for the two teams before an attendance of 11,000, which was the second highest at the ground. The scenario was best described in Tommy Lawton's *Football Is My Business*: 'With 35 minutes to go we led 3-0 and it was money for old rope as they say in the Navy. We lost 7-4. I still don't know where we went wrong that day.'

The timings were as follows: 2-0 in 42 mins, 3-0 (50), 3-1 (70), 3-2 (penalty) then 4-2 (72), 4-3 (80), 4-4 (82), 4-5 (86), 4-6 (87) and 4-7 (89). McCulloch scored two, Hagan and Lawton one each. Arsenal's scorers were Reg Lewis 3, Denis Compton 2, Cliff Bastin and Bryn Jones. Joslin was in goal for Aldershot a week after his guest outing for Palace!

Shell-shocked from this result, Aldershot went to Southampton next time out and lost 2-1, Lawton their scorer. Sadly, even with more new faces in the team, they were still insufficiently recovered by 5 December at Charlton Athletic, losing another high-scoring affair 6-4, having led 2-1 at half-time. One of the new guests was Ernie Muttitt of Brentford, who scored twice, with Tommy getting the other couple plus another that was originally given then ruled out for offside.

At home to Luton Town the Shots went a goal down in six minutes, levelled six minutes later, then rattled in four goals in six minutes, and a further three in ten minutes to lead by an incredible 8-1 at half-time. The combination between the inside-forward trio of Hagan, Lawton and McCulloch was outstanding, with Tommy claiming a double hat-trick, and Hagan and McCulloch one each. Britton added a further goal in the second half, making it 9-2 at the conclusion. Lawton was now the leading scorer in the Football League South with 20 goals, Reg Lewis (Arsenal) had 19 and McCulloch 18.

Portsmouth provided sterner opposition on 19 December and, for the first time, Aldershot failed to muster one signed player, the 11 on duty all being guests, including Wilf Copping, Arsenal's England wing-half. Pompey had the usual half-dozen of their FA Cup-winning team, and goalkeeper Harry Walker had some interesting duels with Lawton by cutting down on the centre-forward's space in which to find a sufficient shooting target. Still, Tommy did manage two goals, while Albert Bonass (QPR winger) scored the other goal for the Shots in the 4-3 defeat. Pompey's winner was unlucky for Herod (Stoke City goalkeeper), who saved well from George Bullock (Barnsley guest) but Willie Martin (Clyde) popped in the rebound. Aldershot were now placed sixth, one place ahead of Pompey in the table.

Lawton was back on Merseyside in Everton colours for the holiday period, entertaining Manchester City on Christmas Day, then playing at Tranmere Rovers on Boxing Day. Used to playing in high-scoring Aldershot games, the genre was switched to Goodison Park against City, where some enterprising forward play resulted in the Blues winning 6-3. Lawton scored a hat-trick, with Wyles, Grant and Stevenson notching the other Everton goals. Jim Currier (of Bolton Wanderers days) with a brace and Northampton Town's Bobby King responded for City.

The following day at Tranmere, Gordon Watson had to play in goal as George Burnett was a no-show. Rovers had beaten Liverpool 3-2 the previous day and were serious about a local derby double. Everton found the Rovers defence in no mood to surrender; indeed, Tranmere were two up until eight minutes from the end when Lawton scored Everton's only response. Dixie Dean had promised he would try to make the holiday matches for Tranmere but was unable so to do. However, instead of him, Arthur Frost (Newcastle United guest) scored two goals against the Reds and the winner against the Blues.

Back down south Lawton played for the Army against the Met Police, a team packed with London professionals. Cullis had to cry off with influenza but the soldier boys were 5-1 up into the second half before the constabulary got a grip and made it 5-5. Lawton bagged a trio for himself, as did Billy Richardson the Birmingham centre-forward – the only 'out of town copper'. Seven of the Army team had played as guests for Aldershot during the war period. Lawton had now taken his tally to 28 goals in 13 consecutive matches for various teams.

Aldershot had Tommy back for the visit of Tottenham Hotspur on 9 January. While there were invariably enough outfield players available whatever the original source, a spare goalkeeper was rarely included. But it happened against Spurs. Joslin's train was 90 minutes late; however, a young Army lad stationed nearby volunteered, claiming Yorkshire youth credentials. Sadly, it was clear that he was not up to the task and at 2-0 down at half-time Ginger Palmer had to take over, with Broome swept out to play on the wing. The Shots lost 3-1 and Lawton's scoring sequence had been broken, as Pat Gallacher (Bournemouth guest and a military policeman) scored the Shots' only goal of the match.

Tommy was briefly back on Merseyside for the clash with Liverpool on 16 January, with Everton having lost to the Reds at Goodison the week before, 3-1. Despite having six of their First Division championship-winning team, Everton were again beaten, this time 2-1 in what was part of the qualifying competition for the War Cup. Critics were of the opinion that the Blues had been unlucky in both matches but results say all that matters. Lawton, only given service in the air, scored Everton's goal.

It was then a change of colours for Tommy, back playing for Aldershot at West Ham the following Saturday, after Chelsea had drawn 1-1 at the Recreation Ground the previous week. Despite having a star-studded line-up at Upton Park, with Britton, Cullis, Taylor, Geldard, Hagan and Cunliffe all available along with Lawton, the Shots were 3-0 down at the break. Goulden hit a fourth goal, then Lawton pulled one back for the Shots. However, Small nipped in a fifth before Britton scored with a penalty kick to make it 5-2 to the Hammers. Richard Dunn then completed his hat-trick for West Ham, before Cunliffe scored the final goal to make it 6-3 in the Hammers' favour, in a match where Geldard was injured in the second half.

Brentford, often tricky opponents for Aldershot, were the visitors on 30 January. Len Townsend put them ahead after half an hour following end-to-end play but Gallacher made it 1-1 at the turnaround. Lawton had the last word with a gem of a strike in the second half, taking a return pass from Palmer and, despite pressure from both Joe James and George Poyser, putting in a rising drive that scraped the underside of the bar in beating the goalkeeper.

On 6 February it was up to Queens Avenue and the Command Ground for the Army v Belgian Army. Hagan and Cunliffe formed the Army left wing, with Tommy leading the attack. It was a Lawton spectacular with four of the goals in a 5-0 victory. Then it was down the road to the Recreation Ground in the High Street the next Saturday with Brighton due.

Aldershot featured yet another different goalkeeper, Daniel Smart, an amateur, who let one in from a corner after three minutes but survived until late on, by which time Hagan had made it 1-1, Lawton had scored and Hagan added a third. Near the end Brighton scored from another corner but it was insufficient as the Shots won 3-2.

It was then off to Selhurst Park for what was to be Tommy Lawton's last game of the season for Aldershot. It wasn't a happy ending either as the Shots were beaten 5-2, Gallacher and Raynor scoring their two goals. Albert Dawes scored a couple for Palace, of course!

Aldershot's last League South match before the cup games was the one in which Tommy would dearly have liked to have been included. It was at White Hart Lane, Arsenal's evacuation home, with the scorching memory of having led 3-0 only to be beaten 7-4 by the Gunners earlier in the season. And it was yet another new goalkeeper for the Shots, this time George

Duke (Luton guest), their ninth custodian of the season! There was also a completely new left-wing partnership as no player of international status featured among the XI. However, the final score was Arsenal 0 Aldershot 1!

A subsequent Aldershot programme referred to Tommy as a great leader and one who would be missed at the Rec. However, there was scarcely a mention of the match in the truncated national press of the period, especially as England were beating Wales 5-3 at Wembley, Dennis Westcott, in Lawton's No.9 shirt, scoring a hat-trick.

At least it was a satisfying day for Lawton against Southport at Goodison Park, where there was a romp of scoring, 10-2 to Everton. The Blues had to borrow Johnny Carey from Manchester United at centre-half, Ron Dellow from Tranmere on the right wing and Jackie Humphreys moved to left-half. After nine minutes Tommy got on the end of a Mutch–Bentham move and went up for the ball with Southport goalkeeper Frank King (ex-Evertonian). Lawton picked up the pieces and scored. Stevenson added another on 14 minutes but Frost – of Newcastle – reduced the arrears to 2-1. Lawton hit his second with a low shot, then Syd Rawlings (Millwall guest) put through his own goal for 4-1 at the break.

Dellow had been limping with a thigh muscle injury but Everton continued scoring when Lawton completed his hat-trick for 5-1, then King had the misfortune to fracture his collarbone. Len Flack (Norwich guest) took over in goal for Southport. Mutch, on 61 minutes, then Lawton's four-timer from a magnificent back-headed effort eight minutes later made it 7-1. Just a minute later, Tommy Fowler – destined for a long post-war career at Northampton – increased the score further, and on 78 minutes Cook converted a penalty. Mutch had the last word for Everton, giving them double figures with eight minutes remaining. Southport at least managed a second to make it 10-2, through Reading's Jackie Deverall, another regular Sandgrounder at the time.

In the League War Cup first-leg match on 6 March, Blackpool took a 15th-minute lead through Dix but a minute later Lawton fed Wyles for 1-1. But that was Everton's best moment and they lost the match 4-1. There were more changes by the Blues the following week for the second leg, amateur Tommy Fairfoull coming in at right-half, Abe Rosenthal and the unusually named Llew Ashcroft borrowed from Tranmere, plus Jackson back at right-back after being on the left wing at Bloomfield Road. But Dix did it again, within five minutes for the Tangerines, only for George Curwen to make it 1-1. Lawton missed an easy one but redeemed himself with a characteristic hanging header from Fowler's centre for 2-1. He then scored his second goal and Stevenson increased Everton's lead to 4-1 to level the aggregate score on 62 minutes. But Blackpool, not beached by any means, responded through Jock Dodds and Eddie Burbanks (Sunderland guest) to paddle on in the cup.

For Everton it was a Lancashire Senior Cup home and away against Southport – surely no problem for Everton – but at Haig Avenue they were well beaten 4-1. Two goals down at half-time, it was soon three when Deverall scored a minute after the resumption. Frost put the icing on the cake for them on the hour. Tommy Jones had been unlucky in the first half, twice hitting the woodwork for Everton, for whom Fowler's goal on 73 minutes was of little consolation. At Goodison a week later Lawton did get a goal, as did Mutch, making sure of a Tommy shot. But Flack scored for Southport and the 2-1 win for the Blues was insufficient to overturn the first-leg deficit.

There was more misery for Everton and Lawton on 3 April at Wrexham as the hosts won 4-1. Tommy finished on the wing after an injury just over his eye. Stevenson was the lone Everton scorer but Tim Rogers scored a treble for the home team at the Racecourse Ground.

Next on the calendar was the Liverpool Senior Cup home and away against Tranmere, initially at Goodison, where another Blues starlet appeared in Billy Lowe, just 16 years old and a Haydock winger. Mutch after 11 minutes, Stevenson after 36 minutes and a Lawton header a minute before half-time put Everton three goals ahead. Although Rovers nicked one in the second half after 64 minutes, Lawton pivoted on a Stevenson pass and made it 4-1 by the end of the first leg.

Tommy missed the return as he had been playing in the National Council of YMCA War Services Fund match for Cyril Sidlow's team against Tommy Jones's XI at Rhyl, attracting 5,000. Sidlow's XI won 6-2 and Lawton scored the best goal of the match, an audacious 40-yard lob! Without him, Everton won 2-1 at Prenton Park to go through to the final of the Liverpool Senior Cup.

Everton had arranged a friendly with Preston North End and during midweek the Liverpool newspapers announced that Lawton would play. However, the Nottingham press was reporting that on 24 April a new ground, which would in the future become familiar to Tommy Lawton, Notts County's Meadow Lane, was to see him in new colours. It was also a local derby against Nottingham Forest. There were no goals for Lawton but County won 2-1. Even so, the *Nottingham Journal* mentioned Lawton's turn of speed and a 'peach of a shot'. Then on May Day Tommy was on duty for Western Command at Newcastle but beaten 4-3 by Northern Command. However, he did notch two goals for the losers.

A change of geographical direction for Tommy saw him playing a week later at Buckley in North Wales for Chester against an Army XI. The players in kit paraded down the little main street before the game, with the Buckley Town Band sounding out, too. The small ground was packed with 500 fans and the Flintshire Red Cross POW Fund was benefiting. Chester, with other guests, won 11-4. Tommy's first goal, a header, was a 'beauty', while another was a clever nod. He then completed his hat-trick and went on to finish with a five-timer.

On 12 May, the second leg was arranged for the Liverpool Senior Cup Final! Everton had lost the first leg 4-1 at Anfield in the absence of Lawton but won the second leg 3-2. Lawton played in the return match but was off colour and received little scope from Frank Rist playing centre-half for Liverpool as a guest from Charlton Athletic.

Just three days later Tommy played for Western Command against Chester and scored with a glancing header from a centre after 25 minutes in the 3-1 win. Then a week later it was time to renew acquaintanceship north of the border on Army XI duty against an Aberdeen Select XI on 22 May. Though Lawton finished on the winning side from the odd goal in nine and was among the goals, the scoring hero of the day was Stan Mortensen, a guest in the Select team and scoring after 4, 52, 71 and 84 minutes. The khaki lads included Britton, Cullis, Jackie Robinson and Hagan, too. Robinson snatched a couple, Hagan one and Lawton's brace came after 15 and 28 minutes from another five-star entertainment affair.

The Scottish sojourn was not over. Reacquainted with Morton, Tommy Lawton this time had Stanley Matthews in the same team for the Summer Cup against Clyde. Tommy gave Morton a half-time lead but the Bully Wee levelled at 1-1.

The replay was a romp – the *Sunday Post* headline said it all: 'Matthews makes 'em, Lawton fires 'em.' Lawton scored five goals after 21, 43, 55, 58 and 62 minutes. It finished 8-3.

In the semi-final St Mirren proved tougher opposition at Ibrox. Six goals were shared, Tommy scoring just one of them. The replay was at Hampden Park and the Buddies edged it 3-2, with Lawton and Billy Steel scoring the Morton goals. However, this was to be the end of English players nipping across the border on jolly-boy outings to play football unless they were legally working in the area or had been posted in the services.

CHAPTER EIGHT

Four Gems Among
England's Pieces of Eight

TOMMY LAWTON was put in charge of area training for
Army Cadets, so the prospect of being available to turn out for
Everton in 1943/44, duties permitting, looked promising. He
started training on a Tuesday evening in August at Chester's
ground and was also selected to play in that club's trial match
for the Whites team against the Stripes. Tommy Jones was also
playing in that game as was the ubiquitous Don Welsh. The
Charlton Athletic and England utility player was among the
goals with a four-timer, but Tommy topped his tally with a nap
hand. The Whites won 11-5.

Everton arranged to play Liverpool in a friendly but, in a
long-standing agreement with Lawton's old club Burnley, he was
loaned out to them for a friendly against the National Police and
Civil Defence team at Turf Moor.

Tommy did get on the scoring list once but only after the
game was out of Burnley's reach, as they were beaten 5-2.
Meanwhile the Reds had similarly steamrolled Everton, who
led 2-0 late on before losing 5-2. Welsh – who else – scored a
hat-trick.

On 28 August, Everton's first league game of 1943/44 was at Blackburn for the Rovers return of Walter Crook after two years out with a fractured kneecap. John Grant arrived as Everton's 12th man but had to play for one-short Blackburn. Stevenson made Lawton's first goal on 25 minutes before Grant of all people equalised! Jimmy McIntosh (one of five Preston players in the game!) gave Everton a 2-1 lead. Newcastle's Tommy Pearson fluffed a Rovers penalty, then Lawton scored his second goal for a 3-1 victory. The *Liverpool Echo* referred to Tommy's leadership as 'excellent', the *Sunday Mirror* describing him as being 'in his stride'.

There were no goals at Goodison in the return with Blackburn a week later. Lawton distributed the ball well and was certainly prevented from scoring at least one goal when his volley was spectacularly turned over the bar by Herman Conway. Everton, who fielded seven internationals – not all their own brand – also brought back music and information on the microphone for the first time since the war started to cheer everyone.

But it was a wretched performance by Everton at Maine Road against Manchester United (Old Trafford had been bombed) on 11 September, not aided by Lawton being held by Bert Whalley. Everton introduced Eddie Wainwright, 19, at inside-forward, signed only a few weeks previously and he showed promise. Four goals down, Mutch pulled one back for Everton on 83 minutes but it was merely a consolation. Lawton was absent on duty the following week and missed the return match, which Everton won 6-1!

On 25 September it was international time at Wembley for England and Wales but Lawton's centre-forward berth was still in the hands of Welsh – Don that is. There was a nice touch for Stan Mortensen, who was getting his international feet wet for the wrong side, being allowed to come on as a substitute for the injured Ivor Powell at half-time as Wales had no 12th man. Don Welsh scored a couple as did Raich Carter, Jimmy Hagan and Denis Compton as England won 8-3. There was not much chance of Lawton regaining an England place at that rate.

That day Lawton was back at Turf Moor against Burnley in Everton colours. Scraping around for players, Everton had to use a youngster, Jack Morley, at right-half, with Martin McDonnell in the centre, as Tommy Jones was playing for Wales. Lawton was made skipper and soon decided to shift Morley to the wing, with Grant taking his spot. The match ended goalless.

Said to be on leave, Lawton was in the Aldershot team facing Tottenham Hotspur at White Hart Lane on 2 October! Hagan, Cunliffe, Britton, Halton and McCulloch were among familiar faces, of course. The match was broadcast on the BBC. Spurs included Briggs, who had assisted Aldershot previously, and Jack Chisholm at centre-half, plus an all-guest forward line including Frank O'Donnell of Preston and Jack Rowley from Manchester United, so the Shots were not feeling merely home alone on the personnel front. Three down at the break, Aldershot scored twice through Lawton, who renewed his partnership with Hagan, but Spurs finished 5-2 winners.

Two days later it was announced that Lawton would be included in the England team to play Scotland at Maine Road on 16 October, with Don Welsh only listed as a travelling reserve! Perhaps the international selectors had been at White Hart Lane, and was this actually the reason for Tommy playing? The entire squad was composed of either Army or RAF personnel.

But Tommy was back on Everton lines for the Merseyside affair with Liverpool the following week at Goodison Park.

A crowd of 28,835 saw another goal-fest amounting to ten. With no Britton, an amateur, Scott Lee, was at wing-half. Stevenson missed an early chance and Liverpool scored twice in eight minutes, Cyril Done the marksman. By half-time they had streamrolled the Blues, Done completing his hat-trick and John Harley making it 4-0. The mastermind behind the forward play was Don Welsh, the discarded England player! It had been an exhilarating performance by the Reds.

Yet Everton reminded the Goodison faithful that they were playing after all. An own goal by Laurie Hughes on 49 minutes and Lawton, with his only real chance throughout, five minutes later made it 4-2. But on 66 minutes Done had his fourth goal and only a minute later the schemer-in-chief Welsh put in the sixth Liverpool strike. There was still time for Everton to respond with a couple of scraps – Stevenson sending the goalkeeper the wrong way after 85 minutes and two minutes later McIntosh making it 6-4 – but it was victory to the Reds.

It was international time at Maine Road on 16 October and a watershed for wartime international matches with an unsurpassed performance by England, widely acclaimed by critics both sides of the border. *The Scotsman* said: 'Scotland lacked the craft of the English players individually and collectively.' Matthews, involved in most of the build-up, was singled out by the newspaper for his outstanding performance. The *Daily Herald* commented: 'The inclusion of Mercer and Lawton brought to perfection the greatest England combine I have seen in a long experience of internationals. Every one of the eight goals was a masterpiece.' The piece was attributed to Albert Booth.

Since the England players had been playing with and against each other for five seasons, there was an overall insight into individual style and ability. There was no need for coaching when familiarity at this level was obvious. On 15 minutes Lawton back-heeled for Hagan to score. Seven minutes later, Matthews found Lawton, who headed the second goal. After 25 minutes, two goals in 30 seconds through Carter and Lawton made it 4-0, three goals having come in four minutes. Tommy's effort almost defied physics as, although in a prone position, he still managed to hook the ball in. This spoke volumes for his physical training! Carter had a penalty chance early in the second half but Joe Crozier partially saved it only for the Sunderland player to fire the rebound wide.

Having already notched their fifth goal, midway through this half, England's sixth and seventh goals also came within a 30-second period, through driving shots from Hagan and Lawton for his fourth. The crowning effort was Matthews's solo. The maestro ambled through, beating the opposition of a shell-shocked Scotland defence from touchline to goalpost before planting number eight into the net.

With Tommy back on Everton duty at the Racecourse Ground, Wrexham on 23 October, the Blues struggled initially and it was against the general run of play that Lawton scored on 30 minutes, adding a second from 20 yards in the first half. He completed his hat-trick when the Wrexham goalkeeper was holding the ball and stepped back on his line for Tommy to conveniently bundle everything into the net! Archie Livingstone (Bury guest) responded for a somewhat unlucky Wrexham.

Western Command played a Cardiff City Guest XI for charity on 30 October at Ninian Park and attracted a 20,000 crowd, but both Lawton and Mercer featured in the local selection while, in goal, Frank Swift was on Command duty. Ernie Marshall scored for the guests from a pass by Billy

Lucas but there were no goals for Lawton. These had to wait a week.

On 6 November Tranmere Rovers, traditionally suspect to Everton's advances, again did not fail to succumb at Goodison. Lawton had put three into the net within half an hour, Tranmere pulling one back to make it 3-1 at half-time. Stevenson and Bentham made it 5-1 soon after the break, followed by Tommy's fourth on 62 minutes. Reading's Gill Glidden replied for Rovers but Lawton made it a nap hand a few minutes later. Jimmy McIntosh rounded off Everton's scoring in the 9-2 victory.

For Western Command against Northern Command at Huddersfield a week later, Lawton hit one goal in their 4-3 win before going back to Everton's line-up on 20 November away at Crewe Alexandra. From a corner in the opening stages, Tommy's hard drive put Everton ahead. McIntosh added one from 30 yards and then, ten yards from the penalty area, Lawton managed his second. In the second half, Stevenson, McIntosh and Stevenson in that order added to Crewe's discomfort before Lawton wrapped it up with two more for a four-timer at 8-0.

How to top this Tommy? Try Aldershot. On 27 November he was back at the Rec in a strong Shots guest list against Southampton and familiar colleagues for Lawton, including Britton, Cullis, Halton, Hagan, McCulloch and Cunliffe. Then came a setback when, despite cries for offside, Billy Wardle (Grimsby guest) put Saints one up. But Hagan soon equalised and within half an hour Aldershot led 3-1 from additional goals from Lawton and Cunliffe. In the second half, Cunliffe and Lawton added further quick efforts, with Tommy firing from all directions, soon notching his third. There was then a 15-minute lull but, supplied with ammunition, Tommy was then unstoppable and hit three in a quarter of an hour. Hagan scored a ninth and Lawton reached the team's double-figure mark and his double treble. It was also Aldershot's first home win of the season! The *Daily Mail* reporter F. W. Carruthers ('Arbiter') at the scene referred to Lawton as 'the best centre-forward for the past 20 years'.

Lawton, with 27 goals, was the leading scorer in the country but his six-goal effort was almost overshadowed in scant sports headlines by the appearance of Aldershot's Ernie Bell at outside-right, recently repatriated from a German POW camp, and one of two of the club's professionals playing in the game, with Jimmy Horton at right-back.

The Army international England v Scotland at Goodison was well attended by 34,779. Injuries were not from rough play but came from unavoidable incidents. Worst affected was Cullis – struck by a ball in the throat just before half-time and taken off. Swift was several times in the wars, too. The Scottish contingent led from 24 minutes through Bill Strauss, Swift injured trying to save. In the second half, Leslie Compton had the misfortune to divert a shot into his own goal on 73 minutes but Lawton received an overhead pass from the other Compton brother, Denis, and scored in characteristic fashion with a left-foot volley on the half-turn. With half a minute to go, Jackie Balmer ran through the defence, veering left and right, recovering from a stumble and deservedly equalising for the ten-man Army in England.

Although designated as a home game, it had been arranged by Everton for Chester to stage the 11 December match at Sealand Road. With a makeshift right-wing pairing, the Cestrian defenders were able more to concentrate on Tommy Lawton. Billy Hughes in the middle had a grip on him anyway. Unquestionably the better side and, as in the match only seven days earlier, Chester again won 1-0, Fred Harris (Birmingham guest) the late marksman this time.

Transformation was not uncommon in wartime football, and the Manchester City game a week later at Goodison showed Everton in better light. Another new wing pairing was on show, with George Makin and Wainwright making an improvement to the team. On 25 minutes McIntosh despatched a penalty and a dozen minutes later the local newspapers described Lawton's headed goal as one 'only he could have made'. Tommy Jones scored a third, then Stevenson a fourth in the second half. City's Frank Swift was injured a couple of times but naturally carried on throughout.

Christmas Day at Maine Road was dominated by the excellent standard of both teams and Lawton's hat-trick in 24 minutes. Billy Williamson (Rangers guest) scored for Manchester City, who were 3-1 down at the break. Peter Doherty then produced a couple for City but Stevenson and McIntosh equally responded as Everton won 5-3. Swift, amazingly, had got a hand to four of the goals but the power had beaten even him. Everton secretary Theo Kelly considered it the best game since the Blackpool affair the previous season.

It was 5-3 again two days later on yet another trip to Chester in a cup qualifier. Lawton and McIntosh each scored a couple of goals, Tommy's efforts being a volley after 24 minutes and a second four minutes afterwards. George O'Neill had opened the scoring for Chester after six minutes and Tommy Astbury levelled matters at 2-2 five minutes before half-time. In the second half, Lawton presented Wainwright with a goal on 57 minutes but O'Neill immediately replied for 3-3. It was left to a McIntosh double to seal the Everton win.

On New Year's Day it was Western Command v Scottish Command at Ayr, which attracted 6,000 and, although *The*

Scotsman considered it an enjoyable performance by both teams, no goals resulted. Lawton had a quiet game, although he did a useful piece of player 'tapping up'! He asked Andy Black (Hearts) if he would be interested in being a guest for Everton. In short, arrangements were made between both clubs for the necessary permission!

Crewe Alexandra became the next Everton victims at Goodison. Lawton opened the scoring after ten minutes, McIntosh added a second on 17 minutes, before a magnificent effort two minutes later from Jack Boothway (Manchester City guest), adept on the right wing but with a penchant for his left foot, too. In the second half Stevenson and McIntosh added goals before a splendid Lawton strike made it 6-0. He had to beat three players to line up his shot on the hour. Wainwright, McIntosh and Stevenson made it nine before Fred Inskip (Forest guest) gave Crewe some consolation.

Punishment detail seemed Crewe's sentence on 15 January even at home, but they produced 25 minutes of enterprising football against Everton and deservedly took the lead through Dick Roberts with a header. This stirred Everton at least – certainly Lawton. On 32 minutes his header was partially saved, only for the power to nick it in off the bar. Ten minutes later, Wainwright's pass produced Tommy's second goal. In the second half, Tommy completed his hat-trick with a perfect volley on 57 minutes and ten minutes later an acrobatic header made it a four-timer. Wainwright scored Everton's fifth and Tommy managed a tap-in for Everton's number six, completing his own nap hand in the process. There was still time for a traditional Crewe at-the-death goal – Jimmy McCormick (Spurs guest) obliging with five minutes remaining.

Liverpool at Anfield would be a test before a crowd of 34,221. Defensive errors cost the Reds dearly early on – Wyles opening for Everton on 17 minutes and Wainwright adding a second on the half hour. The Blues' Cuthey Tatters, limping with an ankle injury, went off and Grant had been receiving repairs for ten minutes, too. But on 35 minutes it was 3-0 to Everton when Wainwright scored his second with a header provided by Wyles and Lawton. Two minutes later Bill Fagan replied for Liverpool but, even struggling with Tatters' injury, Everton crowned a 4-1 victory in the dying minutes with a goal scored by Lawton, described by the *Liverpool Echo* reporter as 'another amazing effort that he often produces'. Tatters' subsequent X-ray revealed that he had played on with a broken ankle!

In the return at Goodison, Liverpool proved to be more dangerous, leading 2-0 inside a quarter of an hour. Welsh was involved in the build-up to both goals, the first scored in four minutes by Nieuwenhuys, the second by Balmer ten minutes later. After Wyles had pulled one back for Everton, Lawton equalised with a power drive that took the goalkeeper's hands over the line with the ball. The *Liverpool Evening Express* earlier referred to Tommy's 'roving genius'. However, a penalty for handball against TG Jones on 65 minutes gave Welsh the Liverpool winner from the spot.

On 5 February, Everton had to borrow Billy Hall, a Liverpool player, to play on the right wing against Wrexham. On 23 minutes, Lawton's speed took him through the Wrexham defence to score the opening goal. Within ten minutes the visitors had equalised through West Ham's Stan Foxall and four minutes later Les Horsman (Bradford PA guest) had headed them into the lead. Wrexham wasted a second-half penalty, again for handball against Tommy Jones, when Albert Malam

(Doncaster Rovers guest) fired wide from the spot. Lawton then hit his second goal with a left-foot shot that was so swift that it went through the goalkeeper's legs, but Arsenal's Gordon Bremner, a Wrexham regular at the time, had the last scoring word on 74 minutes as they won 3-2.

The RAF XI was well represented against Western Command a week later at Molineux, where a best-of-the-season crowd of 22,906 attended. Matthews and Carter, their England right-wing pair, showed as the most impressive. The flyboys were three ahead before Lawton managed to score twice for the Army side. Pryde headed a third for the Command but the RAF's handful came from Doherty and Carter with two goals each and one from Mortensen.

That was a prelude to England taking on Scotland once more at Wembley. This was a royal occasion, too, with the King and Queen attending, plus Princess Elizabeth at her first such event, while 'Monty' himself was introduced to the players beforehand. Matthews conjured the first goal for Hagan on 37 minutes but the advantage was but a minute old before Dodds made it 1-1. An own goal by Archie Macaulay three minutes after the interval was followed by a third England goal from a tidy effort from Lawton. Hagan made it four on 71 minutes and Mercer entered the scoresheet two minutes later. Carter hit a sixth before Dodds had his and the Scots' second near the end in the 6-2 England victory.

Everton against Tranmere at Goodison Park on 26 February saw two milestones. Lawton registered his 50th goal of the season and Everton passed a century of them. Everton new boy Len Wootton figured at inside-right and, for the first time in two years, the half-back trio of the championship team played, with Grant shifting to the right wing. On nine minutes Lawton collected a through ball from Watson, ran in and scored, then Wootton fed Lawton two minutes later for Tommy's 50th. Rovers pulled one back through Watford guest Tom Walters on 19 minutes. A Grant corner confused everyone and found its way in after 35 minutes for the Toffees' 100th goal of the season. Everton then added two more for a 5-1 win, through Stevenson, a minute after the restart, then TG Jones on 67 minutes.

It was just as well that the records had tumbled at Tranmere on the day because Bloomfield Road a week later facing Blackpool was no seaside outing for the Blues. The *Liverpool Daily Post* summed it up with 'Everton will never play so well and at the same time be defeated so heavily'. Blackpool 7 Everton 1! Strangely enough, Everton might have scored first as Lawton grazed the crossbar with an effort. But then the goals flowed at the other end, with Dix scoring two, then Mortensen and Dodds, all within the first 32 minutes. In the second half, Mortensen, Dix and Dodds added to Everton's discomfort before Lawton scored a consolation goal in the 82nd minute with a flashing effort.

He was spared the return at Goodison, where Everton lost 3-1, as he was on Army duty against an FA XI in front of a best-of-season 28,542 at the Victoria Ground, Stoke. West Bromwich Albion's winger Billy Elliott scored twice in 22 minutes for the soldiers but Brentford's Leslie Smith responded for the FA a minute before half-time. A spurt of three goals in four minutes saw Stoke's Freddie Steele score for the FA, then Lawton with a header and Jack Rowley (Manchester United) from a penalty making it 4-2 for the khaki lads. Elliott then completed his hat-trick.

Then it was Lancashire Senior Cup time for Tommy with the visit of Chester to Goodison. Wally Boyes was back for Everton after a year's absence, but Billy Hughes put the Cestrians ahead after just 30 seconds. Everton recovered with a McIntosh penalty after seven minutes and took the lead through Stevenson on 23 minutes. The Irish international scored his second three minutes before the break. In the second half, Jackson, and Stevenson, for his hat-trick, piled on the goals for Everton before Bill Loxham scored Chester's second three minutes from the whistle. George Scales, the Chester goalkeeper, appeared to save his best for Tommy Lawton, but Everton had a 5-2 lead from the first leg.

The Everton No.9 made up for not scoring in the first leg the following week at Sealand Road in the second leg, even though the final scoreline did not do entire justice to Chester. Tommy headed in the first goal on six minutes but Astbury levelled on 19 minutes and Bill Loxham gave the Cestrians the lead eight minutes later. Although McIntosh soon equalised, just before the break Dave McNeil hit a Chester penalty kick straight at George Burnett, which might have changed the complexion of the game had he scored. In the second half it was one-way traffic – Lawton soon nicked a couple, Stevenson scored three and McIntosh hit his second. Lawton completed the scoring with his fourth goal to make it 9-2 on the day and 14-4 on aggregate.

On All Fools' Day, at least the Army had the laugh over the RAF, for once taking an easy 4-0 win, watched by 50,000 at Tynecastle in a one-sided affair that was decided in the first half. West Brom's Elliott scored first on 20 minutes, then Rowley, having intercepted a Hagan effort, made it 2-0 a minute later. Mercer laid one on for Hagan on 29 minutes and Lawton got into the scoring act two minutes from the interval. That completed the essentials of the game.

Everton's Stevenson, injured in the services game, was absent for yet another local derby with Tranmere on 8 April, this one in the second leg of the Liverpool Senior Cup with Rovers already five goals adrift from the first leg. By such standards this was a more sedate-scoring match – one goal in the first half, courtesy of Lawton, and no more scoring until the last quarter of an hour when Tommy, with his second strike, Wainwright and Bentham finished it at 4-0.

On Easter Monday at Goodison it was also the big Merseyside derby with Liverpool. The match counted for the Lancashire Senior Cup first leg as well, and also coincided with benefit cheques day for many players. There was also a reunion in the Everton ranks after some time, with Gillick and Britton playing. It also meant that the Blues' two inside-forwards, Gillick and Boyes, were actually both wingers! Tommy Jones scored from a splendid free kick from a yard outside the box after five minutes, then McIntosh added a second ten minutes later. On 28 minutes, Lawton wheeled to hit a drive with his left foot that Hobson managed to stop, only for Grant to pick up the scraps for 3-0 to Everton, which was the final score.

The second leg saw Liverpool wipe off the deficit with two goals from Mick Hulligan and one from Done, but even after extra time, in which Everton appeared to be lasting the pace better if not scoring a goal, it was agreed that a further match would take place. This was initially planned for the following Wednesday but was eventually played on 22 April, the day of the England v Scotland match at Hampden Park, so there was no Lawton for the decider at Anfield, which Liverpool won 4-2.

Tommy, on the day, was on England duty at Hampden Park for the Sassenachs' fourth win in a row against the Scots and their eighth during the war period. A wartime record at the time of 133,000 attended, with 'Monty' among the array of guest names. Caskie gave Scotland a 19th-minute lead from fully 25 yards but two minutes later Carter fed Lawton, who pivoted to storm a crashing drive in, followed 13 minutes later with an amazing low finish, according to *The Scotsman*, for a second England goal to put them ahead. Hagan headed on for Carter to score on 36 minutes from the edge of the area but there was no more scoring until Dodds did so on 66 minutes from a Caskie feed but England held on for a 3-2 victory.

There was more England-type duty for Tommy Lawton when fronting an England XI against Combined Services at Stamford Bridge, watched by 30,627. The highly rated Britton–Cullis–Mercer half-back line was fielded. Lawton beat Swift early doors but the post got in the way, before Hagan headed England into the lead just before half-time. The services then lost Matt Busby with a torn shoulder muscle. Rowley, from the penalty spot, and Lawton gave the inside-forward trio a goal each, Carter responding for the services, beaten 3-2.

It was then off to Cardiff's Ninian Park on 6 May but this was a poor affair between Wales and England. In the 27th minute Lawton twisted on to a loose ball and hit the target from 20 yards, then Leslie Smith added a second goal on 52 minutes with a fierce shot, while Wales were handicapped by an injury to Walley Barnes.

Everton, having drawn 1-1 at Southport in the Liverpool Senior Cup Final first leg, in which both teams had a player sent off, welcomed Lawton back in a Blues shirt for the second leg a week later. Southport, despite ten guest players on parade, won with a Jimmy Dougal (Preston North End) goal after 20 minutes. Everton had also been forced to field guests in Glidden and Irish international Sammy Jones, a centre-half of Blackpool. So it was a non-scoring day for both Lawton and Everton and the cup was taken back to Haig Avenue with the Sandgrounders.

Tommy had just one more match to go this season, at Anfield with the Western Command taking on the RAF on 20 May. It proved to be an outstanding finale to the season with both teams displaying the highest of entertainment value and standard of play. Unfortunately, the quality of the finishing was not quite as comparable. The flyboys had but five serious attempts at scoring – Dodds found a home for three of them, the first best of the trio. Another had taken a deflection off Sproston to fool Swift. Doherty simply hit the stand roof with his effort. Dodds opened the scoring on 15 minutes, Andy Black of Hearts levelled on the half-hour and, a minute later, the Command edged ahead through Stan Williams (Aberdeen). However, the high spot of the day was, undoubtedly, the effort of Stanley Matthews to score for the RAF. He beat five players in a faultless dribble, only to be thwarted by Swift's save, allowing Dodds to finish the raid. Lawton again missed out in the scoring department but had come close both early and late, the latter when he turned on a ball moving away from him but still managed to hit it close to the mark.

Despite two blank days, Lawton had enjoyed his best scoring season with 63 goals from some 40 various matches. Everton's season had tailed off disappointingly, but among the 46 players used, 18 had played just once. Preston's McIntosh had been the only ever-present for the Blues, eight others had appeared twice and four turned out three times. Tommy's club contribution had been 40 goals in 25 games.

CHAPTER NINE

Super Solo Show Sinks the Scots

WITH THE war moving seriously into the continent of Europe, the availability of players serving in the armed forces began to diminish substantially. In fact, Tommy Lawton's first match of the 1944/45 season was for Western Command against the RAF at Bloomfield Road, Blackpool. In good form, he scored twice in the first half but the flyboys were on top afterwards and earned a 2-2 draw.

But for the first league game, it was at home to Manchester United, where Tommy was given the Everton captaincy, his first time at Goodison, although previously he had captained away. There was a different right-winger in Everton colours in Syd Rawlings, the Millwall player who had played for Southport against the Blues the previous season. The amateur George Makin was on the other wing.

After going close at the start, United had a chance from the penalty spot but George Roughton shot straight at George Burnett, who palmed it away. Then on 27 minutes Rawlings scored on his debut, a lead lasting all of a minute before Albert Mycock equalised. On 37 minutes United led with a comic goal. Roland Bartholomew (Grimsby guest) centred, Burnett missed it and the ball went in off Jim Currier's back! Lawton had been lively despite close attention and produced his best effort in the game when his 20-yard rocket hit the bar, but United won 2-1.

In the return at Maine Road, with Manchester United's Old Trafford still out of commission through war damage, there was a new left-wing pairing for Everton, with Tom Peters (Doncaster guest) and Boyes appearing. There was no first-half scoring despite several efforts from Lawton, and it was Peters who eventually gave Everton a 52nd-minute lead, followed by a second through Rawlings. Bill Bryant scored for United but Boyes added a fine solo effort for Everton to win 3-1.

The Combined Services went to Northern Ireland the following week for two games. On 9 September they attracted a record Windsor Park crowd of 50,000 with receipts of £4,597. There were goals aplenty and flowing football from both teams, yet the result did no justice to the Irish. The Army and RAF players appearing for the services won 8-4 but the scoreline gives no indication of the closeness of the play. Ireland went behind, then led and even levelled again later. Ireland's Paddy Bonnar had a goal disallowed before it was 4-4. The last two services goals came when Ireland had lost defender Hugh Barr with an injury three minutes from time. Jack Vernon also had to have stitches inserted in a head wound after an aerial collision with Lawton. Peter Doherty, the outstanding player on the day, scored all four Irish goals, Carter equalled this with his own four-timer, Mullen scored two, Mortensen one, fashioned by Matthews, and Lawton had the last scoring word.

On the following Monday, the Irish League took on the Combined Services and again, after dominating the first half hour, lost four goals thereafter at Cliftonville. Here there was again a record: 22,000 and receipts of £1,490. Lawton scored twice in the 35th and 44th minutes, fed Edelston for the third, and Mortensen scored number four.

Saturday, 16 September also had a UK flavour, with Wales the opposition for England in another international, this time at Anfield in front of a record 38,483 attendance. England's forward line was the same as the Combined Services against Ireland but Reg Flewin of Portsmouth was introduced at centre-half. It was one of Wales's best performances. On five minutes, Dearson shot firmly in after a corner and Lucas added to it with a splendid left-foot effort with 14 minutes gone. The England wing-halves Mercer and Welsh were all over the place and never in the right one; Swift had an uncomfortable game in goal, too. But England recovered, Lawton heading down for Carter to score, followed by a typical Tommy power header that levelled the game a minute before half-time. But a well-fought second half almost produced a late goal for Wales. Cumner made the opening but Swansea's Tim Rogers snatched at the chance and sliced it wide.

Lawton returned to the colour Blue for yet another Chester occasion at Goodison, though the Cestrians were unbeaten at the time. On 16 minutes Lawton headed down for Wainwright to score but six minutes later Andy Black (Hearts guest) equalised – the same player Lawton had secured earlier for Everton! On 26 minutes Tommy's lethal left foot made it 2-1 and seven minutes later he set up Makin for the Blues' third.

Two minutes into the second half Lawton hit a right-foot shot into the far corner for 4-1 but then the scoring quietened down until Astbury scored another fine one for Chester on 68 minutes. Makin added his second Everton goal three minutes later and on 78 minutes Lawton drew the opposition before slipping the ball through to Rawlings for Everton's sixth goal.

Then a much-changed Western Command team, reflecting the movement of personnel at the time, met Cumberland Services at Whitehaven on 30 September, though there was also a Command XI beating an RAF side at Barnstaple 5-4 on the same afternoon. Yet, at last Lawton got to play with Black in the same team. In fact, he was centre-forward flanked by Black and Phil Taylor of Liverpool. These two scored the goals in a 2-1 win for the Command.

Returning to Everton duty, Lawton featured against Tranmere Rovers at Prenton Park on 7 October, the day after his 25th birthday. Within two minutes he was on the mark with a strong low drive but Rovers equalised through an Alf Hanson (Chelsea guest) header five minutes before the break. Lawton celebrated with two more goals in the second half for a birthday-plus hat-trick. It was a prelude to the international with Scotland at Wembley.

England showed several changes from the team that played Wales. Mercer switched to left-half with Frank Soo at right-half and Arsenal's Joy in between them. A different left-wing partnership, with Len Goulden and Leslie Smith, was drafted in. This was a game of two halves. England could do nothing in the first 45 minutes as Arthur Milne of Hibs scored for Scotland after three minutes and they made matters awkward for England thereafter. Matthews could find no way round the stoic George Cummings, the Villa full-back, and wandered around trying to find an alternative route. The defence was none too sure either and George Hardwick had problems with Hibs' Gordon Smith.

The transformation in the second half was largely due to Lawton metaphorically taking the game by the scruff of the neck. On 56 minutes a long pass from Soo was snapped up by Tommy, who shimmied and by-passed three defenders before cracking the equaliser. It revived England, and five minutes later he headed in a corner from Leslie Smith with split-second timing and direction. Four minutes later he accepted a pass from Matthews and set up Goulden for England's third goal. Three goals in nine minutes had altered everything. Tommy Walker did reduce the arrears on 76 minutes but the flow of the play was still with England. Lawton completed his trio, made another for Carter and, with the Scottish defence still deranged and distractedly glued on the Everton centre-forward, Leslie Smith scored a sixth. With various royal persons from home and abroad, Cabinet ministers and other high-ranking guests among the 90,000 crowd, charity also benefited by £23,000.

Again the day was almost overshadowed by Scotland – incidentally wearing numbers for the first time – including 23-year-old Darlington centre-half Bob Thyne in place of the injured Bill Shankly. As a Royal Engineers NCO on D-Day plus 7, Thyne had been blown up out of a trench, sustaining shrapnel wounds to his leg and fearing he might be unable to play again. He did not let Scotland down but they were beaten by a better team. *The People* began its report thus: 'Tom Lawton of Everton was England's superman at Wembley Stadium.'

Army duties on the field sent the Western Command to Newcastle to meet Northern Command. Again the composition of the team continued to change and, although Swift, Elliott, Welsh and both Phil and George Taylor were included along with Lawton, the result was a 6-1 defeat. With the chief problem at half-back, only late in the match and four goals down did Welsh swap inside-left for wing-half but it was already too late. Lawton managed a goal after 78 minutes.

Seven days on and the Army in England crossed the border into Scotland again for yet another clash with their opposite numbers. At Hampden Park, a crowd of 41,558 saw Willie Fagan give the Scots a 21st-minute lead, but Billy Elliott's typical dash and finish made it 1-1 seven minutes later. It was left to Lawton in the 33rd minute to provide another 'smashing' header, which the newspapers reported as being good enough to win any match and this one in particular. The next day Lawton began a series of articles for the *Empire News* each Sunday.

Into an Everton shirt for only the fifth time in the season, Lawton saved arguably his best goal of the season for the visit to unbeaten Manchester City at Maine Road. On seven minutes Harry Catterick had the City defence in a tangle but it was unfortunate that it was Jackie Bray who put the ball past his own Frank Swift. The duel between the City goalkeeper and Lawton was well contested. Tommy let rip with one that somehow Swift turned over the bar with one hand but England's No.1 had no chance with Lawton's 43rd-minute delivery on the turn from 30 yards, which Swift saw too late because of its velocity. Tommy made Stevenson's goal on 52 minutes and Jimmy Heale scored City's consolation effort 13 minutes later, as Everton won 3-1.

Both Swift and Lawton were required for Western Command against AA Command the following week. Tommy was back at his roots, with the game staged at Bolton's Burnden Park. He starred in it with all three goals for his team, who did well to share a 3-3 draw, as Liverpool's Jack Balmer was taken ill at half-time and missed the rest of the match.

On 18 November Crewe Alexandra handed Everton another shock at Goodison. Led by their new player-manager Frank Hill, the former Scottish international, and including two players named McCormick, Jim the Spurs right-winger and Joe the Bolton inside-left, Crewe went a goal behind to Stevenson after 18 minutes. But ten minutes later Joe McCormick levelled and within another three had put them ahead. Lindley was struggling with a thigh injury for Everton and went on the wing in the second half.

Crewe then had a goal disallowed for offside before Lawton, bursting through, appeared to be overcrowded until he dragged the ball back and hit a right-foot shot into the net on 52 minutes to level the score at 2-2. Tommy Jones at inside-right headed Everton's third goal in 61 minutes only for Frank Rawcliffe (Notts County guest) to make it 3-3 nine minutes later. On 78 minutes Stoke's Albert Basnett put Crewe in front and four minutes from the end Rawcliffe made it 5-3 with a shot through George Burnett's legs to complete the goalkeeper's unhappy afternoon, although skipper Lawton consoled him in the dressing room along with secretary Theo Kelly.

History repeated itself in the return match at Gresty Road on 25 November because ten months earlier Tommy Lawton had scored five goals for Everton against Crewe Alexandra on the same ground. 'Stork' in the *Liverpool Daily Post* commented: 'Four of the goals will vie with anything I have witnessed.' After ten minutes Tommy slipped past Hughes and hit a left-foot shot from 20 yards. Twenty-five minutes later he topped that with one from 35 yards. Within two minutes of the second half starting Rawlings gave him a simple one close in for his hat-trick. Then there was another cracking effort from way out on 68 minutes, and a classic Lawton header two minutes later completed his five-timer. Crewe's sole response came on 59 minutes from Ted Powell in his only outing for them in the war period!

On the Monday following, 'Pilot's Sports Log' in the *Liverpool Evening Express* mentioned as follows: 'Tommy called as I was entering my records. I asked him how many goals next

Saturday? He replied: "I'll try for six – put it down.'" Of course he had only hit five!

Topsy-turvy wartime football was never better illustrated than a week later at Wrexham when Everton, showing just two changes, lost 1-0 to the Welsh side at the Racecourse Ground. Naturally, Lawton was given extra attention and West Bromwich Albion's Billy Tudor kept close attention. Worse for Everton, a minute after Johnny Hancocks (Walsall guest) had scored for Wrexham, Tommy suffered an ankle injury and finished the game on the right wing.

He had been selected to play for the Army against the FA at Bradford but was not fit enough, so Don Welsh – who else? – filled in at centre-forward for him. Tommy was back when Stockport County arrived at Goodison on 16 December short of three players and finished the game short of goals in a 6-1 defeat to Everton. Blues secretary Theo Kelly loaned Catterick and Bentham to their opponents and sent a message round the ground to locate Mike Murphy, a pre-war South Liverpool player who was on leave from the Army. On nine minutes a Lawton special opened the scoring, then Stevenson finished a three-man move involving Tommy on 35 minutes for a second goal. TG Jones contributed one on 59 minutes and laid on one for Lawton three minutes later. Tommy then did the same for Stevenson's second goal on 82 minutes with Makin completing the half-dozen with four minutes left. There was still time for Catterick to score against his own side with a minute left. Mention was made of one save by Larry Gage, the Fulham goalkeeper playing for County, stopping a piledriver from Lawton from 15 yards. A tribute to a paratrooper no less!

The return at Edgeley Park was even easier for Everton, the forward line composed of Wainwright on the right wing with TG Jones his partner. Mercer was at inside-left, Makin on his wing and Lawton leading the line. Jones stole the show with a treble, Wainwright and Lawton scoring a couple each in the 7-0 walkover. Then on Christmas Day against Tranmere, Everton chucked away a two-goal lead presented by Lawton who then contrived to miss twice as many goals in the first half. Rovers were not to be pushed away this time and, with Ernie Richards back from overseas service for the first time and getting a grip on Tommy, at last they triumphed. Everton's loan player Wyles scored twice for them, with Gil Glidden and Alf Hanson scoring the others as they doubled the Blues effort at Goodison.

For Lawton, his next fixture was not until New Year's Day for Western Command against Scottish Command at Ayr. Andy Black was inside-left and Elliott on the right wing. A well-fought encounter was scoreless at the interval but Elliott and Lawton – described by agency reports as 'clever and strong' – hit the only two goals of the game. Jack Snape, the Coventry City centre-half, was praised for his display against Tommy.

Everton affairs were then with Lawton's home-town Bolton Wanderers for the next two outings in the War Qualifying Competition, the Trotters having not played at Goodison for two years. Despite the discomfort of a boil on his neck, Lawton was simmering in front of goal as ever and on the mark after only three minutes following a fine run by Stevenson, with a right-foot cross shot to put Everton ahead. Having dominated the first half, Everton were caught out a minute after the restart when Jones's back-heel went awry and ended with Nat Lofthouse the latest 'Lawton' out of the Bolton school making it 1-1. Shortly afterwards, Jones went back to his centre-half berth that he had been vacating and swapped with Bentham, a move which might have been better from the kick-off. It was left to Lawton to snatch victory in the 78th minute. From a corner, he jumped between two defenders and headed down, the ball just crossing the line.

A week on at Burnden Park and, despite the underfoot conditions, there was an excellent performance by both teams, ending in Bolton's first home defeat of the season. On 20 minutes, Lawton made a goal for Stevenson but the lead lasted just six minutes before young Lofthouse finished a move by debutant amateur Sid Koffman. Five minutes before the break Lawton provided Rawlings with a goal to restore Everton's lead. In the second half Bentham sustained a cut over the eye requiring stitches and had to go on the wing. In the rearranged side he actually made the third Everton goal in the 72nd minute when Tommy headed in his centre.

Next came another big charity match, with an FA XI taking on the RAF at Coventry City's snowbound Highfield Road and, once more, despite the conditions, there was first-rate entertainment and ten goals to show for it. Once again the flyboys had the edge and won 6-4, Mortensen getting a hat-trick. Lawton lacked support apart from Len Shackleton who scored twice for the FA. Tommy's goal came when he collected a clearance, beat George Hardwick and found the net. Neil Franklin was the other FA scorer, while Dodds with two and Leslie Smith were the other RAF marksmen.

Lawton returned for Everton's home game with Stockport County on 27 January only to inflict more pain on the visitors. It also became a milestone in scoring for the Bolton boy who had conquered part of Merseyside. Stockport again had to borrow bodies from Everton – Catterick, Makin and Hill to be exact. It only took a couple of minutes for Catterick to put his old mates a goal down, too, but then there was no more scoring until 25 minutes when Lawton started a move on the halfway line involving three other players, ending with Bentham back-heeling for the onrushing Lawton to score. Ten minutes later he scored with a peach of a header for his second and, five minutes before the break, nodded in his hat-trick. A Jimmy McIntosh penalty made it 4-1 for Everton by the end of the half.

In the second half, after Catterick had notched his second for County, Bentham scored Everton's fifth goal and Tommy headed the sixth on 53 minutes to hoist his historic 400th goal in all matches since his debut nearly ten years previously. Bentham hit the seventh on 73 minutes, then number eight came from a Rawlings header and, as Stevenson was the sole Everton forward without a goal, Lawton provided him with the ninth after 86 minutes.

The early copy of the running report by 'Pilot' in the *Liverpool Evening Express* stated: 'Lawton could not find his shooting boots for from twelve yards he completely missed the ball.' Then came the four-timer!

England played Scotland again, this time at Villa Park, with Company Sergeant-Major Instructor Lawton hoping to add to his 400 career goals against Petty Officer Bobby Brown, the 21-year-old debutant amateur playing in goal for Scotland. Tommy failed in that but had a hand in the England goals anyway. On 23 minutes Albert 'Sailor' Brown headed in a Lawton–Matthews move against his shipmate namesake! On 37 minutes Delaney levelled and for a time Matt Busby was off being treated for injury. In the second half Lawton made one for Mortensen on 57 minutes then Dodds equalised four minutes later. Only in the last 15 minutes did England assert themselves and again Lawton provided Mortensen for his second goal. But

Brown kept his best saves for Lawton – three in particular – and the 400-goal-man also hit an upright.

Derby day, 10 February, on Merseyside at Anfield provided another triumph for the Reds. Horace Cumner, the Arsenal and Wales international, opened the scoring for Liverpool on 15 minutes with a centre that went awry – but into the net. Welsh then hit a penalty against a post and Everton, although hardly in it, managed to level in the 67th minute. Grant crossed and Lawton judged his header, beating three defenders to the ball. However, parity lasted only three minutes before Nieuwenhuys restored Liverpool's lead and Cumner scored his second for the Reds' third goal with nine minutes remaining.

Lawton was then on leave but had received Everton's permission to play for Millwall at Brighton on 17 February, his presence increasing the attendance to around 10,000. However, it did nothing for the Lions' points tally or Tommy's goals as the Seagulls swooped for a convincing 6-2 win at the Goldstone. Then, back in uniform for the Western Command against Northern Command at Molineux, Welsh and Lucas scored for Tommy's outfit in the 2-0 win.

On 3 March, a morning dash from London enabled Lawton to get to the Chester game at Goodison on time. The Cestrians had to make eight changes from the programme team and were in arrears in the eighth minute when Lawton headed in Grant's centre for his first post-400 goal. Bentham hit a second Everton goal nine minutes later, courtesy of Lawton. Meanwhile, the referee missed a handball by Everton's Hill and in the second half the Blues went further ahead when Lawton's left foot found the target, although there was suspicion of offside. A minute later Wolves' Tommy Burden scored for Chester but then Rawlings had a penalty saved by Chester goalkeeper Ray

King on 70 minutes before Stevenson made it four for Everton with six minutes left.

Army and other representative matches would dominate Lawton's last third of the season. At St James' Park, Newcastle on 10 March, the RAF were hard pressed for once with Bert Williams having more to do in goal than Swift. Lawton went closest to scoring with one effort, had a goal disallowed for offside, then went close again when his header struck the crossbar. Despite all this, a disappointing game ended scoreless.

Western Command met London District at Stoke the following week and the match was totally dominated by Don Welsh playing inside-left with Lawton leading the line. The Charlton Athletic player scored all five goals in the whitewashing of the opposition that included Welsh's club colleague George Smith.

With such games coming regularly, Lawton was selected for the short trip to Belgium, now in Allied hands! Under the guise of FA Services the first game was in Bruges on 24 March. The Red Devils were put to the sword 8-1 in comfort, Lawton scoring four, including three in 23 minutes of the second half. Matthews, Leslie Smith, 'Sailor' Brown and Mortensen were the other scorers. The following day Belgium were taken on in Brussels with some changes, including Matthews out with injury. It was a tighter affair but the FA Services won 3-2, Lawton scoring all three, including a penalty!

It was back to earth and Blighty on 31 March – the reality of another Liverpool encounter in an Everton shirt for Tommy at Goodison. Moreover, the Reds had the perfect answer to 'seven-goal Lawton' with Laurie Hughes marking him and Busby acting as a sweeper for anything his colleague missed. Lawton was also suffering from a groin injury and was below his usual effectiveness anyway. One second-half goal from Billy Liddell was enough for a Liverpool win in front of the 51,512 crowd, which bulged at the seams. Many spectators broke in, and the overflow was accommodated on the cinder track by the police.

Lawton's injury kept him out of the next two matches but he was back fit for another clash with Scotland at Hampden Park in a match in which nothing went right for the Scots. They even had Tommy Bogan carried off in the first minute with torn ligaments – though Swift carried him off in his arms – but sensibly Leslie Johnstone of Clyde was allowed as his substitute, although not until 14 minutes later! Waddell did score for Scotland but was pulled back for an earlier free kick and a Lawton effort on 28 minutes was also ruled out, this one for offside. Even so, Carter immediately scored for England and Johnstone levelled on 38 minutes for 1-1 at half-time. In the second half, on 58 minutes, Carter split the Scottish backs, Lawton racing 30 yards to hit low into the far corner for a second England goal. A back-heel from Tommy then allowed Brown to score another three minutes later. After this, Lawton had one goal ruled out mysteriously then Scotland missed a 75th-minute penalty when Swift saved Busby's effort. Scotland then lost Jim Harley for a time, off for repairs. Bobby Brown pushed out a shot from Carter, and Matthews had a tap-in on 79 minutes. Five minutes later England had a penalty, too, so Leslie Smith took it as the only forward who had not scored. Lawton had the last word on 86 minutes with his second goal in the 6-1 win.

But aside of this, those Red Devils in Belgium were up for more and this time it was not the picnic followed by a feast of goals for the FA Services. In Liege, a goal by Wolves' Bobby King ensured a 1-1 draw and the following day there were no goals around in another draw in Brussels. Information about the games proved sketchy, if there was any at all, but this is unsurprising under the circumstances with front-page headlines announcing: 'Berlin's Last Hours'. So it was two blank days for Lawton, who was looking for goals after his seven-up performance on his last visit to Belgium. He was also in for a tough time and had plenty of bruises to prove it, keeping him out of Everton's team on 28 April against Southport.

He was okay by the time England played against Wales in Cardiff on 5 May but it turned out to be Raich Carter's day with a hat-trick as a gallant Welsh team was just edged out 3-2. Carter's first was on seven minutes, then Mercer handled and Cumner equalised from the penalty on the half-hour. Straight from the second-half kick-off Lawton intercepted the ball and found Smith, who passed to Brown. A defence-splitting affair ended with a finely judged Carter lob from 25 yards. On 55 minutes the Sunderland inside-forward completed his trio, though the shot was deflected. Ten minutes from time, Coventry's George Edwards reduced the arrears for Wales, despite the fact that he had been involved in a collision with Laurie Scott in the first half and lost a couple of teeth, while his opponent played the second half in a daze!

Foreign shores beckoned a few days later and Tommy was off to Italy, even landing on VE Day to entertain the troops and, inevitably, cries of 'D-Day Dodgers' and 'Aldershot Commandos' aimed at the Army team selected. This was unwarranted, if understandable, but especially wrong for Tommy Lawton whose flat feet would not have allowed him in the infantry. Despite long, uncomfortable road journeys there was some sightseeing in between. The football in Italy produced laughs on the way as well. Lawton scored five goals in one match and four in another against various Army teams. One of the more difficult matches was against the champions of the Central Mediterranean Forces, which brough a narrow win, 2-0, with Blackburn's Bob Pryde keeping a close eye on Tommy in that one. Overall, the ten games in Italy and Greece produced nine wins and a draw, with a goal ratio of 55 to 11.

Lawton was back, along with Mercer, for the international against France at Wembley on 26 May and was appointed captain. He won the toss. After ten minutes, Soo, Matthews, with a cross, and Tommy were involved in a movement that led to Carter scoring but the French were not unsettled by it. Their combination play was excellent and the twin central defenders, Gusti Jordan and Lucien Jasseron, provided a formidable barrier. A minute before half-time Ernest Vaast equalised from a pass by René Bihel. In the meantime, Leslie Smith had a penalty saved by the spectacular Julien Darui.

Lawton headed England back in front on 79 minutes before the French left it really late to secure a well-earned draw with just 20 seconds remaining. Oscar Heisserer scored from an opening created by Alfred Aston. Heisserer had been a refugee in Switzerland since 1943, having escaped from being press-ganged into the German Army with others from Alsace. He had helped its liberation, too. For his part, Darui had been captured at Dunkirk but escaped, while full-back Maurice Dupuis, a Versailles gendarme, was a rooftop sniper in the Resistance fight for Paris.

CHAPTER TEN

Transferred from Everton to Chelsea

THERE HAD been rumours that Tommy Lawton was to ask to be placed on the transfer list because his wife was unwell and had been advised by her doctor to move south for her health. Clubs immediately started scrambling for his signature. Of those in the south, Arsenal, Chelsea, Crystal Palace and Millwall were among the first to be interested. Nottingham Forest was another club interested, but despite frantic speculation, after two weeks Tommy withdrew his application as his domestic problem had been resolved.

A pre-season visit to Switzerland under the FA Services banner produced a shock for the tourists, beaten 3-1 at the Neufeld Stadion in Berne by the national team. Such was the overwhelming dominance that the Swiss crowd carried Frank Swift off the field at the end because of his outstanding performance. Tommy Lawton was quoted as saying they were the finest combination he had seen. The Swiss led 1-0 at the interval and 'Sailor' Brown was the scorer of the Services' sole goal. Three days later in Zurich the Swiss B team was beaten 3-0 – Tom Finney, Micky Fenton and Willie Watson were the scorers.

No sooner was he back in England than Lawton injured his right knee by falling at the Army Cadet Camp and it was decided as a precaution that he would see a specialist. He thus missed the Celtic benefit match for Mattha Gemmell on 15 August in which Everton lost 4-0. But the club had announced that Lawton would be captain for the team in the coming season with Norman Greenhalgh his deputy. However, on 29 August Tommy was still a spectator when Bolton visited Goodison but was given the all-clear by the specialist and had started training already for the Evertonians' game with Wanderers on the following Saturday.

But little went right for either Everton or Lawton at Burnden Park. The team lost 3-1 after Boyes had given them the lead. Tommy had a terrific shot that hit an upright and in the second half his header rebounded down off the bar and appeared to be over the line before being cleared. Shortly after that he injured his bad knee after stubbing his toe on the turf and faded out of the game.

More woe followed. On 4 September at a board meeting Lawton asked to be put on the transfer list again as he and his wife had been unable to find accommodation in an area that would suit her medical needs. He emphasised that he had no quarrel with Everton Football Club.

At Preston in the next match, Lawton led the attack but appeared subdued. He was brought down for a penalty, which Mercer converted, Wainwright having already scored Everton's opener in the 2-0 win. Then for Tommy it was Victory International time in Ireland at Windsor Park, Belfast. A record crowd of 45,061 paid £4,446 for the privilege. With an early shot, a header and getting a knock from which he recovered quickly, Lawton was lively at the start, but gradually Vernon clamped down on him. However, both he and Carter had goals disallowed for infringements. In fact, it was not until ten minutes from time that Mortensen scored the only goal for England from a Matthews pass, with his shot being deflected in by a defender.

Then on the following Monday, under the cloak of the Combined Services but with only three changes to the team, a new left wing of Wolves' Billy Wright and Watson, with Mortensen taking Carter's place at inside-right, the Irish League needed only one goal of their own for victory at Cliftonville. The all-important goal came from a cross by Bobby Langton, finished off by Linfield's Sam McCrory four minutes from half-time. Earlier, Lawton had been unlucky with a fierce left-foot drive, which cannoned off the crossbar. Then in the 52nd minute, Watson was brought down and Neil Franklin – a strange choice for a spot-kick taker – had his effort saved by the diving Gerry Matier of Glentoran. Not that the Services were inactive. Mercer, Mortensen and Lawton all went close but Matier was in no mood to concede.

Lawton was unable to attend an Everton board meeting to discuss his transfer request but he was available for the Lancashire Senior Cup tie against Liverpool on 19 September. He scored twice in 15 minutes, then Bentham hit Everton's third on 24 minutes before the Reds took over! Welsh had already missed a penalty, so it was Balmer who was entrusted with a second spot kick, reducing the arrears. He added another goal and Les Shannon made it 3-3. Lawton was injured in the last ten minutes.

On 22 September Tommy was expected to play at home to Leeds but he only arrived at 2.50pm and was unfit to play. He had had injections in his right knee to remove swelling. Three days later the club agreed to his request to be placed on the transfer list for compassionate reasons. Millwall immediately expressed an interest in signing him, but Arsenal, Tottenham and Chelsea all said no. Tommy's injury had been aggravated in his recent matches and he was obviously far from fit for football.

On 27 September, the *Daily Herald* queried whether Lawton was the player 'nobody can afford'. It was believed Everton wanted something in the region of £17,000 to £18,000. He was also continuing to have injections in the injured tendon in his right knee. Having been pencilled in for the Army team to play Dundee in a benefit match on 1 October and naturally unable to turn out, it was a surprise when Tommy celebrated his 26th birthday by playing for Everton away to Manchester United at Maine Road.

There was no celebration for either club or player in a goalless draw, the respective centre-halves Whalley and Mercer keeping a tight rein on Lawton and Rowley, respectively. Tommy did manage to create a couple of openings in the first half but nothing materialised. While hostilities may have long since ceased it should be remembered that Lawton – now stationed in Shropshire – like many other players, was still serving in the forces.

It was no surprise that Tommy was omitted from the England team to play Wales at The Hawthorns in view of his recent knee trouble; Newcastle's Albert Stubbins, another prolific wartime marksman, was at No.9. However, oddly enough, along with Rowley, Tommy was selected for the British Army to play the Belgian Army in Brussels on 13 October and the BAOR in Dusseldorf the following day. The Army won 3-2 in Brussels and, thanks to a couple of late goals by Lawton, earned a 2-2 draw with the lads in Germany. These were his first two goals of the season!

Transfer or not, Lawton was in the Everton team to play Sunderland at Goodison Park on 20 October. He proved to be in almost untouchable form with a sparkling hat-trick – which were to be his last goals for Everton. Wainwright made the first, drawing the opposition for Tommy to finish with a slick low left-foot shot after 13 minutes. The second came from a perfectly judged free kick from 40 yards by Tommy Jones that Lawton glided in perfectly. Number three was provided by Rawlings, who stabbed the ball back for a typical Tommy hook shot. The fourth Everton goal went to Jones, with no reply on the day from Sunderland.

George Green's caricatures in Liverpool newspapers were outstanding. His last one of Tommy had the catch line: 'A-Tom-ic Lawton'. In fact, rumours of a move to Chelsea were rife and, in another bizarre twist to the tale, Arsenal sought to approach Everton for his services against Charlton at The Valley. It was refused and Tommy had to watch from the stands, the Gunners misfiring in a 6-2 defeat, with Don Welsh one of the Addicks' scorers! But with no shifting in the transfer scenario, Lawton was in the Everton team at Sheffield United on 3 November. There were eight of their championship-winning team on view, too. But little went right for them. Burnett might have saved two of the four goals put past him, United's left-half Harry Latham, playing out of position in the middle, held Lawton, and Bentham was injured during the game. In hindsight, playing Tommy might not have been the best idea, with his mindset not on Merseyside.

The transfer to Chelsea was completed in a Chester hotel at 11.30am on 7 November 1945 at a fee said to be slightly under the record £14,000 when Bryn Jones went to Arsenal from Wolves in 1938. The announcement between the two clubs, Everton and Chelsea, was not made until 11 o'clock on 8 November. The *Daily Mirror* reported that Tommy's wife was ill in bed at the time of his move and had been the reason for the necessity to find a club in the south, for her health. Tommy received his accrued share of his benefit amounting to £25 from August to November and the £10 signing-on fee at Chelsea.

On the morning of Tommy's debut for Chelsea on 10 November at Stamford Bridge against Birmingham – now City – he travelled in their coach to the ground! The official on the gate had to be told: 'I'm your new centre-forward!' His appearance in the blue shorts of Chelsea from his blue shirt at Everton was personally satisfying for him if not the Chelsea supporters. Birmingham, who had only recently returned from playing in Germany and were minus three players appearing for Wales, scored on six minutes through a fine strike by Wilson Jones but Lawton levelled on 15 minutes from a pass by Reg Williams. However, Jones then scored a second well-taken effort for Birmingham.

In the second half Lawton headed another equaliser but Chelsea conceded a penalty and Arthur Turner won the match for Birmingham, 3-2. Near the end Lawton set up Len Goulden but he crucially missed a sitter. Lawton had drawn the crowd, as the 52,959 was the highest of the season so far. Among the throng were the Moscow Dynamo team, who were due to play Chelsea in three days' time.

By now the fee for his transfer had been reduced to £11,500! The *Birmingham Daily Gazette* had commented on Lawton's goals with a phrase that any debutant would have appreciated: 'Each was a masterpiece of football craft.'

The Russians had had a first-hand account of Chelsea and Lawton. The paid admission for their match against Chelsea numbered 74,496, although the actual attendance was at least 85,000. Spectators ringed the touchline and clambered on to the roof of the main stand, several falling and needing treatment. It was amazing there were no fatalities as the Bridge was bursting at the seams. Chelsea had to borrow two Fulham players with Joe Bacuzzi and Jim Taylor becoming Pensioners for the day.

Limbering up before the kick-off, these super-fit Russians scarcely looked as if they had been digging trenches and filling sandbags outside Moscow when the Germans were on the doorstep of the Kremlin. After presenting the Chelsea players with a bouquet of flowers they dominated the first half with slick movement and players moving here there and everywhere, whatever the position expected of them. In another age it would be called total football. But Dynamo still went in 2-0 down! On 22 minutes, from a Jimmy Bain corner, Lawton fired a shot that Alexei 'Tiger' Khomich could only parry and that, quick as a flash, Goulden, following up, netted. Six minutes later came the second goal when Reg Williams charged down a clearance, had a try and it went in off Ivan Stankevich's foot. Lawton had had a 35-yard cracker that hit a post and another peach of an effort from eight yards, remarkably saved by Khomich, while the Russians had missed a penalty – Leonid Soloviev, the 'penalty tsar', had only hit a post on 34 minutes.

On 67 minutes, Vasili Kartsev got one back for Dynamo and six minutes later Evgeny Archangelski equalised, but Lawton hooked a high ball off several defenders and headed Chelsea back into the lead. The Russians had the last word at 3-3 through Vsevolod Bobrov, perhaps not the occasion for complaining about suspicions of offside.

The Army called and Lawton missed the Spurs game as Chelsea lost 2-1 at a quieter Stamford Bridge. He was back for the return on 24 November at White Hart Lane and it was a leaping Lawton that headed Chelsea ahead after six minutes. He also made another goal for Goulden but Tottenham proved the masters and won 3-2 in an absorbing match.

The goals flowed and the play ebbed from end to end at Griffin Park on 1 December. Brentford, two down in 20 minutes, even led five minutes from time before that man Lawton timed his header to perfection, ending it 4-4. He had also scored the second Chelsea goal after making the first for Alf Hanson.

Two days later, it was across to the other side of London, playing for England Army v Scotland Army at Tottenham. Showing leadership and dash, Tommy went close with a fast-rising effort just over the bar before Edelston gave the England side a 39th-minute lead. Lawton then, through cleverly changing feet, deceived two players before crashing in their second with a low drive. Jimmy Mullen hit the third from Tommy's 40-yard pass. There was no response from the Scots.

Then came the second game with Brentford for Chelsea, with arguably the most outstanding half-back line of the season on duty in Russell–Harris–Foss for the Blues. It was a match of misplaced passes, but at least a terrific eighth-minute strike by Lawton from just outside the area found the net. Durrant levelled but then Harris was injured just before the break before returning later. Dickie Foss made it 2-1 for Chelsea, Goulden added another, then Lawton collected a high ball from Foss and shot Chelsea 4-1 up. Bob Thomas reduced it to 4-2.

There was no rest for some, and Lawton was selected for the United Services team to play the FA XI at Portsmouth four days later. It was designated as an England trial match, too. With Stubbins in the FA team, the No.9 position was either

Mr L. or Mr S. Lawton, who noticeably opened up the attack by sweeping passes to the wings, scored twice for the Services, along with a goal each for Brown and Mullen. Stubbins got the FA goal in their 4-1 defeat.

Reality then came in the League South match at Swansea for Chelsea and Tommy, as the Londoners were two down in three minutes through Bolton's guest for the Swans, Jackie Roberts, and Trevor Ford scoring. Ford had another on 19 minutes before Len Dolding replied a minute later for Chelsea. In the second half, Ernie Jones and Ford made it 5-1 before some semblance of respectability saw Williams score after 71 minutes and Dolding five minutes later to make it 5-3. Lawton had been starved of the ball and Chelsea also had Barnsley guest Harry Ferrier injured and hobbling on the wing.

Back at the Bridge, Swansea proved just as difficult, not that Lawton could be blamed for another defeat. He scored a hat-trick as Chelsea lost 4-3. *The People* reporter referred to Tommy's treble as 'a characteristic Lawton effort, an acrobatic header and a right-foot shot'. Chelsea led in an entertaining game three times – Dennis Coleman, Ford, Roberts, and Coleman again in the dying moments settled the issue in Swansea's favour.

The holiday matches with Millwall provided Lawton with more goals for his collection – five in fact. At Stamford Bridge on Christmas Day, after a goalless first half, Chelsea scored three times, Tommy getting two and Goulden the other one. Boxing Day at The Den drew a crowd of 30,493, who witnessed three goals in the first half and another handful in the second half as Chelsea won 8-0. Lawton netted a threesome, Joe (Ten-goal) Payne, on his first appearance of the season and shifted to inside-right to accommodate the treble-shooter, scored a couple, as did Dickie Spence, with Goulden adding the eighth.

There were as many as seven goals in Chelsea's next outing at Southampton, but the Pensioners didn't get a sniff of one, unless you count the penalty that Goulden fired yards off target. The Saints had to make changes and included Reg Mountford, the Huddersfield full-back. They were also a man short so Chelsea loaned them Peter Buchanan. Inside four minutes Buchanan's corner kick led to Doug McGibbon opening Southampton's account. Ted Bates hit their second on 33 minutes, then McGibbon his second a minute before half-time. McGibbon ran riot with four goals in a 21-minute spell, although in fairness Williams was off injured for half an hour, which did not help the situation. There was a double hat-trick for McGibbon, while Lawton hardly had sight of the ball.

Naturally, it is *still* the Army Mr T. and duty for Western Command against Scottish Command on New Year's Day at Ayr. Lawton was back to form according to reports with two goals in the 4-3 win. Johnny Hancocks and Everton's Wally Fielding scored the other counters for Western Command.

The return of the FA Cup, with a sensible two-legged affair in the early stages from the first round proper to allow clubs to replenish empty larders of cash from during the war, saw Chelsea drawn against Leicester City at Stamford Bridge for the first leg on 5 January. The slippery surface and weighty ball did nothing for the spectacle but after ten minutes Payne headed against the bar and Lawton took care of the remains to put Chelsea ahead. Both players missed further chances and in the second half Charlie Adam levelled for City.

At Filbert Street in the second leg, Payne was absent injured, with Williams taking his place. On 21 minutes Goulden scored and Williams should have added to this shortly afterwards, although he did redeem himself in the second half with a goal in Chelsea's 2-0 win, 3-1 on aggregate.

Then Lawton was on England duty against Belgium at Wembley. A bone-hard surface greeted the teams at the Empire Stadium and England had changes to make with Soo injured. Billy Wright moved to right-half in his place, for an England debut. Matthews and Pye formed the right wing, Brown at inside-left. The earliest action of danger saw Lawton set up Pye but Belgian goalkeeper Francois Daenen saved. Then after 13 minutes Brown scored from 20 yards. Pye did get one in from a Matthews pass, with a left-foot effort. Lawton had a go but the goalkeeper rescued Belgium. Fog descended at half-time but through the mist Tommy hit a post with the goalkeeper motionless. The final score was 2-0.

The fourth round of the FA Cup brought West Ham United across town to Stamford Bridge on 26 January. A crowd of 65,726 turned up to see Alex Machin open the scoring in the first half for Chelsea and Dickie Spence ensure a 2-0 first-leg advantage to take to Upton Park on the Wednesday. Almer Hall snatched one back for the Hammers in the first half of the second leg but the Chelsea defence stayed firm and they reached the fifth round, where they were drawn against Aston Villa.

Tommy Lawton had now gone a handful of matches without scoring. Alas it did not alter at Coventry on 2 February. George Mason, the City centre-half, rarely let him have a sniff of the ball and Lawton also lacked support. Coventry's Spanish pair of Emilio Aldecoa and Jose Bilbao were lively and the former put them ahead on 42 minutes. Harry Barratt made it 2-0 from a penalty shortly afterwards. Tommy finished the match injured and playing on the right wing, too!

Situation normal all fouled up (Snafu) continued for both Chelsea and Lawton in the cup games with Aston Villa. At Stamford Bridge, 65,307 crowded in. Tommy went closest to scoring for Chelsea, lobbing one on to the bar and having a shot hit a post. Ten minutes from time they were awarded a penalty but Payne shot miles wide. Three minutes later Frank Broome gave Villa a precious lead with the home leg to come.

For this one Villa took no chances at Villa Park, with the gate some 10,000 fewer than the first leg in London. Villa detailed four players to keep an eye on Lawton! Clearly they felt there was no threat from any other Chelsea player. Their view was spot on and this time they scored in 49 minutes through Billy Goffin for a 2-0 aggregate win.

On 13 February not even Eastern Command could help the dearth of Lawton goals as Northern Command hit four without reply at Leeds, with Pye helping himself to a quartet of his own. Now surely Luton Town at the Bridge might end the famine. It did, as Tommy scored Chelsea's first goal in the 2-1 win, Williams getting their other goal, while Billy Waugh replied for Luton. However, any continuance of this looked unlikely with Aston Villa due to visit the Bridge so soon after their cup meetings.

But what was possibly developing as a dynamic duo of Williams and, yes, Tommy Lawton, scored again for Chelsea in a 2-2 draw with Villa at Stamford Bridge. Jimmy Bain, back on the left wing for Dolding, was the only change in the Chelsea side. It was not until 9 March that Chelsea had another league match, away to Arsenal at Highbury. With no Payne, the Pensioners introduced Jack Brindle at inside-right, with Williams switching to the other wing to partner Dolding, who came in for Bain. Three goals in the first half settled the scoresheet – Denis Compton for the Gunners, Lawton and Spence for Chelsea.

A week later the tables were turned at Stamford Bridge as Arsenal reversed the scoreline. This time Compton scored twice for Arsenal and Brindle replied for Chelsea, who had made only one change, with Alex White at right-back for Danny Winter. Compton's performance was noted by the England selectors, who appeared to be unhappy about previous occupants of the left wing.

With Lawton's scoring ratio dropping alarmingly by his own standards, the away trip to Kenilworth Road to face Luton might have been considered the ideal fixture to remedy the situation. Even with Goulden back after a lengthy absence for Chelsea, Luton were the winners 3-1. There was no scoring in the first half but later Hugh Billington, the blossoming Luton leader, scored two goals and Freddie Laing their other one, while Foss was Chelsea's lone marksman.

Lawton was then whisked away with the Army team visiting the Continent but was back for the England trial at Wembley between the FA XI and the Army Physical Training Corps (APTC). Eight goals were scored overall – the Army lads scoring five goals to three for the FA XI. Shackleton, Stubbins and Elliott were the FA scorers, while Welsh with two goals, Lawton, George Wardle and Compton netted for the instructors, who contained seven internationals, including a Scot – Andy Beattie an unlikely selection for England! The team to play Scotland at Hampden Park was chosen during the second half.

There was sun after rain at Hampden, but still a hard surface, and the Scots had four new players for an international, including Frank Brennan of Airdrieonians at centre-half, who was taller than Lawton! The newcomer stuck to his task and controlled the aerial threat. But Tommy struck the bar from a Compton pass and remained the one threat to Scotland. Territorially the Scots held the upper hand but in an isolated raid Lawton was only inches wide. With Swift keeping danger at bay it was only in the dying moments that Delaney scored the only goal of the afternoon for Scotland. Shackleton, helping out in defence, fouled Liddell and, from the free kick, Waddell beat Swift in the air and headed down for Delaney to score the only goal in what had been a low-key affair, but a welcome success for the Scots.

Lawton was back on Chelsea duty for the visit of Plymouth on Good Friday and after 18 minutes he played a defence-splitting pass for Goulden to score. On 35 minutes the Rangers guest John Galloway headed a second goal from a corner. It was then off to Portsmouth the following day to be blanked in a 3-0 defeat – from a Doug Reid trio as well. Easter Monday brought another long trip for the return with the cellar dwellers Plymouth, who actually scored first through Tommy Swinscoe, who had played against Lawton in Italy. It was but a token effort, as Lawton made the opening for Goulden to equalise, and further goals came from Machin and Jimmy Argue. Late in the game Goulden added his second in the 4-1 win.

Portsmouth appeared at the Bridge on 27 April, which was also FA Cup Final day. For Chelsea it was their penultimate League South fixture of the season. The scores were reversed from the Fratton Park result, with a brace from Goulden and one from Dolding, all three in the second half. It was the prelude to a brief overseas visit, so there was no time for slacking, Chelsea. It was smartly off to Denmark the next day, to Copenhagen to play KB Copenhagen. Argue scored for Chelsea in the first half but the quicker Danes scored twice in front of their King and Queen.

On 4 May Chelsea's domestic season was wound up at the Baseball Ground against Derby County. The game settled as a 1-1 draw, with Raich Carter, recruited from Sunderland by the Rams in December, scoring for Derby and Lawton getting his first Chelsea goal since that of 9 March at Arsenal. Tommy still finished with 20 league and cup goals and was leading scorer for the Pensioners, despite playing only 26 games for them.

But that was not all for the season. England had two Victory Internationals with Switzerland and France to play, respectively home and away, Stamford Bridge being selected for the first. However, the proposed Billy Walker's XI v Tommy Lawton's XI scheduled for Nottingham Forest's ground for Willie Hall's benefit was vetoed by the FA as it contained players chosen for the Swiss match. It was said to be postponed until September. Hall had recently had a leg amputated.

Switzerland included nine of the team that played against England the previous year and they took the lead just before the hour through Hans-Peter Friedlander. But England were roused from slumber and Carter, Brown, Lawton and Carter again saw England home, 4-1. However, Tommy finished the game with concussion. Interestingly, the Swiss substitute would have amused Sherlock Holmes's aficionados: Franz Rickenbach.

France in Paris were a different outfit in all departments to England on 19 May. More than 75,000 actually attended, 58,481 of them officially for a record and upwards of 20,000 with forged tickets! Jean Prouff opened the scoring on 55 minutes with a shot in off a post, and Ernest Vaast added their second on 81 minutes. Two minutes later Hagan headed England's sole response from a Matthews opening. Franklin was one of few English players who looked the part and Lawton had a quiet match.

CHAPTER ELEVEN

Impressively Resumes
His England Place

THE FIRST big game of 1946/47 was in aid of the Bolton
Disaster Fund emanating from the tragedy in March when 33
people lost their lives and over 400 were injured during the FA
Cup tie between Bolton Wanderers and Stoke City at Burnden
Park, caused by some people trying to gain admission while
others were attempting to leave. Since his hometown club was
involved, Tommy Lawton clearly wanted to play in this England
v Scotland game at Maine Road, Manchester on 24 August but
he had to withdraw because of his persistent groin injury. Frank
Swift, the senior professional, was named captain. Lawton's
place was given to Reg Lewis of Arsenal, who had scored six
goals in the Arsenal trial match the week previously. No full
caps were awarded for the international.

On 7 August, the Chelsea manager Billy Birrell had been
forced to deny that Lawton was about to be transferred to Derby
County. This was perhaps not the best of prospects for continued
harmony at Stamford Bridge. By an odd twist, the Pensioners'
first game was at Stamford Bridge against Bolton and Lawton
was fit to play. Tommy was noticeably playing a deeper role,

more as an inside-forward. After only five minutes, Spence took advantage of a defensive error to open Chelsea's account for the season. But on the half-hour Lofthouse – the 'Lawton-type' discovery from his home town – scored impressively from 30 yards. The maestro responded immediately, as Tommy headed Chelsea back into the lead, before Ernie Forrest made it 2-2 just before the break. In the second half both Spence and Lawton reprised their earlier efforts in a 4-3 Chelsea win.

It was quickly back to earth on the following Wednesday with Manchester United obliterating Chelsea at the Bridge and unlucky to score only three goals. Lawton, playing so deep that he looked more like a centre-half, was still Chelsea's best player even though he missed a penalty for handball on 55 minutes, when United were two ahead. Rowley after 12 minutes and Stan Pearson with a header 20 minutes later had already done the damage, while Charlie Mitten scored their third on 75 minutes.

Chelsea's defensive frailties were further illustrated at Anfield against Liverpool on 7 September in a match of 11 goals! Chelsea were one behind within three minutes through Liddell, four behind at half-time, and six had gone past Robertson before they woke up. Lawton, getting little change out of Laurie Hughes, decided to alter tack by feeding his inside-forwards instead. This produced four goals in 19 minutes – Machin getting two, Argue getting one from a lob that fooled everyone and one more from Goulden. Liddell, Bill Jones and Fagan each scored two for Liverpool with Balmer getting their seventh in a remarkable 7-4 win. It was the day Chelsea signed Tommy Walker from Hearts for £6,000 plus a job and house. Perhaps he could also play in defence?

On the Monday at Bramall Lane against Sheffield United, the Scottish international made his Chelsea debut at inside-right. Argue made way for him, but Chelsea stuck with the same defence. The newcomer showed up promisingly and made Lawton's goal. United led twice through Harold Brook and Walter Rickett but Dolding was the other Chelsea scorer, and 2-2 was a relief for the Londoners.

Walker's home unveiling came on 14 September against Leeds United. Drizzle produced a wet surface at Stamford Bridge for his home debut and the Scot quickly recovered from missing an open goal by slotting one in from a Dolding pass. Walker proved industrious and, according to the *Daily Herald*, would be able to relieve Lawton of his role as 'director of approach work'. The game was no spectacle, and patrons leaving early would have missed the other two Chelsea goals, one from Walker and the one he made for Lawton. However, Lawton damaged an ankle and had to cry off for the international trial and the return with Manchester United. His trial place went to Albert Stubbins, recently transferred to Liverpool from Newcastle. The date of the Leeds match was also the day of Tommy Lawton's *Football Is My Business* book launch.

Lawton returned to Chelsea colours for the trip to play Grimsby on 21 September, which provided the Mariners with their first win of the season, 2-1. Lawton did get the Chelsea goal but, by now, despite the substantial outlay on players, this had produced two wins, two draws and three defeats. Whoever the scribe was who said pre-war Chelsea were consistently inconsistent might well have extended it.

England had an extended weekend of internationals in Ireland, initially against Northern Ireland, with just two players who had played pre-war for their country, Raich Carter and Tommy Lawton. A record attendance of 57,111 meant that Windsor Park was swelling in all directions and referee Webb, the Glasgow engine driver, decided on a bit of shunting, moving everyone from pitch encroachment before a start was made. Carter scored within two minutes, then Wilf Mannion added two more for 3-0 at half-time, both Lawton initiated. The first came from Tommy's pass, the second from a rebound after the Chelsea centre-forward had hit the bar. Tom Finney scored on the hour and Mannion completed his trio a minute later for 5-0. Lawton, who had had an excellent match, scored in 80 minutes from a 'thank you' pass from Mannion, and Langton made it seven shortly afterwards. Lockhart scored twice for Ireland late on in the 7-2 win for England.

Sightseeing across the border provided a prelude to the following Monday's match at Dalymount Park in Dublin against Eire, soon to become the Republic of Ireland. Finney did his prospects of eventually taking Matthews's place on the right wing no harm with the only goal on 82 minutes. Mannion's shot was parried and Carter allowed the ball to run for the Preston plumber to save England faces against the more dominant Irish lads.

Chelsea's trip to Middlesbrough and Mannion at Ayresome Park was costly after three minutes when Fenton scored for Boro. Lawton had a shot blocked close to the line but it was Mannion who added to Boro's score. Despite Tommy's heading being described as 'brilliant', Chelsea fell further behind in the second half before Middlesbrough eased up and Goulden hit a couple for Chelsea, including one from a penalty, but the score ended 3-2 to Boro.

Chelsea's highest attendance of the season, 67,935, awaited Stoke City. Goulden was out injured and Machin switched to his inside-left berth. The visitors were the first to score, on 35 minutes, Freddie Steele with a header. Four minutes later

Lawton hooked the ball over the goalkeeper to level by the break. Thirty seconds after the restart Tommy slotted his second after a move involving Spence and Walker. The Potters responded, with Alec Ormston netting twice, on 49 and 58 minutes, then Jock Kirton and Ormston again, for a convincing 5-2 win, adding to the Pensioners' misery.

Goulden was back to play Portsmouth at Fratton Park and there was a debut for Jimmy Macaulay, a civil servant and part-timer, at left-half. After three minutes Lawton fed Spence for the opening goal. Under pressure for most of the half, there was little change subsequently but it was a good day out on the south coast for Chelsea when Lawton scored again to secure the 2-0 victory.

Chelsea named an unchanged team for Arsenal's visit to Stamford Bridge on 26 October, and there was an encouraging performance by both Chelsea and Lawton. The final result was 2-1 to the Blues from a brace by Tommy in reply to Reg Lewis scoring for Arsenal. Inside four minutes, Bernard Joy slipped Spence and quickly transferred the ball to Lawton, who put Chelsea in front. The same two Chelsea players continued to give Arsenal problems throughout. At this stage of the season, the Gunners had taken only eight points from a dozen games compared with Chelsea's 11 points.

At league leaders Blackpool, Chelsea opened in lively fashion, Lawton producing a lovely header that Doug Wallace had to go full length to save. Spence missed a reasonable chance, then it was Jimmy Blair who opened the scoring for Blackpool on 20 minutes. Walker and Lawton kept testing the Blackpool goalkeeper but were unable to break through and the match ended 1-0 to Blackpool.

With the same team at home to Brentford, Chelsea wasted two easy opportunities in the first ten minutes, with high-priced inside-forwards Goulden and Walker the culprits. It was left to Lawton to score eight minutes from the interval. Walker atoned in the second half and Bain scored too, but Dai Hopkins hit one for Brentford on 63 minutes and managed his second in the last minute as Chelsea edged it 3-2.

Lawton had been chosen for England against Wales at Maine Road on 13 November. Wales were struggling for players, with injuries upsetting their plans. On seven minutes Lawton, Langton and Carter combined for Mannion to open the scoring. Five minutes before half-time Mannion made the opening for Lawton to convert, then in the second half Tommy repaid the compliment by making one for Mannion after 65 minutes as England won easily 3-0, though by general acceptance wing-half Ronnie Burgess of Wales had been the best player on the field.

Lawton hit another milestone at Sunderland three days later when he scored his 100th goal in peacetime football in his 125th match. Spence also scored at Roker Park, where Chelsea won 2-1.

Aston Villa sustained early pressure from Chelsea at Stamford Bridge on 23 November but the tactics employed by the Blues were restricted to a long ball in Lawton's direction. Once Villa sniffed this tactic out, George Edwards scored after 17 minutes but, after a flurry of corners, Spence scrambled one in for Chelsea a minute before half-time. Con Martin headed a second Villa goal on 50 minutes and Leslie Smith made it 3-1 after 73 minutes, as Chelsea lost at home, 3-1.

A midweek diversion of an England friendly against the Netherlands at Huddersfield gave Lawton a chance to recharge his scoring batteries. The dyke was breached on 20 minutes with Tommy shooting hard and low to score the first of five England goals in 15 minutes. Lawton headed in a Finney lob, then it was Carter, Mannion and Lawton for his hat-trick. On 37 minutes Co Bergman replied for the Dutch, then Piet Kraak, their swamped goalkeeper, managed to save a penalty from Hardwick, before Finney made it 6-1 on 44 minutes. The quieter second half saw Carter scoring on 71 minutes, then Lawton for his four-timer seven minutes later. There was a consolation for the Netherlands with the appropriately named Kick Smit netting three minutes before the match ended, 8-2. Harry Johnston of Blackpool gained his first cap, having played with Tommy for Lancashire Boys in 1934.

Willi Steffen, the Swiss international full-back, an amateur and ex-Swiss Air Force pilot, made his Chelsea debut at Derby County the following weekend, the latest in the paraded stars taken on at Stamford Bridge post-war. The rain brought with it unpleasant conditions, which was just as disappointing as the result for Chelsea. Chelsea took the lead when Walker scored, although there was a suspicion of offside about it and it was certainly against the run of play, but Angus Morrison levelled matters on 40 minutes. Frank Broome took on Steffen and beat him for a second Derby goal and Morrison obtained his second in the Rams' Raich Carter-inspired 3-1 win – their first in seven weeks – while Leon Leuty kept Lawton quiet.

Tommy's old club Everton arrived at the Bridge on 7 December, including half of the team with whom he had played. Chelsea had another new signing – winger Johnny Paton, who cost £7,000 from Celtic. Lawton flashed an early header just wide but it was Everton who crazily took a 23rd-minute lead through Jock Dodds. He tried his luck from 35 yards and somehow it skidded in off Bill Robertson's legs. Dodds should have added a penalty five minutes before the break after John Harris had brought him down, but he tried a trick run-up, only to make a hash of the actual kick, which Robertson saved at the second attempt. Chelsea saved the day through Macaulay ten minutes from time, before Lawton had a shot which just cleared the crossbar, to leave the match at 1-1.

At Leeds Road, Huddersfield, came Chelsea's best result for three months, winning 4-1. Lawton and Spence scored in the first half, before Lawton went on to complete a proper hat-trick. However, the real test would come a week later when fired-up league leaders Wolves were at Stamford Bridge, with Dennis Westcott in fine fettle leading their attack.

As it happens, Westcott missed his train and Jesse Pye played centre-forward! Precious little good it did Chelsea though, as Mullen scored for Wolves on 18 minutes and then made one for Willie Forbes a minute later. The duel between Cullis and Lawton was interesting. Tommy cut the confrontation likelihood by turning this way and that, skilfully feeding Walker and Goulden when it would normally have been a role reversed. Lawton did sweetly put away Chelsea's sole reply with a text-book drive from a Walker pass, but Chelsea went down at home again.

For Christmas Day, hosting Preston North End, Chelsea introduced Harry Medhurst in goal, aged 30, who had been swapped with Joe Payne, who went to West Ham United. However, there were no seasonal presents for the Pensioners as Finney and Jackie Wharton scored for Preston. Lawton was again the sole marksman for Chelsea in another 2-1 home defeat. The following day at Deepdale, Chelsea introduced Bobby Russell, who had been a welcome wartime right-half guest signed from Airdrie two years previously. Paton scored and Jimmy Garth netted for Preston in a 1-1 Boxing Day affair.

Lawton was back in hometown Bolton two days later. The town's latest 'Lawton-replica', Lofthouse, had the misfortune to receive a kick on the head and was carried off early on. Paton scored for Chelsea on 25 minutes but Russell, due to be married in a couple of days' time, sustained a broken leg before half-time. In the second half, depleted Chelsea conceded a penalty and Lol Hamlett equalised for another 1-1 draw. At this stage, Chelsea's prospects of finishing as high as halfway in the league looked unlikely.

Into 1947 and the visit of Liverpool produced a 59,226 crowd at Stamford Bridge. The *West London Observer* remarked that Chelsea had changed tactics from 'pretty – ineffective', presumably meaning pretty ineffective, to swinging the ball about. It yielded results. Paton had one ruled out for offside, before his centre was swept into the net by Lawton on 27 minutes. Balmer made it 1-1 on 36 minutes but soon after the interval Tommy had his second with a lovely drive from Spence's corner. Near the end a Spence header was partially stopped only for Goulden to make it 3-1 and a welcome home win.

Then on 11 January Chelsea hosted Arsenal in the FA Cup. The attendance was a huge 70,257. Bryn Jones was effective for the Gunners with his long direct passing and a minute before the interval lined one up for Ian McPherson (DFC and bar) to score. Lawton had missed a couple of chances but it was Walker with a curling drive that levelled it a few minutes into the second half. Arsenal switched Jones to the wing, bringing Jimmy Logie inside to his normal position without any improvement. Steffen deputising for Harris at centre-half had a grip on Ronnie Rooke in the 1-1 draw.

Four days later at Highbury, Harris was back and Steffen resumed on the left flank for Chelsea. Defences again dominated and it was not until the last ten minutes that there was any scoring. On 81 minutes Ronnie Rooke put Arsenal ahead but only three minutes later, after work by Spence and Goulden, Lawton scored the leveller, with extra time played out with no further goals. Chelsea wanted the third attempt to be played at Wembley, as 53,350 had watched the replay, and interest was clearly capable of filling the Empire Stadium. But Tottenham's White Hart Lane was chosen as the venue.

However, before that, Chelsea had to go to Elland Road, Leeds on 18 January, three days after the Highbury clash, for a league engagement. Gerry Henry put Leeds ahead from a penalty, then Lawton, from his only chance in the game, equalised in the second half. However, United pressure close to the end provided Davy Cochrane with the winner after Medhurst had stopped two certain goals. It was Leeds' first win in ten weeks.

Just two days later, Monday, 20 January, 59,590 attended the FA Cup second replay at White Hart Lane against Arsenal. The Gunners' targeting seemed more in range and Logie hit the bar, before they were awarded a penalty for handball after just three minutes. Lewis merely fired well wide, letting Chelsea off the hook and handing them the initiative. On 23 minutes Lawton's perfectly judged header from Paton's cross put them ahead. Two minutes later he had his second from a rebound. With Leslie Compton unable to hold Tommy, the England centre-forward had two more shots, one knocking George Swindin over, the other catching George Male full in the face. The 2-0 victory meant that Chelsea were next drawn at home to cup-holders Derby County the following weekend.

A frozen pitch at Stamford Bridge in that dire winter was the setting for the fourth-round tie. Chelsea made a change, with Reg Williams, having just recovered from a cartilage operation, given the right-wing berth, but the Blues went behind to a Jack Stamps goal. Then Williams, apparently well offside, nodded in for 1-1. Lawton then managed to elude Leuty, and with his back to goal and the ball at his feet, seemingly unable to manoeuvre, he pivoted on his left foot and hit it with his right for 2-1. The *Nottingham Journal* remarked: 'It is this type of goal scored in spite of the closet marking which stamps him as the great player he is.' Good enough to win a game maybe, but the Rams, not inclined to relinquish their hold on their trophy, still denied Chelsea victory. In the dying moments Broome's cross lined Raich Carter up for a sitter. Despite the ball bouncing awkwardly, Carter's athleticism enabled him to score in off his right hip! In the 78th minute Lawton had had a goal disallowed for offside; it was clearly not their day, as they faced another replay.

Four days later at the Baseball Ground was the stuff of legend, an Aesop fable likely to be scoffed at – not amusing for one team. After just five minutes, Alec Grant, the Derby goalkeeper, slipped on the frozen pitch and dislocated his left elbow. Frank Broome went in goal. A strapped-up Grant returned at outside-left. The tie was to last 510 minutes overall and was decided in the ninth minute of extra time when the unbelievable happened. Grant crossed for Reg Harrison on the other wing and his return was put in by Stamps. Near the end, Lawton had an effort scrambled off the line by Broome – looking suspiciously over the line. Chelsea had previously complained about the choice of referee who they claimed lived too near Derby! It is worth noting that through taking teaching exams, missed because of war service, Grant was a part-timer getting just three old pence a week, the lowest sum a professional could be paid!

Returning to league action against Charlton at The Valley on 1 February, Chelsea found themselves two goals down in 13 minutes, both scored by Bill Robinson. A dozen minutes later Lawton found Walker, who reduced the arrears with a fine effort. In the 27th minute Lawton headed in the equaliser from Paton's cross, then in the second half, with just seven minutes remaining, Goulden converted a penalty for Chelsea's 3-2 win.

At a still icy Bridge for the visit of Grimsby on 8 February, defences were at their best, considering the conditions. Three times the ball was in the net and on each occasion the referee ruled offside. Twice Tommy Lawton was denied and once Harry Clifton for the Mariners, as the match ended goalless.

At least there were plenty of goals to be seen at Stoke City the following week but unfortunately only one for Chelsea and six for their opponents. Even without Matthews, suffering from a carbuncle on his leg, Stoke were too much of a handful for Chelsea. On two minutes the maestro's replacement George Mountford forced Medhurst into action but Johnny Sellars buried the rebound. In the fifth minute Ormston scored and, shortly afterwards, Syd Peppitt popped one in, followed by Ormston for his second on 12 minutes. Alex Machin at last gave Chelsea some hope with a lobbed goal, only for Frank Baker to net City's fifth. Six goals overall had come in just 16 minutes. Peppitt hit his second goal on 27 minutes but Chelsea then came more into the picture. Lawton missed a chance then forced a save with a header but then Stoke came close to a seventh goal near half-time. Lawton tried to get Chelsea moving in the second half and distributed in all directions but received little support, but at least there was no more Stoke scoring!

There was then some league respite for Tommy, chosen for the Football League against the Irish League at his old snowy stamping ground of Goodison Park. The shaded side was worse than the rest of the pitch for the first meeting here of these two opponents since 1938. Lawton, feeling at home again, set up Mannion, who forced an early save. Then on seven minutes, the recovered Matthews found Lawton, who headed down for the Burnley amateur winger Peter Kippax to score with just seven minutes played. On 18 minutes it was 2-0, Lawton putting away a first-timer from 15 yards. Meanwhile, Matthews delighted the crowd with one dribble in and out of his own penalty area!

Harry Johnston was the defensive star of the Football League team and Lawton was an effective and error-free leader. He scored his second goal on 52 minutes but four minutes later the Irish responded through Eddie McMorran. Bert Wright made it 3-2, only for the impressive debutant Kippax to score his second as the Football League won 4-2.

However, with his groin injury playing up again, it was no real shock to find Tommy not selected for the Football League against the Scottish League. He also missed Chelsea's fixtures at Arsenal and at home to Blackpool. Williams took his No.9 shirt and scored in both! Tommy was back for the Brentford match on 15 March at Griffin Park.

During his injury absence, there were rumours that Lawton might be the high-priced centre-forward wanted by Newcastle United, but there was little factual evidence for this as Tommy had not too long ago become a father and was settled in the Kenton area of London.

On Tommy's return to action, although Brentford forced the pace plus several corners and George Smith switched to centre-forward, hitting a post, it was Chelsea who took a 30-minute lead, Lawton finding Paton, who lobbed Joe Crozier in the Bees goal. Chelsea's second goal came midway through the second half in a snowstorm, with Machin the scorer in the 2-0 victory.

Sunderland's visit to Chelsea produced a game of missed chances, the Pensioners being most at fault with Walker and Lawton the chief culprits. Chelsea were the better side in the first half with fine approach work ruined near goal. But Goulden, from a penalty, and Lawton, with a header from Goulden's cross, scored in reply to Jackie Robinson for Sunderland, who had all the play after the interval, having caught the lack of finishing habit from their hosts.

At Villa Park on 29 March the home team proved too good for Chelsea. Transfer-listed Johnny Dixon was the architect behind Aston Villa's two goals. The first on nine minutes gave Ford a goal and five minutes before half-time Dixon supplied Dickie Dorsett with his counter. Chelsea were well beaten on the day, with the attack unable to get itself into gear, although Lawton did provide Walker with one opportunity before the Scot was stopped in his tracks.

The heavy Easter programme did not start well either for Chelsea, with Blackburn Rovers taking the points back to Ewood Park on Good Friday after a 2-0 win. For Chelsea, the *Daily Mirror* wrote it off as 'one of their worst days'. After Billy Rogers had hit a post, Jock Weir stuck the rebound home and Jackie Oakes hit their other goal. With Pryde denying any space for Lawton there was no life in the Chelsea attack. However, within 24 hours, it was a different complexion on Easter Saturday, with Derby County, conquerors of Chelsea in the FA Cup, back at Stamford Bridge.

It was Willi Steffen's last game for Chelsea, as he was returning to Switzerland to work with his father's company. He was allowed to toss-up with Raich Carter at the start. On six minutes Goulden set up Lawton for the first goal, then Walker's overhead kick laid one on for Tommy to slam number two into the net. In the second half Goulden increased Chelsea's lead to 3-0, the final score.

Then, with Syd Bathgate in Steffen's left-back position, the trip to Ewood Park on Easter Monday also turned out well for the Pensioners. Lawton and Walker scored for them, while Verdi Godwin composed Blackburn's singular response, as Chelsea gained revenge for their Good Friday defeat.

The last home international of the season at Wembley brought Scotland, still hoping to snatch the title, but needing to win against England, the more likely to land the first post-war title. Within 15 minutes the Scots led through Andy McLaren, and with Lawton having arguably his poorest game in an England shirt, the nearest to an England goal came when Carter hit the angle of post and bar. However, Tommy cleverly back-heeled an equaliser and close to the end might have done better than shoot straight at the goalkeeper from five yards although he was probably well offside at the time. The draw was enough for England, before an attendance of over 98,000, bringing receipts of £34,200.

Huddersfield at Stamford Bridge on 19 April had three-quarters of the play against Chelsea but had two goals ruled out for offside. They then lost to arguably the one decent effort by the Pensioners to get a result when Walker scored famously with 15 minutes to go. Lawton was still suffering a post-Scotland disappointment. Two days later he started to ease himself back into it, concentrating on distribution, while the now alert Walker scored a hat-trick in the friendly against Hearts at the Bridge. Machin scored the fourth goal with Johnny Urquhart replying for the visitors.

The prowling Wolves invariably presented Tommy Lawton with a problem. It had happened before when he was at Everton. Chelsea went to Molineux on 26 April and the goals flowed as freely as ever. On five minutes Hancocks put Wolves ahead, then Spence levelled on 29 minutes, before Westcott entered the frame with a couple on 30 and 41 minutes, the second hoisting his 35th in the league during the season. Chelsea were losing 3-1 at half-time then, within ten minutes of the resumption, three goals were fired in as many minutes – Goulden and Machin for Chelsea, with Forbes scoring another for Wolves for 4-3. Then came the day's best goal – a spectacular Lawton header on 61 minutes from Paton's opening. Back roared Wolves, scenting victory, with further goals through Hancocks and, in the 87th minute, Forbes making it 6-4.

Even though his previous international outing had been disappointing, Tommy Lawton was chosen for the Great Britain team to play the Rest of Europe at Hampden Park on 10 May. There were five from England, three Scots, two Welshmen and one from Ireland. Team GB would wear blue with a specially designed crest. But before that on 3 May France met England at Highbury.

The French were physically obstructive but it was an accident on 23 minutes when both Jean Gregoire and Lawton went for the same ball in a mid-air collision. The Frenchman sustained a cut over his left eye, Tommy one over his right. After plaster repairs Lawton was back after ten minutes, his opponent returning five minutes later. After 50 minutes Finney scored for England, then Lawton went close before Mannion made it 2-0. Tommy also forced Julien Darui into a smart save before, on 77 minutes, Carter made it three in front of a crowd of 54,389.

If that was a continental hors d'oeuvre, the main course had two and a half times more spectators at Hampden's vastness, 133,000. Naturally, since most of Europe was only just restarting first-class football, the expected GB victory was understated. But many ticket touts became rich overnight. Billy Steel provided Mannion with the first goal on 21 minutes but Gunnar Nordahl of Sweden made it 1-1 three minutes later after the Dane Carl Praest had outwitted George Hardwick. The Czech, Walter Ludl, strangely handballed when there was no danger and Mannion banged in the penalty on 33 minutes. Mannion then fed Steel a minute later, and in the 37th minute Lawton made sure of another Mannion target aim, for 4-1 at half-time. With a quarter of an hour remaining, Lawton pressurised Caro Parola, the Italian centre-half, into putting through his own goal and ten minutes later Tommy headed in a Matthews cross for a final score of 6-1.

The match had been arranged ostensibly as a welcome back to the home countries into the FIFA fold again, but in reality the world governing body was skint and would have been overjoyed if a third of the £30,000 raised had been offered. So a chance of taking control of FIFA had gone forever.

A tour for England to Switzerland and Portugal was rainy at the first venue, there was extreme heat at the second, but after the worst winter ever to disrupt football in the UK, neither was too arduous. Admittedly the pitch was small in Zurich and it rained. The Swiss were speedy and, after a disallowed goal, scored on 27 minutes through Fatton. Just before half-time Lawton poked a foot at a Mannion pass that appeared on target, and Langton appeared from nowhere to make sure, only to find the French referee Victor Sdez declaring it offside!

It was then off to sunny Portugal and a Wimbledon-perfect pitch at the National Stadium in Lisbon on which to perform –

surely England could have no excuses. Stan Mortensen was given his first real cap. Within just 17 seconds if you please, Lawton took a Mannion feed and scored with an oblique crashing drive. After two minutes Tommy gave Mortensen a debut strike for number two, then on 11 minutes Lawton scored again, first-time from a Finney pass. Finney then had a goal for himself on 21 minutes, before Lawton completed a hat-trick via an upright on 38 minutes from Finney's cross. Lawton's second goal had been England's 700th in internationals.

Matthews provided Lawton with his four-timer on 59 minutes, then supplied Mortensen's second a couple of minutes later. Two more Mortensen efforts, on 74 and 77 minutes, provided him with a hat-trick, then a fourth for an amazing debut. Matthews rightly earned his own effort with five minutes left for 10-0. The Portuguese FA suspended their entire team!

CHAPTER TWELVE

The World's Most
Expensive Player at £20,000

THERE MAY have been four goals in Lisbon, but Lawton was said to be jaded and unwilling to go on Chelsea's tour of Sweden, although his presence was clearly of paramount importance to both hosts and tourists. Tommy asked for a transfer with the knowledge that, if on the list at the time, his England place would be forfeited. He was left out of Chelsea's first two league games of 1947/48, but come 30 August, Lawton was at No.9 against old adversaries of the previous season, Derby County at Stamford Bridge; the programme notes mentioned that the directors were to consider Tommy's transfer request.

Some 59,919 appeared for Lawton's return and, although Leon Leuty, the Rams centre-half, attached himself closely to his task of containment, Tommy managed a couple of headers that went close, then in the 34th minute he fired in from a Spence pass from 15 yards. It proved to be the game's solitary goal.

On the following Tuesday, the club announced they were not prepared to agree to Lawton's transfer request and he was selected to play at Huddersfield Town on 6 September. The previous day, Blackburn Rovers had expressed an interest in signing him. At Leeds Road, Huddersfield, Chelsea failed to beat a team that had to play with a half-back in goal, due to Bob Hesford injuring his right hand. For 50 minutes, tiny Georgie Green kept the Pensioners at bay. Walker did eventually score for Chelsea but Peter Doherty, Vic Metcalfe and Billy Price produced a trio of goals for Huddersfield to win 3-1.

Obviously, the stand-off between Chelsea and Lawton was achieving nothing for either party, but Tommy was chosen for the home game with Sunderland on 10 September. The England selectors were watching, with international fixtures on the horizon, and they decided to choose Lawton again, who gave a much improved display against the Roker Park boys, even though Dolding scored Chelsea's only goal against the run of play just before half-time. Tommy Reynolds made it 1-1 early in the second half.

Bolton Wanderers at Stamford Bridge on 13 September produced another 1-1 draw, Ken Armstrong from half-back saving Chelsea. But three days later, the Chelsea directors said they would let Lawton go, preferably in part-exchange for a wing-half and centre-forward. Nottingham Forest, Stoke City, Blackburn Rovers, Derby County and Tottenham Hotspur had all expressed interest. Even Mrs L told a reporter: 'Where Tom goes I will be happy, but I prefer the south as I have felt much better since living here.' The Lawtons resided in Kenton, north-west London, near Wembley – the house worth £4,750.

At Sunderland the next day, Tommy Lawton had just one chance in the game and took what was the winner for 3-2. The other Chelsea goals came from two-shot Jimmy Bowie, a wartime discovery from the Navy. Then with Lawton already picked for the England team to play Belgium in Brussels, the selectors could scarcely invoke their policy of not choosing transfer-listed players! All was forgotten within around 72 seconds when Matthews found Lawton, who headed in. On 15 minutes Mortensen made it two, Matthews and Lawton involved in the build-up. Then the mercurial Matthews contrived to be at the base of another England goal, when the Belgian goalkeeper fumbled and Finney headed home. Jef Mermans snapped one for Belgium on 33 minutes, though its destination was via Hardwick's limbs, giving Swift no chance. Twenty-two minutes later, Victor Lemberechts headed in off the woodwork as a fightback looked possible. However, a Matthews free kick was headed in by Lawton on the hour, followed by another 'Wizard of Dribble' cross giving Finney his second goal. It was 5-2 and a tour de force by Blackpool's Stanley Matthews, feted in the Belgian press.

Lawton was in Chelsea colours at Wolverhampton – never a happy hunting ground in his days at Everton. There was just one goal in the game, for Wolves in the 26th minute from Willie Forbes. The *Birmingham Daily Gazette* considered that Lawton had appeared subdued during the match. There was also a time limit on his proposed move and while the club were considering offers – said to be around £17,000 but not high enough – the Ministry of Labour would enter the play! Of course, in 1947, the Players' Union had succeeded in obtaining a minimum wage for the first time – £7 in the season and £5 in the summer for all players over 20. The maximum was raised to £12 and £10 respectively, too.

A further week on and Tommy was still in Chelsea attire for the visit of Aston Villa to Stamford Bridge. There was another new recruit to the Pensioners in Bobby Campbell from Falkirk, who responded brilliantly, scoring two goals, the first after 20 minutes, the second a quarter of an hour later. In between,

Johnny Dixon had put one in for Villa. Then Lawton, who had been menacing a Villa defence overly concerned with the offside trap, fell twice for it. Armstrong turned provider, putting one across for Tommy to score and then the rejuvenated leader added a second with the last kick of the half. Ford converted a penalty for Villa in the second half in Chelsea's 4-2 win.

Whatever deadlines had been imposed on Lawton he was still a Chelsea player on 11 October at Anfield against Liverpool. A crowd of 51,359 saw the former Evertonian on his return to Merseyside. He went on to have a quiet game, which was dominated by the Reds. Bob Priday scored for Liverpool after three minutes and Albert Stubbins had a second before half-time. Billy Liddell added a third towards the end of the second period.

Lawton reported sick with a chill, having not looked too well at Liverpool, and it was only later in the week that the Chelsea club doctor reported he would be fit for England against Wales in Cardiff. There, a record 55,000 crowd squeezed into Ninian Park on 18 October. Four days earlier, Chelsea manager Billy Birrell had restated the club's position over the England centre-forward, that they were only interested in a straight swap. It would seem, at that time, a wing-half would suit their current needs, as goal-getting Ken Armstrong seemed to have slotted in well at No.9. However, the likelihood of a straight exchange was unlikely, as any deal needed serious financial adjustment.

But England, quick and clever, achieved three goals in 16 minutes to win the game with Wales, 3-0. After the fit-again Lawton pivoted and shot, Sidlow saved, only for Finney to open the scoring a minute later. Matthews squared the ball to Mortensen, who made it two and Lawton got into scoring mood again when he sent a right-foot effort stinging past the Wales goalkeeper.

The following week, more clubs lifted their heads above the transfer parapet for Lawton and among the dozen or so were Arsenal, Derby County, Portsmouth, Sunderland, plus Notts County. Figures offered appeared to be now in the £15,500 to £17,500 range, occasionally with a player exchange liable to reduce the final amount. Mrs Lawton reiterated her happiness with the south of England to the *Daily Mirror*, though again with the bottom line of going wherever her husband played. She now had their daughter Amanda to consider and hated packing and unpacking. There was also the family pet dog to consider! She also added that she had few friends in Derby and none at all in Nottingham! Oops!

Chelsea left Tommy out of any team on 25 October. Instead, he took the family shopping in London. He was, though, selected by the London FA to play in a friendly against Diables Rouges in Brussels the following week, but Chelsea decided to give Lawton a run-out in the reserves away to Arsenal in view of his selection for England the following Wednesday. Tommy's presence produced a London Combination attendance at Highbury of 23,000! He also got the biggest cheer when he headed a goal and helped winger Ken Suttle to the best of the four goals on the day in the 2-2 draw. None less than Bryn Jones, still the record transfer man at £14,000, scored one of Arsenal's goals!

Fireworks in the transfer market continued to have a damp squib look even on 5 November. Moreover, the football was not exactly sparkling at Goodison Park, Lawton's former HQ, for the England game against Northern Ireland. Mortensen and Mannion both missed chances, the 'M' formation clearly not functioning at first, and there was no scoring until the second half, when, on 54 minutes, Ireland's Doherty made one for Davy Walsh. Referee Peter Fitzpatrick, the Glasgow blacksmith, then appeared to drop something from a great height on Irish hopes when awarding a soft penalty incurred by Vernon on Matthews, but Ted Hinton saved Mannion's effort. On 84 minutes, Billy Wright, although having appeared to handle, fed Mannion, who atoned with an equaliser. In stepped Lawton, with his trademark half-turn and 15-yard drive making it 2-1. England's lead was to be dashed in the dying moments when Doherty dived spectacularly at Eglington's centre for a dramatic 2-2 finish. Frank Swift helped carry the dazed Doherty off the field.

At long last, on 13 November, the transfer to Notts County, a Third Division (South) club, was completed for Lawton, with Bill Dickson moving in the opposite direction to Chelsea in part-exchange. But it was subsequently revealed that the fee for Tommy was a staggering £20,000. A separate cheque had been made out in that amount, while the document for the makeweight wing-half was £2,500. Included in Lawton's transfer was a business opportunity and some provision made for his wife and child once his playing days ended. This was almost certainly the clincher. The player himself received £300 accrued share of benefit and the usual £10 signing-on fee. Reasonable moving expenses were also to be paid. Mrs Lawton had viewed some 14 properties in the area, ranging from £2,000 to £5,000.

The signing ceremony took place in a Paddington hotel in such secrecy that only seven reporters, six photographers and five small boys turned up. Notts County had made it clear that Tommy Lawton was signed as a 'player-tactician' and not simply someone who could put the ball in the opposition's net. He would have his work schedule clearly laid down to meet that expectation.

There was widespread criticism about the whole affair, from sceptics saying the club would not reap any financial benefit for their intention of spending some further £100,000 on players, to a question raised in the House of Commons for Aneurin Bevan, Minister of Health to requisition the 14 houses offered to the Lawtons, as elsewhere a man and wife were having to live in a billiard room.

With the business engagement and a newspaper column, the addition to Tommy's footballer's wage would bring in a further £20 a week for the Lawtons. But the football took over in a couple of days and the interest in his debut at Northampton was encouraging for the Notts County directors. Within four minutes, Lawton soared above the Cobblers defence to head a storybook opening for his new club and expanding career. Some 18,272 had watched at the County Ground, double the average gate, with many queuing early, traffic diverted and space found for 27 buses containing Notts supporters. Tommy produced his 'head flicks and rasping drives' according to the *Nottingham Journal*, but they had to be content with a 2-1 win, Jack Marsh being their other marksman after Archie Garrett had bundled ball and goalkeeper Harry Brown in for the Northampton equaliser.

Tommy was still an England centre-forward, and next up was Sweden at Highbury, for Wednesday's international. Lawton was involved in the first goal, for which Phil Taylor was the initiator before Lawton passed to Mannion, whose low delivery gave Mortensen the chance on 12 minutes. The Blackpool striker was then sandwiched by two defenders eight minutes later and Lawton despatched the penalty with power and pace. The Swedes then reduced the score a minute later through Gunnar Nordahl. The margin went back to two goals when Lawton created an opening for Mortensen on 26 minutes; however, with the Swedes putting thinking caps on at half-time, they sorted their defence out. It helped elsewhere, too, and when Hardwick tripped Nordahl, Gunnar Gren converted the spot kick for a 3-2 scoreline with 68 minutes gone. But two minutes from time, Mortensen's left foot completed his hat-trick as England won 4-2. Lawton had come through his 'Third League' cap well, though Mannion had been man of the match.

For Tommy's home debut in Notts' black and white, it was a colourful occasion against Bristol Rovers at Meadow Lane on 22 November with 31,450 inside, nearly 10,000 more than the average gate. A special postal delivery had to be made for the good wishes to Lawton and a telegram even came from Bob Hughes, the Horsham centre-half, who would be marking him in the FA Cup the following week!

But when Vic Lambden headed a fine goal for Rovers after just three minutes, surely the script had not been scrapped already? But on 17 minutes, Lawton latched on to a deflection off a defender and snappily sent a telling drive into the net. Tommy continued to be the livewire in attack, but it was no one-man affair, for it was Jackie Sewell who scored after 24 minutes and again just before the interval for a 3-1 lead to Notts. Soon after the break, Lawton notched his second goal with a low shot and later Vic Lambden, the Rovers leader, added his second.

Horsham, the Sussex County League amateurs, in the first round proper of the FA Cup for the first time, made the best start possible at Meadow Lane on 29 November, scoring in 90 seconds through right-winger Ron Smallwood, a 29-year-old ex-Army cook. It lit the gas under Notts and the goals fairly sizzled in. Lawton began it, finishing with a hat-trick, as did Sewell, with Marsh getting a couple and Tony Freeman the one over the eight in the 9-1 win. Notts skipper Lawton thanked the Horsham players 'for a really fair and sporting game'. Horsham took a share of the 24,815 gate – around £1,000. From a home game they usually averaged £35. The Notts chairman insisted both teams autograph the ball, which he presented to Horsham.

On 5 December, the Notts players went to the Odeon to see newsreel footage of the tie, and the theatre manager arranged for Tommy to address youngsters in the audience during the refreshment interval. The next day a friendly was arranged with Port Vale at Meadow Lane and 11,791 even turned up for that. The Valiants gave Basil Hayward, serving in the RAF at the time, the task of marking Lawton. He did a fair job. Vale scored on 34 minutes through Alan Martin. A fairly quiet Lawton flashed a header that was only just nodded over the bar by a defender and, on 39 minutes, Sewell made it 1-1. In the second half, Tommy sprang into life and from a lengthy centre helped on by Sewell produced a Lawton text-book header for a 2-1 lead on 52 minutes. Alf Bellis made it 2-2 11 minutes later.

In the next round of the FA Cup, Stockton almost did a 'Horsham' early, although not as quickly, when Leicester opened the scoring for them. From then on, the Ancients were under siege and the guardian of the redoubt was goalkeeper Jim Barron who defied everything – or nearly everything. Handicapped by an injury to Bill Baxter, who had to hobble on the wing, Notts still had all the play. Eventually a goal was scored, Lawton's effort being stopped but not cleared up by Barron, and Sewell equalised. Bill Thompson, a fitter at Horden Colliery, had enhanced his prospects of landing a league club in keeping Tommy Lawton in check. There was talk of the replay being held at Middlesbrough rather than Stockton, which came to pass.

With 34,261 at Ayresome Park, it was a pay day for Stockton if nothing else. They were behind in three minutes to Horace Cumner's strike, then five minutes later it was two, when Lawton headed in from a long centre. Although the Stockton outlook improved on 18 minutes through Pears, and Notts' Baxter was a passenger on the left wing after injury, County redoubled their efforts. Lawton skimmed the bar with a header shortly after Barron had briefly injured himself in a flying save from the Notts skipper. Then Stockton lost Jones to injury ten minutes before half-time and, with a minute remaining in the half, Lawton scored with a classic header. In the second half, he completed his hat-trick on the hour. Notts drew Birmingham out of the hat for the next round.

Boxing Day at Meadow Lane provided a record Notts crowd of 45,116 for Swansea Town, who took a 20th-minute lead via Sam McCrory. Freeman equalised before half-time and Notts then took command. On 57 minutes, a flashing hook shot by Lawton made it 2-1 and he scored a second with a scorching header 17 minutes later. Marsh and Sewell near the end made it 4-1. But among four Notts players injured in the game, Lawton was found asleep in the dressing room suffering from concussion and was taken home in an ambulance! Recovering within a couple of days – part of which was spent in a dark room – he missed the 1-1 return with Swansea, along with the other three casualties.

Tommy was appointed area manager with a firm of typewriter manufacturers based in Belgium. One of the Notts directors had business connections there. Lawton was to visit the country and learn the language. On a football note, he was pronounced fit for Bristol City at Ashton Gate on 3 January, but was confined to a spectator's role as Notts were forced to concede ground to the opposition. He had what was described as two difficult chances, one a header that went outside of a post, the other a stinging drive that cannoned off a couple of defenders' legs. There was only one goal, by Len Townsend for City on 15 minutes, which pleased the 35,287 crowd, City's best for a decade. It was Notts' first defeat since their new centre-forward had arrived.

It was then FA Cup time at St Andrew's facing Birmingham City. Coachloads and special trains ferried Notts fans, and there was even a bus with off-duty coppers. Also, Mrs Lawton, who never watched her husband playing football, fronted up among the 55,000. Tommy had a quiet time by his standards but distributed the ball well. The first Notts goal from Bill Corkhill was a free kick that Jack Wheeler fumbled, but Marsh scored a second, which was well worked. Young decorator's apprentice Freeman, on the Notts wing, was marked by Dennis Jennings, who was playing professionally before the lad was born. Following this 2-0 win, was it a reasonable draw in the next round away to Swindon?

On 17 January, Reading were well beaten 5-1 by Notts at Meadow Lane, in what was a personal triumph for Sewell, who scored a hat-trick. This miner, limited in his availability for training, was outstanding. Marsh and Lawton were the other scorers with a crumb of comfort from Ronnie Dix replying for the Biscuitmen. Was it an aperitif for the cup?

A week later at the County Ground, Swindon, there was a record gate of 27,130, including some 6,000 Notts supporters, but it provided a huge disappointment for the travellers as the 1-0 defeat could have been much worse. With a confidence born of 13 games undefeated, Swindon were in command. With criticism that Notts had changed the team from the previous cup match not the answer, the performance on the day was poor. Lawton was starved of any service and the inside-forward trio, so devastating against Reading, was insignificant on the day.

There was also no joy at Walsall in the league on 31 January, where a ground record 20,383 at Fellows Park watched a disjointed Notts get in a tangle. Lawton tried to spark things with a header and another drive, but on 56 minutes Johnny Devlin was brought down by two defenders and converted the penalty himself. On 72 minutes, Ken McGowan made it 2-0 to the Saddlers. Three minutes before the end there was a touch of class from Lawton as he headed down a free kick, controlled the ball and shot right-footed for Notts' sole reply.

If that had been a wretched affair, there was another setback the following week when Leyton Orient visited Meadow Lane. Kept in check by some outstanding saves by Stan Tolliday, the visiting goalkeeper, there remained criticism of Notts' tactics. Lawton showed fine distribution, but there was no end product. Wally Pullen scored first for Orient, Lawton flashing in an equaliser just after the break. From then on, gaining in confidence, the Londoners added further goals through Vernon Chapman, Pullen again and Frank Neary. It was Notts' heaviest defeat of the season and they were fifth from bottom in Division Three (South), with Orient two places lower.

Rumours spread after the match that Lawton had immediately demanded to be placed on the transfer list. These were instantly denied. When Tommy signed for Notts County in November they were fourth from the bottom with 17 points, a dozen behind the division's leaders. It was a concern and clearly considerable responsibility would fall on the still rated England centre-forward. Tommy Lawton would have to subjugate his predatory instincts as a goalscorer, using his tactical know-how for the benefit of the team – and quickly.

The revival in the Magpies' fortunes actually began on 14 February at Exeter City's St James Park ground without Lawton, who had been sidelined with gastric flu on the Thursday beforehand. Albert Parks was switched from the wing to inside-left and scored the only goal of the game. Notts looked a much better-organised outfit.

Marsh was rested against Newport County and a fit-again Lawton led the forwards. After he had gone close with a rasping cross drive, he put Notts ahead with one of his customary net-finding headers from a Lyman centre. Dougie Hayward levelled from a penalty and the Magpies defence had to have their wits about them with Bryn Allen causing problems. But Sewell restored the advantage and it was late on that Lyman and Sewell, with a 'Lawton' header, made it 4-1. The following day, manager Arthur Stollery and Lawton were hoping to fly to Belgium to watch an Army player, but snowstorms put the flight off. The Health Ministry then ordered Wembley Borough Council to return the property it had requisitioned in December in Mount Stewart Avenue, where the Lawton family had resided, to Chelsea, for the use of two of their players!

Against Port Vale on 28 February, the information gathered from the previous friendly match was put to good use. Unchanged from the Newport match, Sewell and Lawton scored the Notts goals, while the much-sought-after winger Ronnie Allen responded for the Valiants in what was their first home defeat of the season, perhaps further proof of the Magpies' revival.

But Lawton was in the toils again, this time with an abscess on his chest, which meant he missed the home victory over

Swindon Town. He was still suffering the after-effects the following week and was next fit again for the Crystal Palace home match on 20 March, where he was watched by the England selectors.

An expectant crowd of 30,558 watched, hoping the team's recent improved form would continue. Lawton, despite being well policed by a couple of defenders, did provide three headers, which needed Dick Graham's alertness in the Glaziers' goal to prevent intrusion, plus a characteristic back-flick nod that almost caught the custodian out. Eventually the keeper was beaten in the 73rd minute by Lyman.

On Good Friday, the attendance shot up at Meadow Lane to 35,689. The match developed into a scrappy affair with Southend United taking a 34th-minute lead through Cyril Thompson, a former POW in Germany. His colleagues took few prisoners themselves and several Notts players were nursing bruises afterwards. The hard surface and light ball made carpet-football unlikely. Despite meagre support, Lawton managed to level the scores, shaking off three persistent defenders, then headed the winner from a free kick.

A return to Lawton's wartime stamping ground at Aldershot proved an unhappy reunion as there was a Notts hangover from the Southend match. Wind spoiled the match but the Magpies did nothing to suggest that they were worthy of a draw. The only goal was a penalty tucked in by the Shots' Alf Rogers, still in the Army Catering Corps. Another Alf – centre-half Rowland – another one-time POW after being taken at Gazala, succeeded in ring-fencing Tommy and also received support from other defenders. Sewell almost snatched a late leveller, but Eric Searle made a flying save. The 12,750 crowd was the club's second highest.

The return at Southend on Easter Monday was an all-ticket 17,613 attendance. George Goodyear put the home crowd in a good mood with a goal after ten minutes, then on the half hour Lawton, quietly effective, made the equaliser for Doug Pimbley. Two minutes before the interval, a high ball saw Frank Sheard rushing back and goalkeeper Ted Hankey, moving forward, finished in a heap, the ball going into the net from the centre-half's attempted header away. Both teams appeared tired after their various holiday exertions but Notts won 2-1 and moved up to tenth in the table.

Next up were Northampton Town at Meadow Lane and the unfolding picture in the *Nottingham Journal* pinpointed Notts' problems in its headline: 'Notts need – class inside man'. If it had not been for Lawton's performance in this match, perhaps not even a draw would have been the outcome, let alone a 3-2 win. The still England centre-forward provided a fizzer of an effort from the edge of the area and a masterly header from Sewell's centre. The other Notts goal was a Harry Lowery own goal. Tommy Fowler and Dave Smith scored the Cobblers' two goals.

Preparing for England duty, Lawton missed two club games. Against Scotland at Hampden Park *The FA Yearbook* described the match 'as full of drama as it was empty of science'. Now, come on, no sitting on the fence. The first England goal was against the run of play and without an opponent touching the ball after it left Swift. Lawton received the ball, gave it to Stan Pearson, who transferred it on to Finney, dashing in for the finishing line. Nineteen minutes after half-time, Lawton passed to Mortensen for the second England goal. Otherwise, it was a rough and tumble affair, best forgotten, although Lawton's excellent use of the ball was duly noted.

In midweek Ipswich Town were visiting Meadow Lane, although Tommy came out of it with concussion sustained just after half-time when he went for a header, the ball striking his temple and putting him in a daze for the rest of the match. Then it was off to bed afterwards. It was clearly not his day, as his 22nd-minute penalty attempt after handball rose fiercely over the bar. Ipswich won 1-0 from a spot kick by George Rumbold.

Lawton was unfit for Saturday, 17 April, but declared fit for the third home fixture in succession against Brighton & Hove Albion five days later. His return sparked much needed life back into Notts, with his thoughtful tactical sense and foraging producing dividends for a team lacking consistency. Pimbley opened the scoring on five minutes, and on 40 minutes Sewell made it 2-0. Marsh on 68 minutes and Cumner nine minutes later gave Notts a welcome 4-0 win that moved them up to eighth.

Two days later at the seaside for the return clash at the Goldstone Ground brought a record 19,572 crowd for the venue. The outstanding feature was provided by Seagulls goalkeeper Harry Baldwin, who saved penalties from Howe and Cumner. He got away with another incident when Lawton had a goal disallowed, despite his cracking effort from the edge of the area hitting the bar and clearly bouncing over the line before Baldwin retrieved it. But Tommy scored one goal in each half and Cumner managed a third, while Tony James replied for the 3-1 losers.

At Carrow Road, Norwich on 28 April there was another record crowd – 37,863. Gates were locked with many disappointed and police had to ensure the safety of spectators swelling the barriers. On the hour, a superb power-struck 30-yard right-foot drive from Lawton won the rain-drenched game for Notts.

On 1 May Notts wrapped up the season at Meadow Lane, sharing six goals with Watford. Again, it was a mishmash home performance from Notts. Dave Thomas put Watford ahead on ten minutes, then Lawton equalised. Moving to the right of goal, he crashed one in with his left foot on 24 minutes, then laid one on for Freeman in the second half, only for Johnny Osborne and Taffy Davies to put Watford ahead again. Only a penalty from Sewell in the dying seconds saved a point for Notts, who finished sixth in the table having been fourth bottom when Lawton arrived.

One more match beckoned for Lawton – the England international at the Stadio Comunale in Turin on 16 May against Italy, celebrating the Italian FA's Golden Jubilee match. Tommy was leading arguably the best forward line produced in the era – Matthews–Mortensen–Lawton–Mannion–Finney. Swift was captain – the first time the armband had been handed to an England goalkeeper. Rain gave way to the early evening sun and heat. Swift, winning the toss, shrewdly decided to kick against the sun. He anticipated problems when it would appear lower in the sky for the second half.

An early strike did give England a crucial advantage. After only three minutes, Mortensen caught Valerio Bacigalupo, the Italian goalkeeper, out by feigning a cross and shooting in from a difficult angle to open the scoring. The Italians played long and direct football but had some outstanding individuals. However, the Blackpool striker was also involved in the second goal after a splendid run, eluding Carlo Parola on the way and giving Lawton the opportunity to score powerfully with a low drive 20 minutes later.

England assumed complete control in the second half and overcame the vigorous tactics of the Italians. Finney volleyed number three on 72 minutes from Mannion's feed and hit the fourth, too, a couple of minutes later when put through by Mortensen. Teamwork had won over some outstanding players in the Italian team. Swift was busy, particularly in the early stages, and saved three shots that he had no right to get anywhere near. It was a fine ending for an accomplished England team, perhaps the sun already setting on it, but the Third Division centre-forward had not looked out of place in it.

Vittorio Pozzo, the long-standing Italian coach, agreed that England had been the superior team on the day. Italy were still the World Cup holders.

CHAPTER THIRTEEN

Boom Time Everywhere, Especially at Notts County

EXPECTATIONS FROM the outset at Torquay United on 21 August 1948 were dashed immediately, although the cause was not generally known until after the match. In the opening minutes, a clash of heads between Lawton and a Torquay defender left Tommy with slight concussion and he played for the rest of the game in a half-speed daze. A high wind, rain and a greasy ball spoiled the football, but Torquay were much the better team. Jack Conley on 28 minutes and Hugh Cameron 11 minutes later gave the home team a 2-0 interval lead. Sewell reduced the arrears in the second half, but 'Digger' Ebdon sealed it at 3-1 on 55 minutes. Lawton was ill in the dressing room afterwards and was taken to bed in his hotel before returning to Nottingham the following day.

However, he was fit for Thursday's home game with Walsall, with the crowd of 35,319 getting a first glimpse of left-winger Tom Johnston, signed from neighbours Forest for £8,500. He was outstanding, but although Notts won 2-0, A. E. Botting, in the *Nottingham Journal* report, wrote them off with the headline: 'Not Good Enough For Promotion'. Johnston's free kick on 51 minutes went in off the head of Saddlers defender Norman Male, while the newcomer's other effort appeared to be handled in by Sewell trying to make sure! Lawton cracked the crossbar with a typical effort.

At Meadow Lane against Bristol Rovers, there was a crowd of 33,747 inside and the police allowed youngsters on the running track. A dull first half was brightened by a Lawton-made goal for Marsh on 34 minutes but there was a transformation after the interval. Tommy, now schemer-in-chief it seemed, made two more goals as well as getting one himself. After Sewell and Johnston – the latter following a Lawton whack off the bar – made it 3-0, Tommy made it a Notts quartet, the three goals coming in a six-minute period. George Petherbridge scored Rovers' consolation near the end.

At Fellows Park for the Walsall return, Sewell was on target on ten minutes, heading in a nod from Lawton, a lead Notts held until just before half-time when Harry Brown fumbled one and Johnny Devlin scored into the open goal. Although the injured Sewell was a passenger on the left wing, he still contrived to score a replica second goal for the Magpies. But then it fell apart with two late penalties converted by Devlin for his hat-trick, one for handball, the other for an infringement. Notts had now played two away games and lost them both.

Away day number three came at Newport County and the general opinion was that the days of Lawton spearheading the attack were on the wane, as his central role required a decoy and schemer. He succeeded in drawing opposing defenders to him while opening gaps for other forwards, which worked for Sewell's goal after 30 minutes. Eric Houghton added to the score two minutes later and Marsh five minutes before the break to give Notts a 3-0 lead. Within ten minutes of the second half the score was 3-3 after Billy Lewis scored on 50 minutes, then Bobby Harper and Reg Parker salvaged a point for the Ironsides!

Defensive changes were made for Notts hosting Ipswich Town on Thursday, 9 September. Within two minutes Lawton had scored. Jennings equalised for Ipswich before Tommy shook off three defenders to restore Notts' lead. Sewell added another one and Dave Bell put through his own goal before Lawton headed in a corner for 5-1 at half-time! So the architect was not neglecting the final product after all. On the hour, Lawton made the sixth for Marsh, but a minute later John Dempsey scored Ipswich's second. Houghton on 78 minutes then Lawton sweeping in Houghton's pass made it eight, before, finally, Tommy sold a dummy for Johnston to score for 9-2. Notts were now the top scorers in the four divisions, but only had seven points from six games!

Two days later the euphoria evaporated, though expectations had surfaced again in the opening seconds when Lawton scored with a flying header. Shell-shocked Swansea Town, the league leaders, might have drifted further behind when Johnston missed a couple of chances but they decided to keep tabs on Lawton. There were always a couple of defenders ready to pounce on Tommy, and on 55 minutes a Billy Lucas–Stan Richards–Sam McCrory move provided the equaliser and kept the Swans at the top of the Third Division (South).

Wednesday provided an away game at Ipswich, who were still sore from the pasting of nine goals and were determined to stamp some authority. They did so on three minutes when Bill Jennings hit one in off a post. Notts made it 1-1 when Ipswich centre-half Matt O'Mahony, under pressure, sliced into his own net. In the second half Lawton made it 2-1 with a header from an Eddie Gannon lob, but Ipswich sensed they still had something and Tommy Parker scored twice, on 65 and 79 minutes, for Ipswich to gain revenge with a 3-2 win. It left Notts looking to strengthen their defence.

What prospect for the away-day hoodoo being banished at Reading? Lawton was in his schemer-in-chief role from the start. Houghton, with a direct free kick from outside the area, settled everything down early. Fred Evans soon snapped a second goal and near the interval Johnston made it 3-0. Tony MacPhee hit Reading's goal early in the second half but Evans scored his second for a first away win for Notts of the season, 4-1.

Lawton was chosen for the England team in the friendly in Copenhagen on 26 September, missing two club games. With his role now becoming more and more of a tactical focus and pass-master at Notts, just how would this work for England for whom he was still pencilled in as the spearhead? It became only too obvious that it was a testing time in Denmark.

Tommy and Matthews were the only two forward survivors from the previous international. Hagan was on the right of Lawton, Shackleton on the left and Langton on the wing. Neither Hagan nor Lawton, thanks in part to his new role at Notts County, as well as playing in Third Division football, would figure for England again. True, Lawton went close once and had a goal disallowed for an infringement by Shackleton, but on a wet and slippery surface, performances by the forwards drained away and with it Tommy's England career. The Danes had had a couple of goals disallowed but it ended 0-0.

Including unofficial wartime international matches for England, Tommy Lawton had made 46 appearances in an England shirt and scored 47 goals. Excluding the wartime matches it was 23 full caps, 22 goals.

Tommy's next league appearance for Notts County was at Watford on 2 October. Marsh was declared unfit on the morning of the match so Evans was at inside-left next to Lawton. Dave Thomas opened the scoring for Watford, then Evans earned a draw after 51 minutes. Lawton, shadowed by a couple of players, needed someone to take a holding role to allow him to work the ball, but at least it was a rare point away from Meadow Lane.

A long trek to East Anglia to play struggling Norwich City a week later provided Notts' heaviest away defeat of the season, 3-0, despite a new addition at centre-half, Alan Brown, signed from Burnley. Norwich went ahead after only five minutes through Oscar Hold and they were faster on the ball throughout. Lawton was poorly served and City's other goals came from inside-forwards Les Eyre and Noel Kinsey. Promotion for Notts County seemed some distance away already, as they were currently seventh in the league table.

There was yet another switch against Exeter City at a rain-soaked Meadow Lane, where 36,615 watched the inconsistent Notts County team featuring another signing in Hold, snapped up from Norwich. The £50,000-rated Magpies still took 26 minutes before opening the score, incredibly through the newcomer. But goalscoring honours were to be shared by Sewell and Lawton with four each in a remarkable 9-0 victory. The *Western Morning News* picked out Tommy as man of the match. His shrewd use of the ball and space, allied to finishing power, made the now ex-England centre-forward outstanding. Six goals came in an 18-minute spell. Lawton's last was the best. Shrugging off a challenge, he side-stepped two other defenders, sold the goalkeeper a dummy and walked the ball in – nine goals for the second time in the season and the Grecians' worst defeat in 28 years.

Could this form be transferred to away games? Naturally not! At Millwall seven days later, Notts suffered a 3-2 defeat. At The Den, Sewell gave them an early lead but two fine headed goals by Jimmy Constantine put them on the back foot, until a Houghton–Lawton opening produced a fine right-foot leveller from Johnston. However, the Lions were the predators and George Fisher scored their winner.

At least the next match was at the sanctuary of Meadow Lane, with Lawton's old wartime guest team Aldershot the visitors. Held up by outstanding defensive performances by the highly rated Alf Rowland, the Shots centre-half, who impressed again, along with goalkeeper Ron Reynolds, Notts had to be content with misfiring until Lawton provided Sewell with the first goal on 20 minutes. Johnston scored the second just before half-time and the Magpies had to be content with 2-0.

Lawton was declared unfit on the morning of the Leyton Orient match on 6 November with a groin injury and the doctor said Tommy might be out for six weeks if he risked playing. Notts lost 3-1. But Lawton was fit again for the visit of Port Vale a week later, a depressingly gloomy day, with the football matching it. Johnston accepted Lawton's thoughtful opening a minute before half-time, then Walter Aveyard hit a stunning leveller for the Valiants on 59 minutes. Johnston fed Hold to score to give Notts the 2-1 win. Placed seventh in the Third Division (South) table, nine points behind the leaders Swansea Town, Notts County had scored 51 goals, ten more than any other team in the division. However, until the haphazardness was eradicated and away performances improved, promotion still seemed very unlikely.

Another predicable defeat came at Bristol City on 20 November and, naturally, three more goals lost in the process.

A goal behind to Vic Barney in just 30 seconds, there followed one for Don Clark and a third on the hour for Sid Williams, Johnston replying for Notts. There was again little service to Lawton, who was held mostly by Denis Roberts, who had been given a free transfer before the war by Notts County! With less than half the season gone, the question remained: where next for Notts County? That would be at home to Port Vale in the FA Cup.

It was the comfort of Meadow Lane for the cup and, with wing-halves Eddie Gannon and Bill Baxter getting a grip on matters, Notts looked better. There were chances at both ends but no goals until the second half. On 55 minutes Lawton opened the scoring and, with eight minutes left, knocked in his second goal after George Heppell had blocked his first attempt. It was surprising the Notts captain had managed much at all. Having suffered slight concussion in the early stages, Lawton was violently ill after the match and had to be taken home by Baxter. Alan Martin responded in the 86th minute with a Vale penalty for handball but Notts hung on for 2-1 and went through to the second round.

It was a seaside excursion to Brighton on 4 December and the odds on a defeat and conceding three goals looked good. Yes, the result was 3-2 and all too predictable. Eddie Gannon was on Republic of Ireland international duty, Doug Pimbley replacing him at the Goldstone Ground. Within just a few seconds Micky Kavanagh had scored for Brighton and George Lewis volleyed a second. It became three when Lewis added his second and only then did Notts get themselves into the game. Sewell had a goal disallowed and at last the Magpies started having a serious peck at the Seagulls. Johnston and Hold both scored but the efforts were too late to salvage a point.

Barrow in the FA Cup at home provided a Lawton goal on nine minutes but this did not herald a flood of biblical proportions, and Eddie Miller even equalised. Over-elaboration by the over-eager did not help Notts but eventually Johnston scored twice, and it was only when most patrons had exited or were thinking of so doing that Miller scored a second goal for Barrow. So it was 3-2 again but this time in Notts' favour and the worry of a next round tie at Plymouth Argyle.

Torquay United, who had started Notts' season and the trend of conceding three goals on their travels, were at Meadow Lane on 18 December. Hold was Notts' first marksman, then Sewell hit a second goal from Lawton's flick-on, before Sewell buried his own rebound. Johnston scored number four, the trio of goals coming within a few minutes of each other. Only daring saves by Derek Davis in the United goal prevented more. Lawton headed the fifth Notts goal on 80 minutes.

On Christmas Day at the County Ground against Northampton Town, would Santa be kind on an away day for Notts? Certainly, if the curse existed, special dispensation was put in place at Northampton when goals from Sewell and Hold edged out Garrett's one for the Cobblers. Even better came on 27 December at Meadow Lane at the all-ticket return match with the Cobblers. Since goalkeeper Roy Smith had been signed from Sheffield Wednesday, the defence had looked more stable. Lawton moved around to unsettle the opposition throughout and on 38 minutes he headed down for Hold to open the scoring. Sewell added a second goal in the 2-0 win. Amazingly, at the same time, only three goals had been conceded in as many games.

Perhaps 1949 would herald a change of fortune in the offing for Notts County. On New Year's Day at Bristol Rovers they had to make do without Lawton, who had been injured in a car crash the previous Thursday night at Macclesfield on the way from Liverpool in company with Baxter. Both were treated for shock, and Lawton needed a stitch in the back of his head. He left himself out of the Rovers game: 'I didn't think it fair to the team or the crowd.' Baxter played, and yes, it was another 3-2 defeat away for Notts, still lying in seventh place, 11 points adrift of the league leaders.

On 8 January, Notts were in the FA Cup third round at Home Park, with Plymouth Argyle's all-ticket crowd of 40,000 having to wait until the second period of extra time for a goal – then it went to Notts County. A Johnston corner was challenged for by Lawton and the Argyle goalkeeper Bill Shortt, but Sewell's headed touch won the tie for Notts. Hold had been limping for most of the game. 'We earned our win,' said Tommy afterwards. Liverpool were picked out in the next round, at Anfield.

Newport County arrived at Meadow Lane on the back of an unbeaten six-game run. The avalanche that followed could not have been expected. Johnston, off a post, scored Notts' first on 14 minutes, Sewell scored a couple on 18 and 23 minutes, before Lawton added a fourth three minutes later. Sewell completed his hat-trick in the 29th minute, Johnston scored again on 35 minutes and Houghton five minutes before the interval, taking it to seven first-half goals.

After a breathing space, Sewell made a personal four-timer with the best goal of the game on 64 minutes. Lawton scored his second four minutes later, then Eddie Carr replied for Newport! Lawton finished it off with, according to the *Nottingham Journal*, 'a couple of gems' in the 87th and 89th minutes for his four-timer in the 11-1 victory. Pimbley, the only forward not to score, had one ruled out for offside!

All was clearly well and good at Meadow Lane, yet the prospect of table-toppers Swansea Town at the Vetch on 22 January was unlikely to unfold a similar tale, and there was a sea of mud for good measure. On the offensive from the kick-off, on 30 minutes Stan Richards surfaced to put the Swans in front. Five minutes later Frank Scrine headed their second. Strangely, an own goal by the Swansea centre-half Reg Weston was ruled out and wily Billy Lucas then scored their third goal. Johnston's header was a consolation only for Notts. Lawton, well policed throughout, produced one fine effort – a rocket free kick that just went wide.

Lawton was back on Merseyside for the FA Cup fourth round against Liverpool on 29 January, with 61,003 watching, close to Anfield's record attendance. Here, Notts gave arguably their best away display of the season but lost 1-0 to the First Division side. Both goalkeepers, Cyril Sidlow for Liverpool and Roy Smith for Notts, played outstandingly. Unfortunately, the one goal came from a free kick in the 57th minute when Cyril Done tapped aside for Billy Liddell to score, with Smith unsighted for the shot. In response, Lawton encouraged all Notts players up to force an equaliser, but it was not to be.

It was a subdued affair against Reading at Meadow Lane on 5 February, the Biscuitmen always snapping at any chances offered. It was not until the 58th minute that Lawton's header down to Sewell resulted in a goal, in off the bar. Encouraged by this, Notts looked livelier and Lawton twice headed close but it remained 1-0.

On 12 February, Southend United managed to prevent the Notts players from scoring for the first time at Meadow Lane in the season, but it was thanks entirely to the goalkeeping of Paddy Nash in the Shrimpers' goal. The nearest to a Notts marker came late when Lawton was sent sprawling in the penalty area. However, the referee was unmoved and the match ended goalless.

On the following Tuesday, Notts announced the resignation through ill health of manager Arthur Stollery, following on the departure of trainer Tom Ratcliffe the previous Saturday. Wilf Fisher became secretary-manager with Bill Corkhill assisting on the training side as well as playing.

Notts County clearly lost their bearings a week later at Selhurst Park, maybe thinking it was Meadow Lane. They won 5-1 against Crystal Palace and Johnston took his total of goals to 21 for the season. His first two came after long centres from Houghton on the opposite wing. Evans added a third from a Lawton flick-on. Johnston completed a hat-trick in the second half and Lawton sealed the nap hand with a typical header. Johnny Thomas scored Palace's response and his team played like one about to seek re-election.

On fire, Johnston had another treble, this time at Watford's expense on 26 February at Meadow Lane. His first was a header, the second a right-foot drive and the third he edged in following Lawton's shot against an upright. Evans was the other Notts marksman in the 4-0 victory. Lawton's roving commission allowed himself space to distribute cleverly and now only 13 more goals this season were needed and the century would be hoisted for the first time for the world's oldest club, with a split of two-thirds to one-third home and away. Although the team was likely to end no higher than mid-table, the local newspapers at least seemed to be more optimistic after a handful of wins.

In the next match, Norwich City proved a virulent outfit at Meadow Lane and led at half-time through George Morgan. In addition, Ron Ashman had hit the crossbar for the Canaries.

It took a painstaking 56 minutes before Ken Nethercott in the Canaries goal was put off his perch by a wonderful outside-the-box drive by Lawton. Evans then gave Notts the lead which they kept.

However, the good-life flavour dissipated at Exeter City within a week. The *Western Morning News* considered that Notts had been 'outplayed'. Duggie Regan gave the Grecians the lead and only Roy Smith kept the score down, but when Jim Clark sliced a Sewell effort into his own net, Notts had an unexpected leveller. But they were handicapped by an early injury to Aubrey Southwell. Second-half goals from Peter Fallon and Regan's second produced the all-too familiar three goals conceded on their travels by Notts. Lawton had striven to enliven matters without success in the 3-1 defeat.

Not content with a trio conceded away, Millwall took the treble chance at Meadow Lane on 19 March. The match was otherwise notable for two Magpie debutants – Harry Chapman from Aston Villa at right-half and Joe Praski, a French-born outside-right, from a Scottish junior club. There was also the first penalty awarded to Notts in the season and Houghton converted it. However, Willie Hurrell scored two for the Lions and John Short their other counter in their 3-1 win, while Lawton was again forced to plough an unresponsive furrow.

Finally, relief came at Aldershot – a squeaky win from a scrappy affair, hanging on after Johnston's header had given Notts a 24th-minute lead and being under pressure for the last 20 minutes. Despite the forward formation being back to normal and Lawton's promptings, the life seemed to have departed the Magpies' attack, but at least it was a welcome away win.

Against Leyton Orient at Meadow Lane on 2 April, Notts featured another newcomer, Irish amateur international Terence

McCavana at right-back. There was also the return of out-of-favour Alan Brown at centre-half, with Oscar Hold at inside-left, plus, amazingly, another penalty! Houghton converted again five minutes before half-time. Wally Pullen made it 1-1 and it was left to Johnston's late cross drive to gain Notts the points. Lawton plugged away as usual and Sewell continued to play a withdrawn role in midfield.

Next up was Port Vale for the third time in the season, this one the first at Hanley, with Notts wearing old gold. On 12 minutes, Walter Aveyard's opening gave Alan Martin a goal for Vale, which proved to be the only one of the match. Despite the strenuous efforts of Johnston, Sewell and Lawton to get on terms, nothing approaching a glittering response was achieved. Indeed, a second Vale goal-bound shot in the dying seconds was ruled out, as the referee had blown in transit!

An attack of fibrositis caused Tommy to miss the next two games, returning on Easter Monday at home to Bournemouth. On three minutes, Evans's goal broke Notts' scoring record with their 98th of the season, one more than in 1930/31. However, they had precious little else to cheer, with two Doug McGibbon penalties put away and an Alec Blakeman effort for Bournemouth. The only other response from Notts was a 31st-minute goal from Lawton, who should have been given a second-half penalty when upended. Bournemouth won 3-2 – what else?

At Swindon on 23 April, luck deserted Notts. On 15 minutes, Bert Howe fell awkwardly in trying to stop Maurice Owen from scoring and broke his leg in two places. Notts battled well under the circumstances, Lawton adopting a total football role, at wing-half one minute, on the left wing the next. But Morris Jones scored a second Swindon goal, then had a penalty saved by Smith. Near the end George Hudson made it 3-0.

At their last home game of the season the crowd was down to 19,478. The first goal of the match was one conceded on 20 minutes to Brighton's Kevin McCurley. Then a few seconds before the interval, Lawton's header, from a Johnston opening, hoisted Notts' 100th league goal of the season, although the 1-1 draw meant that they were now destined to finish below halfway in the league table.

Notts' last fixture of the season was at Southend United's Greyhound Stadium and the betting on the final score would probably have amused the bookmakers. Southend won 3-2! A Jimmy McAlinden penalty and a goal from Frank Dudley after a defensive error had Notts two down, before Sewell replied after a brilliant step over by Lawton. However, Southend had their third counter from Morris, then Hold provided the other Notts goal. The Magpies finished exactly halfway in the table, taking only ten points from away games and scoring only a third of their overall total of goals on their travels.

On 25 May, Eric Houghton, a month short of his 39th birthday, retired, swapping his No.7 shirt for the managerial hat at Notts County, with Fisher resuming as just secretary. Meanwhile, during the summer, Tommy presented a trophy for Long Eaton Speedway and played in charity cricket matches.

CHAPTER FOURTEEN

Third Division (South) Champions with Points to Spare

A NEW Notts boss for 1949/50 and the first match was against Southend United, the last opponents of the previous season. Another newcomer was paraded at Meadow Lane in Billy Evans, ex-Aston Villa, at inside-left, with Fred Evans taking Houghton's old right-wing position. Played in a heatwave, Notts opened the scoring on 24 minutes after Lawton and Sewell had combined to feed Fred Evans. Sadly, there were two misses from the penalty spot, the first when Sewell shot wide and then Johnston giving Ted Hankey in the Southend goal an easy stop. Sewell did manage to score the second Notts goal from a splendid piece of sleight of foot by Lawton before the crowd of 33,507.

The first away test of the season came at Norwich City, never the easiest of venues but surely the jinx of away-day horrors was unlikely to continue? Well, with 14 minutes remaining, the score was the ominous 3-2, but this time in Notts' favour. But hold hard, because two goals in three minutes through Johnny Gavin in 78 minutes then a fine Les Eyre header gave Norwich an unexpected win 4-3. They also had two goals disallowed.

Notts had scored first from a typical Lawton right-foot drive before Allenby Driver made it 1-1. Len Dutton then put City ahead from a penalty following handball by Baxter on 35 minutes. In the second half Billy Evans headed in after more clever Lawton work and Sewell's left foot finished a splendid run and cross by Johnston, but all to no avail.

Then it was West Country ways to Bristol Rovers on the following Saturday. Under the cosh from the word go, Smith and Baxter held the Notts defensive line before, on 32 minutes, Lawton back-heeled to Fred Evans, Sewell moved it on quickly and Tommy hooked in from waist-high on the turn. Tommy was playing deep in this match and spraying passes effectively. Johnston was the next marksman. His oblique shot was only half saved and trickled in, then Lawton scored number three on 58 minutes, running through and lobbing the goalkeeper.

Revenge-seeking Magpies, desperate to swoop on the Canaries, were at Meadow Lane on 1 September and, while Notts went nap, they were far from dozy. The *Daily Herald* thought Norwich had been unlucky to lose 5-0. Their football was orchestrated by a Bryn Jones who was slower than of yore but he was still an effective schemer. Yet Notts had the finishing touches. On two minutes Fred Evans scored and, with Lawton probing for openings, Bill Evans scored their second goal on 27 minutes. Sewell presented Johnston with number three on 71 minutes and Lawton headed in Fred Evans's corner for the fourth. Evans scored his second in the last few seconds.

With 34,606 at Meadow Lane two days later, Notts had to immediately overcome the handicap of injured players against Bournemouth and were down to nine men for a time, with Baxter and Chapman needing treatment off the field. Chapman, who received a kick in the mouth, went to outside-left and there was a general reshuffle. Lawton opened the scoring, somehow heading in while being sandwiched by two defenders. He also scored Notts' second goal, on 65 minutes. They were now top of Division Three (South).

On Thursday, 8 September the England selectors arrived at Meadow Lane to see Tommy Lawton, with Exeter City the opposition. Neither Baxter nor Chapman were fit, so Johnston stayed left-half and Geoff Stone was in at centre-half. On 21 minutes, Johnston belted in a free kick for the Notts lead and three minutes later Lawton headed their second. Exeter replied with goals from Regan and Charlie McClelland within seconds of each other and, on 59 minutes, Regan gave them the lead. Lawton supplied Johnston with his second goal on 81 minutes for a 3-3 result. It was said afterwards that Lawton had again suffered slight concussion during play.

Tommy recovered during the week, but several other casualties were absent for the next match, although their replacements did well at Crystal Palace, especially Bobby Crookes at inside-right. Bill Evans took a Lawton pass to open the scoring on 28 minutes, then ten minutes later Johnston hit number two. Palace replied just before the break through Jack Lewis, but Notts won the match 2-1. Reports reckoned it was a good advert for the Third Division.

A week on, with Watford at Meadow Lane, visiting goalkeeper Geoff Morton distinguished himself. Sadly, his only error resulted in Jackie Sewell, back after a two-game absence, registering on 50 minutes. Two crashing drives by Lawton in the first half lifted the 33,962 crowd, but they had to be content with the 1-0 win, keeping Notts top of the Third Division pile.

At Elm Park on 24 September, Notts managed to spoil Reading's home record, again needing just one goal for victory.

Bill Evans headed in from Johnston on 29 minutes. Lawton was praised for his excellent use of the ball, keeping the Notts attack moving. After two 1-0 victories, for the first day of October there was a return to the Notts heavy brigade of marksmanship, with Leyton Orient on the receiving end, giving goalkeeper Pat Welton a barrage of a debut.

The England selectors were in the stand for the game. Sewell soon opened Notts' account, Bill Evans added a second on 28 minutes and Sewell scored again to make it three just before half-time. A minute after the restart, Lawton headed in Johnston's centre and Evans hit his second on 55 minutes. A splendid volley from a corner was a Lawton speciality but George Sutherland managed one for Orient, only for Johnston to grab Notts' seventh with three minutes left.

Away days thus far had seen no return to the countless setbacks of the previous season, but at Newport County it was the hint of a return to poor performances by Notts. With their best post-war gate of 21,425 urging them on, Newport made it difficult for the Magpies to swing into action. Worse followed when, following a corner, Danny Newall fired in a shot that left Smith unsighted in the Notts goal, masked by a bevy of defenders, with only 19 minutes remaining. But it was a wake-up call. Notts looked a different team from then on and five minutes from full time they managed to salvage a draw when Sewell headed in from Johnston.

Bristol City visited Meadow Lane on 15 October and Notts paraded new man, Tommy Deans, ex-Clyde, at right-back, with Southwell moving to outside-right and even scoring the third Notts goal! Lawton put Sewell in for the first on three minutes and, after Tommy's effort was cleared, Sewell snapped up another goal in the 35th minute. Lawton only managed to hit the bar when it looked easier to score but did put the fourth Notts goal away after a typical second-half burst through. Arnold Rodgers, City's £8,000 recruit from Huddersfield Town, had City's consolation effort in their 4-1 defeat.

It was mud pies at Brighton and hailstones at one point, too, but a bespattered Lawton told the *Daily Mirror* reporter: 'Our best of the season.' This came after being two goals down to Johnny McNichol and Billy Morris. Tommy scored twice, one from a penalty. Johnston snatched the winner in the last seconds. Notts were now three points clear at the top of the table with a game in hand over second-placed Northampton. They had also scored 37 goals, the highest in the four divisions.

The gates were closed at Meadow Lane on 29 October, with a 42,676 crowd for the visit of Walsall. After Sir Stanley Rous had watched Lawton at Brighton, it was the turn of Arthur Drewry to look at the former England centre-forward. Without scoring a hatful of goals, Lawton was active enough with a header, a shot over the bar, then bringing Jack Lewis full length to save another nodded effort. Indeed, the fine Walsall goalkeeper kept an unbalanced Notts team from scoring for some time. New signing, ex-Derby County player Frank Broome, was on the right wing. With precious little attacking, Walsall eventually broke away and scored after 54 minutes, with a scrambled affair from Gordon Medd. It looked good enough to win until the dying moments, when Walsall centre-half Reg Foulkes appeared to handle and referee G. C. Iliffe of Leicester awarded a penalty. He was engulfed by a swarm of the Saddlers' players, but after consulting a linesman signalled to the spot. Lawton obliged, though many in the ground had gone home by then.

Fireworks, quite naturally, were expected on 5 November at The Den against Millwall. The Lions' crowd, never short of expressing their opinion, gave the verbal full blast and were encouraged when Constantine headed their team in front on seven minutes. It lasted but a minute before Lawton flicked in Sewell's pass. Sewell, in better form than for some time, scored twice, while Johnston and Bill Evans struck the woodwork. Millwall lost Johnny Johnson with concussion in their 3-1 home defeat.

Swindon Town, at a windy Meadow Lane the following week, suffered the misfortune of losing goalkeeper Frank Boulton just after half-time with a leg injury. Albert Young took the jersey. However, they were already two down to penalties, one on 30 minutes and another just before the break, Lawton netting both. Close to the final whistle he completed a hat-trick, with a header from Broome.

There were no goals at Plainmoor but a bumper crowd turned out for the match at Torquay United, 13,824, a club record. Despite there being no goals, there was plenty of attractive attacking from both teams, and some expert defending. However, there should have been one goal for Notts. Lawton's effort was going in, when in a scramble it struck the hand of one of his colleagues! There were also two incidents in the first half when Victor Rae, the London referee, denied Notts penalties. This was in the wake of Lawton addressing a meeting of referees in Croydon and criticising them!

The next week saw FA Cup action, and Tilbury faced the Third Division (South) leaders at Meadow Lane with a collection of dock workers, expecting to lose but intent on enjoying the experience. Their team and supporters received a generous welcome. On the back of a 17-match unbeaten run, the Essex men played decent constructive football and their goalkeeper Tommy Scannell was equal to two typical hard drives from

Lawton. Then Tommy scored on 28 minutes, Sewell adding a second five minutes later. On 61 minutes Lawton fed Broome for number three and the winger added his second and Notts' fourth near the close.

Then came the long-awaited derby with Forest at the City Ground, the pundits deciding the outcome would depend on the contest between their rival captains, Horace Gager, the Forest centre-half, and Tommy Lawton. It was a cleanly fought, hard and fast game, just edged by Notts. The Magpies took the lead on 28 minutes from a corner by Broome, headed in superbly by skipper Tom. Lawton was also involved in their second goal on 61 minutes, when he pulled the ball back with Johnston and Broome both lurking. Johnston was the first to react. Tommy Capel scored for Forest with three minutes remaining in a contest that enhanced Nottingham's sporting stature.

Rochdale hosted the FA Cup second-round tie against Notts on 10 December. The Magpies even received a good-luck telegram from Tilbury. But it was Cyril Brown, a former Notts player, who caused a stir when he opened the scoring after 31 minutes. A bit of a snowstorm and a muddy pitch was not encouraging for on-the-carpet stuff but Johnston levelled from Lawton's pass on 53 minutes and Tommy flicked the winner in from Sewell to send the Magpies through.

Notts were on the rocks at Southend in a gale-force wind, with the United manager Harry Warren owning up to 'four attacks and two goals', but this was enough to win the match. Injury-hit Southend gave Reg Davies, 19, his debut and he scored 12 minutes before the end. Freddie Morris soon added a second. Lawton, watched by two defenders throughout, went close several times, one effort beating Ted Hankey in goal but the wind carrying it over the bar. Another of his fizzer free kicks whistled past the goalkeeper but went just wide. It was only Notts' second defeat in the league but they remained four points clear of Northampton at the top of the table, and still with a game in hand.

On Christmas Eve, Bristol Rovers arrived in Nottingham for what was to be the start of a three-match bonanza for points. Johnston, suffering from ear trouble, was rested but Lawton soon heard cheering when he forced Rovers goalkeeper Jack Weare full length with one save and had another effort just as close. Goals had to be forthcoming and Fred Evans, then Broome, ensured a 2-0 Notts start for the festivities.

On Boxing Day, Ipswich Town visited and 40,192 were at Meadow Lane, expecting more of the same. Broome was absent, injured, but Johnston was back. Sewell scored on 47 minutes and the fit-again Johnston scored a second on 72 minutes to seal the win. That day also saw the attendance record for one day broken, with 1,226,098 watching Football League matches.

At Portman Road the following day, only a penalty save by Smith prevented Harry Baird from putting Ipswich ahead, though it was straight at him. Actually, after the infringement, the ball had gone in! On the hour Lawton set up Sewell for the first goal, Johnston added a second from Tommy's centre on 72 minutes and the two combined for Tommy to add a third a minute later. Lawton made it 4-0 with a waist-high volley with eight minutes remaining. Along with Middlesbrough, Notts were the only team to obtain six points from three matches.

A visit to the south coast changed things on New Year's Eve when the Magpies found slim pickings amongst the Cherries at Bournemouth. In fact, what they had were flying saves by Ken Bird, celebrating his 200th league match in the Bournemouth goal, keeping out a couple of stunning headers from Lawton.

This was Notts' only real response to early goals from Alec Blakeman and Jack Cross, plus a third in the second half from the latter. This was not the welcome to 1950 that Notts would have wished for but they remained clear at the top of the table.

On 7 January at Meadow Lane, Burnley arrived for the FA Cup third-round fixture, a mid-table First Division team that would give a clearer indication of Notts County's ability to rise from the Third Division. There was an encouraging enough start for the Magpies, as Lawton set up Johnston for the opening goal on 17 minutes. The lead was maintained, despite being under pressure, until Notts conceded a penalty on 43 minutes, with Reg Attwell levelling for Burnley.

The score remained the same, giving the 44,000 in attendance, about a quarter of the number comprising visiting supporters, some dual interest, until a devastating last six minutes when Burnley rammed in three goals through Harry Potts, Billy Morris and Jack Spencer. Lawton suffered a thigh injury during the match, but at least Notts could now concentrate on winning promotion.

However, in the immediate period they had to do without Tommy, who missed the next two matches, resuming on 4 February against Reading, with 36,183 watching his comeback. On 33 minutes Sewell scored from a Chapman centre, then 20 minutes later Broome made it 2-0. In the 63rd minute, Lawton hit the third Notts goal with a low drive and on 70 minutes Johnston made it 4-0. However, by then Notts had had Sewell carried off injured and Broome was limping. They had signed Peter Robinson, the Chesterfield captain, so perhaps he would be needed.

Two weeks later it was another venture to London, with Leyton Orient intent on using route one to find a way through.

It worked in the 16th minute when Sutherland put them ahead but Notts were still probing, with Lawton showing excellent use of the ball. It was not until five minutes before the break that Sewell equalised, Johnston then added a second on 48 minutes and the outstanding Broome scored their third on 72 minutes. Eight minutes before the end Johnston scored his second goal for 4-1, and the Magpies also hit the woodwork five times after the interval!

Newport, with the memory of shipping 11 goals at Meadow Lane on their last visit, were struggling again this season, and lost goalkeeper Harrison Fearnley with a shoulder injury in trying to save Notts' fourth goal just before half-time. Sewell scored twice in the first 16 minutes, the second delightfully after a Lawton set-up. Tommy converted a penalty when fouled and Johnston hit number four.

Fearnley, with his arm in a sling, played on the wing in the second half, with Dougie Hayward going in goal. Lawton headed in from Sewell, Bill Evans scored, then Sewell collected a hat-trick with Notts' seventh. On the morning of the match the *Nottingham Evening Post* ran a story that many local amateur players were crying off when Notts were at home because they wanted to see Tommy Lawton play and were using various excuses for being unable to turn out! Notts now led the table by five points and had a game in hand, while no other league side could match their 73 goals.

At Ashton Gate, it proved an off day for Notts against Bristol City in more than one sense. Sewell pulled a right thigh muscle, became a passenger after treatment, then retired. Bill Evans finished limping on the wing, too. A goal down to Rodgers after 37 minutes, Notts still managed to keep going until the last 20 minutes when these depletions took their toll. Alec Eisentrager, the former German POW, scored a couple and George Lowrie the other counter as Notts slumped 4-0, only the second time in the league season they had conceded as many.

For Brighton at Meadow Lane, Notts had Chapman in Sewell's No.8 shirt and Alec Simpson at right-half. Des Tennant, under pressure from a Notts attack, passed back but Baldwin was absent from goal and the ball trundled in with 20 minutes on the clock for Notts' first goal. Chapman headed in Johnston's high ball for a second Notts goal on 34 minutes. In the second half, on the hour, Lawton characteristically brought a high one down and his trusty left foot hit a third goal. Eric Lancelotte immediately scored for Brighton, but on 69 minutes Johnston netted from a Broome cross. Cyril Thompson, signed from Derby, scored on his debut for Brighton in the 79th minute, the match ending 4-2.

While 'Little John' in the *Football Post* was pointing out the reluctance of players to join a Third Division club, mentioning Wolves' Dennis Wilshaw and Arsenal's ex-Walsall forward Doug Lishman, on the same day Notts were taking on the Saddlers at Fellows Park. By half-time Devlin had scored twice for Walsall and in the 63rd minute Foulkes hit a third, though Smith had made a partial save. The final rites seemed appropriate, but no – the Magpies fluttered into life with ten minutes left. Broome's high centre was headed in by Lawton, who fed Simpson for a second goal. He had switched with Chapman. Finally, Johnston levelled at 3-3!

Struggling Millwall put up a gutsy performance at Notts on 25 March and, in truth, Notts were not firing on all cylinders in what proved a scrappy encounter. But it was Simpson, revelling in his new inside-forward role while Sewell was recovering from injury, who scored twice. His first goal came from Lawton's thoughtful pass after six minutes and again in 69 minutes with a header. The 2-0 victory left Notts four points clear of Torquay, with a match in hand.

Down in the West Country at Swindon, never a happy hunting ground for Notts, they had Sewell back but looking unhappy at outside-right. Again it was the in-form Simpson who carried on his recent net-finding mission with a goal on 12 minutes. This lead lasted just 120 seconds before Bob Peart headed in. Swindon should have taken full points for, in the dying seconds, Joe Simner missed an open goal. However, the post-match good news for Notts was that closest rivals Torquay had lost for the third time in a row so, barring a collapse, Second Division football looked likely at Meadow Lane, even with eight matches left.

With the Easter programme likely to resolve the promotion issue, Notts hosted Port Vale on Good Friday. Illness and injury meant that Johnston and Sewell were absent, but they still took a two-minute lead when Simpson provided Wally Boyes with the opener. On 25 minutes Lawton shook off two defenders to hit a scorcher and moments later Simpson made it three, his fourth in the last trio of games. Lawton had a headed goal disallowed and Stan Polk scored one for Port Vale in the second half, the match ending 3-1. Meanwhile, Torquay lost for the fourth consecutive time and were due at Meadow Lane the following day!

Torquay had the better of the first half at Notts and scored through Ron Shaw on 23 minutes. Lawton replied during an improved second half from the Magpies with a rocket of a shot. The point obtained in front of a crowd of 43,906 left Notts County three points off the Third Division (South) championship.

However, Easter Monday away to Port Vale produced a reverse of the scoreline of three days earlier. Another rearrangement was needed in the Notts team due to injuries and Robinson was given his debut. Vale took the lead on 21 minutes with a Cliff Pinchbeck header, Mick Hulligan added a second and another was nodded in by Pinchbeck to make it 3-0. Lawton did get on the scoresheet for Notts, but Vale hit the woodwork twice afterwards. The Magpies were making hard work of claiming the title, with Southend still in with a chance of nipping the prize.

At Aldershot, there was more misery for Notts and, but for Smith in goal, the 2-0 defeat might have been worse. Charlie Billington, the Shots' 21-year-old centre-half, had a grip on Lawton throughout and Charlie Mortimore, their England amateur international centre-forward, scored both goals, the first with a header, the second with a lob, which he confessed later was meant as a centre! Meanwhile, Southend had won away at the other Nottingham side, who County played next.

Perhaps all this was designed to make the local derby with Forest on 22 April the deciding match! In its aftermath, A. E. Botting in his *Nottingham Journal* report began with: 'Forest played the football, Notts scored the goals.' There were two goals and these brought Second Division fare back to the Magpies after 15 years. The record crowd of 46,000 saw a nervous Notts team, despite it being back to something like a normal line-up. In the 58th minute a Johnston corner was headed in by Sewell, with the other defenders too busy concentrating on Lawton. But Tommy did score two minutes later from Deans's free kick, with a characteristic glance of the head. Handshakes abounded at the end of a hard, clean game, which was well refereed by J. W. Topliss of Grimsby, as the *Journal* saw it.

Northampton Town, who had provided Tommy with his debut for 'Lawton County', fulfilled a fixture on Thursday, 27

April. He celebrated with both goals in the 2-0 victory. On 11 minutes, he took advantage of some hesitancy in the Cobblers' rearguard to score his first, and four minutes from the end his long stride took him past the opposition to finish with a flick past the goalkeeper.

On medical advice, having been told to take things 'very easy', Tommy missed the return 5-1 drubbing at Northampton, the Clyde friendly and the draw at Exeter City. But Notts finished with a seven-point lead over both Northampton and Southend, while Forest finished fourth, and early pacemakers Torquay fifth. Lawton was leading scorer with 31 goals from 37 league games, while Sewell had 19 goals from 32 appearances and Johnston 15 from 37 outings.

CHAPTER FIFTEEN

Tough Time in the Second Division

NOTTS COUNTY'S return to the Second Division could not have been more disappointing. Three defeats in the first three matches, no goals scored and no Tommy Lawton, struck down by rheumatoid myositis in the back. He recovered to play against Queens Park Rangers on 31 August when, despite twice leading, Notts had to share six goals due to defensive errors. After Johnston hit a post, a Lawton–Johnston-inspired move gave Billy Evans the first Notts goal of the season from a 38th-minute header. On 57 minutes, Don Mills hit an upright and Bert Addinall put the rebound in to equalise. Crookes restored Notts' lead, only for George Wardle to level again. With ten minutes left, Addinall added his second, but immediately a flick by Lawton gave Broome the equaliser.

Two days later, hosting Birmingham, it was City who scored after 30 seconds following a rare mistake by Roy Smith in goal, which led to Billy Smith converting. For the rest of the match Notts were in the ascendancy, except when it came to finishing. Lawton worked tirelessly, Johnston and Billy Evans struck the woodwork but it still came to naught as there were no further goals.

At Filbert Street, Crookes was held up in traffic so Billy Evans kept his place. Thirty seconds – this time into the second half – and Lawton split the defence for Johnston to score for Notts. On the hour Bert Barlow made it 1-1 for Leicester City, for whom Arthur Rowley hit the bar. Lawton came close at the end with a header, but at least it was another point for Notts.

On 9 September, there was better news at Grimsby Town. In the previous *Football News*, Lawton had written about the bad luck Notts had been suffering, and his change of tactics against the Mariners helped, at least in this game, to change it. He adopted a deep-lying role and it paid off. Broome scored on five minutes, Johnston on 30 minutes and a revitalised Sewell scored twice on 38 and 76 minutes. Billy Cairns grabbed a late Grimsby consolation but Notts had won a match at the seventh attempt!

Masterminded by the wily Peter Doherty, it was Doncaster Rovers who ruined Notts' hopes of a first home win. His ploy of ignoring the numbers on shirts fooled many, including the press of course! Anyway, Bert Tindill opened the scoring for them on 59 minutes and Doherty himself headed a second 12 minutes later. Broome managed a goal for Notts on 82 minutes. Lawton schemed as best he could, yet the overall performance was disappointing in the 2-1 defeat.

Next was Preston North End at Meadow Lane and Notts paraded new £25,000 centre-half Leon Leuty from Bradford. Charlie Wayman opened Preston's account on 29 minutes, Angus Morrison making it 2-0 just 11 minutes later. Eddie Quigley landed number three, but Lawton contrived to feed Simpson for Notts' reply on 70 minutes. However, this 3-1 home defeat meant that just four points had been gained from nine matches and a return to Third Division fare looked a distinct possibility. Even so, 44,195 represented the best attendance at Notts thus far. The *Daily Mirror* reported that Lawton still 'chased the ball like a schoolboy'.

Sewell was surprisingly dropped for the visit to Bury on 30 September, Notts' first time there since 1935. Ken McPherson was given his debut. Lawton again reverted to a foraging role as well as managing to crash a shot that bounced off a post, but Notts had to be satisfied with a point from the goalless draw.

Then came another visit to a former familiar ground of yesteryear, a week later at Bramall Lane against Sheffield United. Injuries necessitated recalls for Corkhill and Bart Purvis. Lawton soon slipped into his withdrawn position and, after 24 minutes, a Sewell–Broome–Robinson move led to the recalled Sewell scoring. Corkhill was then accidentally knocked out but recovered. On 46 minutes, another combined attack, this time involving Broome and Lawton, enabled Sewell to score again. The Blades battled away, though their cut and thrust was restricted until eight minutes from the end, resulting in an own goal by Robinson trying to head clear. Notts held on for their second win of the season, both away from home.

On 11 October, Notts County met Chesterfield in the Creswell Colliery Disaster Fund match and won 4-1. Lawton was involved in the first two goals, scored by Billy Evans and Sewell, who also added Notts' third. Tommy opened his account for the season with a strong shot off the upright. Jack Marsh, ex-Magpie, was the Chesterfield scorer.

Still chasing that elusive home league win, Notts faced cellar dwellers Luton Town. On 26 minutes, George Stobbart put Luton in front and Bob Morton then added another. Lawton tried to rally Notts, but it was not until ten minutes from the end that he headed down for Johnston to reduce the arrears. Five minutes later, Tommy headed against the bar and Sewell was able to retrieve a point. Notts, third from bottom, had only two points more than Luton.

At Southampton, a first-half injury to Sewell, who was forced to hobble on the wing, thereafter, upset Notts at The Dell. Early in the second half, Eddie Brown scored the only goal of the match for the Saints. The nearest to a positive response from the Magpies came through Lawton's efforts, one of his forceful free kicks hitting a post. It was the 13th time in the season he had struck the woodwork without luck! He also went close with a blistering half-volley just over the crossbar.

Against Barnsley at Meadow Lane on 28 October, Notts took a 36th-minute lead through Johnston. Lawton then received a blow on the head but, despite being dazed, was influential throughout. In the 74th minute he even notched his first league goal of the season, though he could barely remember doing so later. Leuty, who had kept Cecil McCormack in check, had the misfortune to slip, allowing him to score his 20th goal of the season, but the winning hoodoo at home was erased. 'Little John', in the *Football Post*, commented: 'Lawton led the line magnificently.' Imagine what he might have achieved had he known what was happening!

At Griffin Park, the England selectors were present, watching both Leuty and possibly Lawton. Brentford took the lead after 20 minutes, the Notts defence, expecting offside, not playing to the whistle and Jackie Goodwin running through to score. Fourteen minutes later, Crookes found Broome who equalised. Lawton, switching from left to right to avoid two markers, centred for Johnston to score on 56 minutes. A minute from the close, Broome scored a third Notts goal. Lawton's best efforts had been a 40-yard pile driver that just missed the bar and another shot that Alf Jefferies had to tip over.

Blackburn Rovers scored in an unusual manner five minutes after half-time, away to Notts County on 11 November. Corkhill, in clearing, caught the back of the retreating Eddie Crossan and the ball bounced back in! It took until ten minutes from the end, after continuous Notts pressure, for an equaliser to arrive. The referee was unimpressed when Lawton had his legs taken away in the area, but he awarded a penalty for handball soon after, though only after a word with a linesman. Broome salvaged a point from the spot.

A knee injury meant no Lawton in action for the trip to Leeds United, but in the 38th minute Sewell scored what was his 96th goal for Notts, equalling Tom Keetley's total of pre-war goals. It was enough to take the points – seven from the last four games.

Lawton resumed against West Ham United at Meadow Lane on 25 November. However, Notts went behind on 19 minutes when Terry Woodgate's attempted cross caught Gordon Bradley in the Notts goal poorly positioned, and the ball found its way in. A couple of minutes later the redress was sorted when Sewell found Lawton, whose left-foot drive made it 1-1. On the hour, Sewell scored his 97th Notts goal to set a new club record, Lawton and Evans having made the opening. On 75 minutes, Lawton raced through but Ernie Gregory parried his effort before the Notts skipper made no such error with the follow-up. A minute before the end, Billy Evans made it 4-1, the season's best at home.

Three days earlier, Tommy had sent a good-luck telegram to Nat Lofthouse, ex-Castle Hill School in Bolton, having signed an autograph for the lad years before when encouraging him.

A grateful Lofthouse scored twice on his debut for England against Yugoslavia.

But playing in the old black and white stripes at Swansea Town, it was a case of change of colours, change of luck for Notts. Not only did Dai Thomas score within six minutes for the Welsh team, but Jack O'Driscoll added a second on 22 minutes. It was not until the 58th minute that Broome replied for the Magpies, who went down 2-1.

Another old opponent, Hull City, fronted up minus player-manager Raich Carter, yet were still able to score through Alf Ackerman a minute before the break. Not until much toiling for an equaliser did one appear for Notts when Lawton headed down for Leuty to score his first Notts goal. But Ackerman responded again with 15 minutes to go and it was left to Tommy to retrieve a point, taking Broome's pass and from just inside the area shooting home with 87 minutes gone. It was said to be Lawton's 400th goal in league football, though this must have included wartime regional matches and conflicted with statistics revealed when at Everton!

Next, it was off to Highfield Road to face Coventry City's unbeaten home record, where it was more akin to dancing on ice. It was left to Tommy Lawton to pirouette his way into scoring on the tricky surface. In the first minute Ted Roberts fouled him. From the free kick, Lawton was the quickest to react to put Notts ahead. On 15 minutes, Harry Barratt lost the ball, and Johnston found Tommy who, though outside the area, crashed in a second goal. Notts continued in the ascendancy until Bryn Allen pulled one back for City in 63 minutes, but their record had gone by then.

There was not much greenery at Meadow Lane on 23 December against Cardiff City, with liberal sprinklings of sawdust on the hard surface. On 32 minutes, Lawton and City goalkeeper, Phil Joslin, went up for the ball, only for Johnston to retrieve the aftermath, scoring for Notts. Neither side gained superiority. Crookes twice hit the bar for Notts, then in the 76th minute, Roley Williams levelled. In the last minute, an error by Bradley led to Cyril Grant scoring Cardiff's winner, thus completing the double over Notts.

Saltergate, Chesterfield, was a skating rink on Christmas Day, which hampered controlled football, but it was considered that a mere one chance by each team should have resulted in a goal. The culprits were the respective Jackies – Hudson for Chesterfield and Sewell for Notts. Lawton had a quiet time with defenders on top in the goalless affair. In the return on Boxing Day at Meadow Lane, Notts looked brighter, giving Ray Middleton a busy afternoon between the Chesterfield sticks. Lawton offered chances to his colleagues, but it was not until a controversial penalty that Notts scored the only goal of the match. In the 52nd minute, Tommy was bearing down on the Chesterfield goal when he was brought down. The Spireites protested it was outside the box, but the referee insisted. While Lawton was receiving attention, Leuty put the penalty away for two points.

On the morning of the Birmingham City match at St Andrew's, Clifford Webb, writing in the *Daily Herald*, referred to a 'semi-official' approach by a London club for Tommy Lawton. For the football, there was snow on a frozen pitch and the Notts players wore knee guards. The much-wanted Lawton was lively, yet Birmingham scored first on 20 minutes through Jackie Stewart. Tommy's back-heel led to Sewell levelling from 20 yards some 13 minutes later. Crookes made it 2-1 to Notts just before the interval. After 73 minutes, Broome and the City goalkeeper, Gil Merrick, collided and it resulted in Sewell scoring into an open goal – off a post! Four minutes before the end, Crookes scored his second and the four goals for Notts was twice as many as City had conceded at home in the season so far.

Southampton in the FA Cup proved doughty opponents for Notts at Meadow Lane in another unchanged home side. Lawton brought the Saints' goalkeeper into early action, but Eddie Brown scored twice at the other end on 11 minutes then three minutes afterwards, the second following Ted Bates hitting the bar. Eric Day added to the misery on 49 minutes, before Broome scored Notts' opener on 58 minutes. Even so, five minutes later Day had another for the Saints. On 70 minutes, Leuty converted a penalty and five minutes from time Simpson hit Notts' third goal, one short of earning a replay.

A twisted knee kept Lawton out of the 3-2 win over Grimsby, in which Sewell reached his 100th Notts goal, and the defeat at Doncaster by the same scoreline. In both games, Broome deputised at centre-forward. Tommy was also unable to play in the friendly against Everton at Goodison Park on 27 January when Notts lost 3-2, with McPherson at centre-forward. But both Leuty and Lawton were back for Notts at league leaders Preston North End. After six minutes, Finney picked up a defensive clearance to put the hosts ahead. Lawton, switching the attack as usual, sent in a high ball from the left that Johnston caught on his head, then fired a left-foot effort as it dropped to make it 1-1. That was on 25 minutes, but parity lasted just five more before Morrison restored Preston's lead. Strong claims for a Notts penalty near the interval were ignored. Preston clearly had the edge and on 60 minutes Wayman made it 3-1 after a three-man move.

Lawton's former club Everton came to Meadow Lane for a friendly return and, according to the *Liverpool Echo*, Tommy was 'uncommonly quiet'. He played inside-left with McPherson leading the line. Ex-Magpie Oscar Hold opened the Everton scoring on 27 minutes, then Eglington scored two more as Everton won comfortably 3-0.

On 17 February, the return with Bury was played. In the interim, intruders had broken into Notts County's offices and among items stolen were four of Lawton's gold medals. Meanwhile, Tommy was forced to scotch rumours of a transfer when questioned by *The People* reporter. Heavy rain in the country made Meadow Lane a mud bath and certainly conditions influenced the first goal. Robinson put the ball through and as Andy Goram, the Shakers' goalkeeper, came out to gather, it stuck in the mud, giving Lawton a gift on 21 minutes. Within two minutes he had scored again, this time with a cross shot. Only 60 seconds later, Billy Evans made it 3-0 for Notts. Ken Plant then pulled one back for Bury on 33 minutes. In the second half, Leuty shot a penalty wide, but Johnston added a fourth for the Magpies, before Fred Worthington scored Bury's second effort with eight minutes left.

Sheffield United then arrived at Meadow Lane with hopes of a double for Notts. However, there was a shock in the first minute when Lawton went up for a ball with Latham, suffered a head injury and was taken off. He returned after 25 minutes. Notts included 17-year-old Don Roby on the right wing and he was in action among the ten men while Tommy was patched up. Sewell soon put Notts ahead in the second half and Lawton still managed to be influential despite being groggy, prior to retiring 15 minutes from the end. In the last five minutes, Sewell and Johnston made it 3-0 for Notts. After the match, Lawton was diagnosed with concussion and could remember hardly anything from the game.

Tommy missed the next two games, then, on 14 March, he was granted a divorce in the courts at Nottingham because of his wife Rosaleen's misconduct with a Notts County director. Tommy did not play at Barnsley in the 2-0 defeat, where the England selectors were watching Leuty. Jackie Sewell was also absent thanks to his record-breaking £34,000 transfer to Sheffield Wednesday, but Tommy resumed on 24 March at home to Brentford. Broome put Notts in front on 14 minutes at Griffin Park, but two minutes before the interval the Bees stung twice in a minute through Fred Monk and Billy Sperrin. The latter added another goal on 64 minutes, before Johnston reduced arrears to 3-2 seven minutes later. Despite this defeat, there was no question about Notts County's plight, although prospects looked bleak.

At Maine Road, it was a goalless draw on the following Monday, with the same 11 turning out for Notts, though Broome was back on the right wing. Another scoreless affair was then played out at Blackburn Rovers and yet another at home to Leeds United but the points gained meant that Notts were safe from relegation. However, the general feeling of unhappiness over the departure of Sewell soured many supporters. It was reflected in the clipping of around a third from regular attendances at Meadow Lane.

Next came a game of two halves at Upton Park with Notts on top in the first half, scoring twice, both goals involving Broome and Lawton and scored by Johnston. On 25 minutes, Lawton headed down to Broome, whose pass reached Johnston. Five minutes later a Broome free kick was nodded on by Tommy to Johnston. The second half was a complete change. Harry

Hooper on 52 minutes, Gerry Gazzard six minutes later and Bill Robinson on 75 minutes gave West Ham the lead. Ten minutes from time Robinson scored a disputed fourth with another Hammers player standing on the goal line.

Two days later Notts hosted Third Lanark and lost 4-2. Another friendly at Buxton on the following Wednesday lacked both Lawton and Broome, both still injured. Notts won 2-1. Broome was fit for the home league game with Swansea but neither Tommy nor Johnston was able to turn out. Broome scored first, then Crookes, the Retford schoolmaster, added a second for Notts, eventually edging it 3-2 with a rare goal from Harry Adamson. The gate was only 17,787. Lawton was also missing for the 1-0 loss at Hull and the goalless draw at home to Manchester City. He resumed on 5 May with Leicester City visiting Meadow Lane for the last match of the season.

Not for the first time, Notts chucked away a two-goal lead, after Crookes on 20 minutes then a neat one from Lawton – only his ninth of the season – six minutes later, both scored before the second-half collapse. Derek Hines, Arthur Rowley and Bert Barlow did the damage for City. However, after a difficult season, Notts had recovered to finish 17th in the league.

For the Festival of Britain match against FK Austria, there was only one change for Notts, with Smith in goal. Crookes was the Notts scorer in a 1-1 draw. Then on 23 May, Tommy Lawton's house was sold for £6,100, as another chapter in his life ended.

CHAPTER SIXTEEN

Back to London in Brentford Colours

THERE WAS one new face, or rather return of an old visage, in Ian McPherson, back from Arsenal on the Notts right wing to face Coventry City at Meadow Lane at the start of 1951/52. Spreading the ball about constructively, City impressed until Broome found an opening for Crookes to score for Notts on 39 minutes. Lawton produced a fine header just over the bar near the interval but was getting little change out of Martin McDonnell at centre-half. Crookes should have had another goal from a Tommy set-up and, on 63 minutes, Ted Roberts headed Coventry level. But Crookes scored the winning goal with a header from a free kick on 72 minutes in front of 34,001.

At Vetch Field, unchanged Notts scored first through Lawton on 18 minutes. After he had beaten two defenders his shot was too hot for the goalkeeper to handle. Swansea improved in the second half – Ron Turnbull hit an upright and Alf Bellis earned a 1-1 draw on 76 minutes. Then on the following Thursday, 30 August, with Barnsley in Nottingham, Lawton slotted home a penalty with ease on 40 minutes. A revitalised Broome then scored brilliantly a minute before the break. Johnston added a third on 51 minutes and Broome scored his second four minutes from the close. The Tykes were without Cec McCormack at centre-forward as they went down 4-0.

Two days later at home to Bury, it was Lawton who put Notts ahead after only two minutes. Tracking to the left of the goal, he fired powerfully enough to shake goalkeeper Andy Goram's hand on the way in. But the resourceful Shakers levelled through Harold Bodle on 18 minutes. Notts then had two goals disallowed – one a header from Lawton – and it was not until the 62nd minute that Tommy nodded in a winner. *The People* reporter considered Lawton to be on international form already!

Next to suffer in the Notts revival were Hull City, with one-time England centre-half Neil Franklin facing ex-international centre-forward Lawton. Tommy missed a penalty after ten minutes but he provided an opening for McPherson to score, then notched one of his own from a header before Johnston and Broome made it 4-0. Promotion was already the talk of Meadow Lane.

At Luton Town on 8 September Notts made just one change, Harry Adamson coming in at left-half for the injured Simpson. The only other change was that the Magpies wore claret and blue – was that unlucky? While the inside pages of the Nottingham *Football Post* were splashing: 'Grand Form of Magpies', elsewhere the match description was offering a sadder tale. After 34 minutes Notts had conceded as many goals as in the previous five games. Willie Davie after 12 minutes, George Stobbart three minutes later, then Jack Taylor put the Hatters on top. Stobbart added his second four minutes before half-time. There was a respite in the second half during which Lawton forced Bernard Streten into a spectacular tip over the bar. Yet Luton still added two more in the last ten minutes through Bert

Mitchell and Taylor for 6-0. Leuty had looked out of sorts in a shaky Notts defence.

Three changes followed for the next match at Barnsley, one being Ray Brown the Scottish amateur international being given his debut on the left wing. Notts went ahead after 20 minutes when Lawton made the opening for Crookes. McPherson was upended in the penalty area but no penalty was given. This was to prove decisive, as six minutes later John Jarman, the Tykes debutant at right-half, who had previously stopped Lawton progressing, hit a long pass to present Eddie McMorran with a goal, while Notts claimed offside. Harry Hough was kept busy by Lawton, fending off powerful drives but it was Barnsley who went ahead on 60 minutes with the same Jarman–McMorran combination. McPherson and Brown both suffered injuries and Barnsley's Maurice Hudson sustained a broken nose as Barnsley hung on to the 2-1 scoreline.

Some 44,087 attended at Meadow Lane for the local derby with Forest on 15 September and there were more alterations for the injury-hit Magpies. Leuty, suffering from gastric flu, was replaced by Baxter. After 14 minutes, Colin Collindridge scored for Forest. Lawton was then held back by Gager but no penalty was awarded, and on 51 minutes Forest added to their score through Jack Love DFC. With often three defenders hovering around, Lawton was having a tough time but the team revived with two goals in two minutes near the end through Broome and Crookes to earn a draw.

At Hull City, Lawton was again receiving praise, scoring two fine goals in the first 25 minutes, initially from a free kick outside the area that Billy Bly touched but could not stop, and the second when he controlled Deans's pass, pivoted and drove on the half-turn, again from distance. Syd Gerrie scored for

Hull but Johnston added a third for Notts to complete their first double of the season, all with the injured Simpson limping on the wing.

Two days later little went right for Lawton, with Queens Park Rangers getting away with a goalless draw at Meadow Lane. He had the best two chances, the first from which he shot wide and the second he hit too close to Stan Gullan, the overworked Rangers goalkeeper.

Then on 29 September at Ewood Park there was another mix-and-match Notts line-up but Leuty was back at centre-half to face Blackburn Rovers. Blackburn included Albert Nightingale, an early bird signed that morning from Huddersfield Town, at inside-forward. He saw the Magpies eventually taking flight after a disjointed display, conceding goals to Les Graham on 15 minutes and Joe Harris five minutes from the end.

At Griffin Park against Brentford the following week, Lawton was unfit, suffering from bronchitis and a touch of fibrositis, so the entire Notts forward line was composed of wingers! A goal eight minutes from the end by Ken Coote gave the Bees the points.

Lawton was again absent against Doncaster Rovers at Meadow Lane. The Magpies introduced Scottish schoolboy international Reg Wylie at inside-left. The only goal of the match was a splendid shot by Crookes just after the interval, handing two welcome points to Notts.

It was hoped that Tommy might return against his old club Everton, who had been relegated from the First Division in the previous season. This would be the first Notts meeting with them in league competition since the 1920s and Tommy was fit to play. The 49,604 crowd at Goodison afforded him a tremendous welcome, despite his having left the club for

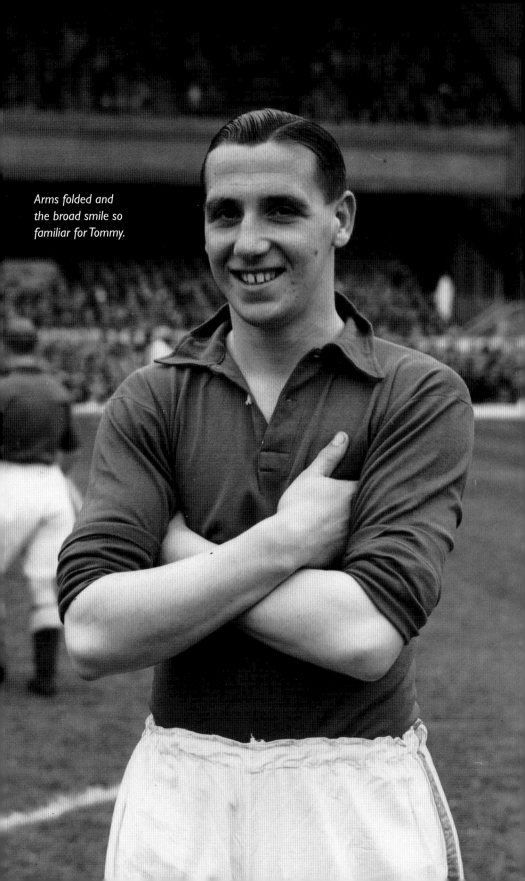

Arms folded and the broad smile so familiar for Tommy.

Jackson.   Geldard.   Cook.   Dean.   Lawton.   Stevenson.   Dougall

Watson.   Jones.   Mercer.

Everton 1937/38 Tommy is in the middle row fifth from left with Dean on his right.

Wembley 1942 and Scotland visit for the Aid to Russia international. Lawton heads home ignoring the arm of Jerry Dawson and the goalkeeper's pained expression.

In 1945 Moscow Dynamo say it with flowers to an embarrassed Chelsea. Tommy is fifth from the end of the row.

Skipper of England, Tommy leads the team out against Switzerland in the Victory International.

Tommy shows off his trademark hanging header during an England game against Ireland.

The Great Britain forward line against the Rest of Europe: left to right: Stanley Matthews and Wilf Mannion (England), Tommy Lawton, Billy Steel and Billy Liddell (Scotland).

Tommy shrugs off a full-scale lunge from Millwall's Walter McMillen.

£20,000 of No 9 talent at Notts County. Tommy prepares for action.

The line-ups in Turin 1948 prior to England's stunning 4-0 win over Italy.

Tommy chases a second goal against the Italian goalkeeper Valerio Bacigalupo.

Brentford's directors well outnumber Tommy on the signing-up occasion.

Red stripes for Tommy Lawton and still looking for goals with Brentford.

Chelsea, and young autograph hunters had to be shepherded away. But it was some Wylie magic that made Notts' first goal for Jimmy Jackson on 16 minutes. Both Wylie and Lawton fashioned Crookes's second goal on 28 minutes. John Willie Parker replied for Everton on 40 minutes before Jackson took the game by the throat in the second half to strike in the 50th, 70th and 73rd minutes for an outstanding four-timer in Notts' 5-1 victory over Lawton's old club.

After such an outstanding display at Everton, Notts then lost their home record against Southampton. They were again without Lawton, who was suffering from a pulled muscle. At one stage, five minutes before half-time, they were losing 4-0 but then Jackson scored one, Broome notched a penalty and Crookes scored on 79 minutes to restore some pride in the 4-3 defeat.

At Hillsborough on 3 November, it was a repeat of the Luton debacle and conceding six goals. Lawton returned but for once was dwarfed by the fledgling Derek Dooley – 6ft 3in and 190lb. In only his seventh game for Sheffield Wednesday Dooley scored five in the second half after ex-Magpie Sewell had opened the scoring on 44 minutes. The Magpies' topsy-turvy season continued and they had now slipped to ninth in the table.

Bradley returned in goal for the Leeds United visit, otherwise the team was unchanged. Lawton asked to be relieved of the captaincy and Leuty took over. Tommy was lively and Jackson scored for Notts on 26 minutes but the second half belonged to Leeds, who scored through Frank Fidler and Eric Kerfoot to win the match. In the gathering gloom the referee called for a white ball, but darker clouds covered Meadow Lane as the team dropped further down the table.

At Millmoor, no improvement was shown against Rotherham United. Jack Shaw scored for the hosts just before half-time, and a penalty from Norman Noble with 15 minutes remaining, produced the vital statistics for table-toppers Rotherham United, while Lawton and others tried to put a more positive ending to midfield endeavour.

Then Notts County sensationally signed Cec McCormack, a touch over 5ft 7in, as a centre-forward replacement for Lawton (watching Forest at Hull). They paid £24,000 to Barnsley. Tommy Lawton's days at Meadow Lane looked to be numbered less than his shirt. A goal after just 30 seconds from Jackson enlivened a small drenched crowd of 19,452 for the visit of Cardiff City, but Stan Montgomery headed an equaliser on 79 minutes. McCormack's debut was costly, too, as he suffered a fractured rib.

The rumouring set was in operation with suggestions that Lawton might be going to Hull City as player-manager, but they only wanted him as a player. Even so, five changes were made for Notts' trip to Birmingham City, including Lawton back at centre-forward and Geoff Brunt given his debut at right-half. Manager Eric Houghton was unwell and unfit to travel. Notts' approach work was let down by occasional wayward distribution. Behind to a Billy (W. H.) Smith goal on 18 minutes, he scored again five minutes after the restart and it was another defeat for Notts County, lying 14th in the Second Division.

Leicester City visited next and there were more Magpies changes, but they made a bright start, with Lawton involved. Crookes, with a splendid opener, slotted neatly on nine minutes, only for Fred Worthington to level six minutes later. Crookes reset Notts in front on 65 minutes but this lasted but a few minutes before Derek Hines equalised. Reg Halton converted a penalty for City, though Smith got a hand to it, and, when Broome was upended in the area, Notts were not granted a similar award. Another home defeat was not aided by poor finishing.

McCormack resumed away to Coventry City, but it was not long before a switch, with Lawton at inside-right and Broome at inside-left. Anthony Allen, ex-Forest, was at right-back for Notts. Broome from close in scored on 23 minutes off his chest, with City cries of 'hands'. This goal was all Notts had to show until a second near the half-time whistle when McCormack netted from McPherson's centre. Only when the winger was injured and had to retire in the second period, did Coventry get going and Roberts hit a post. But it was Notts' first win in eight matches.

Swansea opened the Christmas holiday period at Meadow Lane and were trailing after five minutes, Broome scoring. It became two goals on 21 minutes with an uncanny replay of the previous match as McPherson's centre was headed home by McCormack! Lawton almost spoilt the familiar story but his headed effort was cleared off the line.

On Christmas Day there was a continuation of the improvement, especially in attack, where the deployment of Lawton deeper was reaping benefits, in particular for McCormack. He scored his third goal in successive matches in this one against Sheffield United at Meadow Lane. Adamson and McPherson added two more, with Harold Brook responding for the Blades. However, in the Boxing Day return at Bramall Lane, Notts, with Leuty at left-back for the injured Deans, went down to a solitary goal by Brook.

Much the same line-up began well enough against Bury on 29 December and a slick move involving Lawton, McCormack, then Crookes, resulted in Broome finding the net off a post after 15 minutes. It was steadily downhill from then and two goals in two minutes just after the hour from Bodle and Plant gave the Shakers the two points.

The *Daily Mirror* questioned whether Lawton might be interested in succeeding Freddie Steele as player-manager of Mansfield Town. Meanwhile, Luton Town were at Meadow Lane, with that earlier six-goal reverse still echoing around the ground. The Hatters were ahead on 18 minutes through Jack Taylor but, four minutes later, Lawton's chest controlled the ball and the pass was made to McCormack, who made it 1-1. Five minutes before the break Tommy made McPherson's goal. Back came Luton with Taylor and Bernard Moore scoring before Crookes made it 3-3. On 73 minutes, Broome put Notts back in the lead, only for Taylor to head Luton level again four minutes later. With two minutes left, Lawton fed Crookes, whose centre was headed into his own goal by Syd Owen for an unexpected 5-4 win for Notts.

Early January brought the third round of the FA Cup and the first time in this round for Stockton, four years after forcing a draw with Notts in a previous tie. Deans was injured and Leuty was at left-back, with Baxter in the middle. Broome scored for Notts on 15 minutes but Stockton then hit the bar. However, McCormack headed a second Notts goal a minute before half-time and the same player fed Lawton on 59 minutes, Tommy producing a ferocious drive from outside the area for a third goal. With eight minutes left McCormack was brought down and Broome scored from the spot for a comfortable 4-0 victory.

The 40,005 all-ticket local derby at the City Ground developed into a pulsating all-action affair, with promotion-chasing Forest just edging it. Yet Notts led from a free kick taken by McCormack, the lead lasting two minutes before Wally Ardron scored for the Reds. On 22 minutes, a Lawton-Crookes move ended with Broome scoring for Notts to retake the lead. In the second half, Lawton was poleaxed by a ball hit at his midriff and needed attention. Clearly not right afterwards, he went off. Although he later returned, he appeared groggy. In the 48th minute Bill Morley equalised for Forest. However, their winning goal on 77 minutes was fortunate, as it seemed that Ardron controlled the ball with his hand before scoring.

There was more switching of players and positions at Queens Park Rangers on 26 January, with a covering of snow and some icy patches making football difficult. Notts scored on 20 minutes after McCormack's shot was blocked and Lawton finished it off. Into the second half, Harry Gilberg made it 1-1 and, shortly afterwards, David Underwood brought off a spectacular save from Lawton. McCormack restored Notts' advantage on 67 minutes and seven minutes later it was another Lawton record. Receiving from Crookes, he scored his 100th goal for Notts County. Crookes then made it 4-1 on 76 minutes.

Frost and snow meant there was a morning pitch inspection at Meadow Lane for the fourth-round FA Cup tie on 2 February against First Division title chasers Portsmouth. More changes were made to the Notts line-up. In the sixth minute, Marcel Gaillard scored for Pompey, before three minutes later Lawton headed in Crookes's centre to level things up. Albert Mundy put Portsmouth ahead again on 14 minutes and Dougie Reid made it 3-1 five minutes before the interval. There was no further scoring and the *Portsmouth Evening News* considered that Notts had been outplayed in every position.

Back in Second Division action at Meadow Lane there was a minute's silence for the passing of King George VI followed by 'Abide with Me'. The players wore black armbands. Visitors Blackburn Rovers took a sixth-minute lead against the Magpies through England amateur international Bill Holmes and, although Notts pressed for the equaliser, the Rovers rearguard was stoic and there were few chances. The best came three minutes from the end when a powerful drive by Lawton hit and laid out John Campbell, which was just as well as goalkeeper Reg Elvy was out of position.

Before the match with Brentford, there was speculation that Notts' opponents, seeking a new centre-forward, would have Jesse Pye, ex-Notts, signed for the match. It was not so, and the Bees were stung when Lawton headed down for Broome to score on 14 minutes. Tommy went close with one effort before driving in Notts' second goal on 20 minutes. Johnston made it three but Billy Sperrin replied with a fine effort for Brentford near half-time. In the second half, McPherson on 49 minutes increased Notts' lead before Sperrin hit his second goal. Eight minutes from time, Ted Gaskell saved Broome's penalty but not the follow-up, as the match ended 5-2 to Notts. The Nottingham *Football Post* referred to it all as 'the old Notts County'.

With a free Saturday, Notts played Middlesbrough at Ayresome Park in a friendly match and Crookes opened the scoring on 11 minutes after Lawton had drawn the defence. It was not until late in the second half that Wilf Mannion forged a goal for Harry Bell and added a second for himself as Boro won 2-1.

There was more of the same early marksmanship at Doncaster Rovers when, after three minutes, Lawton headed down for McPherson to score. On 16 minutes, Tommy finished off Crookes's header for a second goal and nine minutes later produced a perfect pass for him to hit Notts' number three. Rovers responded with a goal by Arthur Adey on 55 minutes, but Crookes, on 67 minutes, and Lawton, three minutes afterwards, running on to a pass by Crookes, made it 5-1. Tommy Lawton was foraging everywhere and had been outstanding.

Everton at Meadow Lane produced a dour defence-dominated display by both teams in what was to prove an interesting last game for Tommy Lawton in the Magpies' black and white. There were no goals and few opportunities for either side.

Then, apparently after lengthy negotiations, on 13 March the Notts board agreed to transfer Tommy to Brentford for £15,000. He travelled to London, with his old team heading for Southampton. The most surprised man was Notts' manager Eric Houghton, who told the press: 'I knew nothing about it.'

Lawton, now 34, was appointed Brentford captain against Swansea Town at Griffin Park and a record crowd of 31,000 was present. He almost scored in the first minute, but the Swans surfaced first on the scoring tack through Frank Scrine. Ken Coote equalised before half-time when, from a free kick, Lawton's flick of the head went to him. On 65 minutes Tommy repeated the feat, this time his nod from the free kick landing nicely for Billy Dare to put away. Dare added a second goal seven minutes later. It was Brentford's first league win in almost three months. The *Daily Herald* mentioned a 'Midas Touch', although there was no more power-packed Lawton shooting – 'clever headwork and canny distribution'. The *West London Observer* headlined: 'Lawton puts sting in Bees' attack.'

A week on at Coventry City, there was a repetition of the free-kick scenario. Lawton again headed on for Dare to score, on 73 minutes, but by then Coventry had netted twice through George Lowrie and Eddie Brown. A week later, 29 March, the visit of West Ham to Brentford was started but eventually called off due to a blinding snowstorm at 1-1.

At Bramall Lane, Lawton belied his years, turning the clock back with a 25-yard thunderbolt of old to put Brentford ahead. Sheffield United equalised through Fred Smith, then the Bees turned hovering to penetration with three goals in the last 15 minutes via Johnny Paton, Dare and Tony Harper. It was the Bees' best post-war away win.

It was United one day, then table-topping Wednesday at Griffin Park on Good Friday, and the leggy red-haired Dooley was on target with another hat-trick for the Sheffield club. The *Daily Mirror* referred to Lawton as 'forlorn and hungry', waiting for a chance. Brentford again had a large attendance due to the attraction of the Wednesday goal machine and, of course, Lawton. Wally Bragg and Dare did score for Brentford and Tommy managed near the end to bundle the ball in but it was ruled out for an infringement as Brentford lost 3-2.

Barnsley were at Griffin Park the following day and there was more Yorkshire relish for the Tykes, who scored first through Michael Parkinson's favourite player, Skinner Normanton. The Bees managed to snatch a draw when Jackie Goodwin found the net on 67 minutes. Then Easter Monday brought the return at Hillsborough against Wednesday, who completed the double against Brentford. Sewell scored with a fine cross drive on 35 minutes, then there was an unfortunate back pass by Roddie Munro that went in, too. Lawton did flash one of his 'specials' but Dave McIntosh in the Owls goal was lucky to flap it away. Any lingering promotion hopes had long since evaporated for Brentford.

Relegation was more the concern of Hull when Brentford called on 19 April and, on six minutes, Lawton made a goal for Dare. On 20 minutes, the Tigers, in Carter's last home game, clawed an equaliser through Bill Harrison. Then two errors by

Brentford goalkeeper Reg Newton allowed first Jim Duthie, then Denis Durham to score for Hull, before Eddie Burbanks added a fourth. But Eric Stanger in the *Yorkshire Post* praised Lawton. 'There is much good football left in him yet,' he wrote.

The rearranged West Ham match went some way to prove that point. The Hammers took the lead when a 30-yard free kick from Terry Woodgate hit Derek Parker on the way and diverted out of Newton's reach. However, ten minutes later, Fred Monk raced down the wing and hit a cross that Lawton despatched with express delivery in the air, beating Ernie Gregory all ends up. It was Tommy's first goal for Brentford as the match ended 1-1.

Then came the second of three successive home games to end the season with Blackburn Rovers visiting Griffin Park. Defences ruled, but on 65 minutes the deadlock was broken when England amateur international Bill Slater picked up a clearance and rifled in a left-foot shot from 25 yards, his first goal for Brentford. Ten minutes from time Eddie Crossan scrambled one in for 1-1. Doncaster Rovers then wound the season up for Brentford and it took 87 minutes before a goal arrived. From 35 yards out, left-back Frank Morrad, playing his first senior match of the season, belted one that gave Ken Hardwick no chance in the Rovers goal. It was the Bees' second home win in the last ten matches and they finished tenth in the league table.

Following this, Brentford played five games in Iceland but there was no Tommy, so the Prestwick airport sign – 'Welcome Tommy Lawton' – was completely redundant.

CHAPTER SEVENTEEN

To Arsenal at Last at the Age of 34!

TOMMY MISSED Brentford's 5-1 friendly win over Hayes in May and was spotted at Alford in July by a fan who obtained his autograph and noticed the miniature football on his ignition key. Lawton was again in the news on 8 August, cited as co-respondent in the divorce court, involving Mrs Gladys Mary Rose. Then, 11 days later, on the eve of the new season, Jackie Gibbons the secretary-manager of Brentford resigned. Jimmy Bain was appointed acting manager with the *Daily Mirror* speculating that Tommy might become player-manager.

Lincoln City opened at Griffin Park in 1952/53, the Bees welcoming back Leslie Smith from Villa. Ron Greenwood held prolific-scoring Andy Graver, the Imps goal machine, and 17 minutes from the end Jackie Goodwin scored from a Lawton-inspired opening. Tommy feinted to shoot before slipping the ball to him.

Unchanged at Huddersfield on the Wednesday, there were no goals, but there were four on the Saturday, shared with hosts, Hull City. Dare scored on 15 minutes for Brentford, Viggo Jensen levelled from a penalty on 40 minutes, adding a further goal on 75 minutes, before Fred Monk's penalty three minutes later levelled things up. The *Yorkshire Post* noted Lawton's 'calm assurance'.

Tommy opened his scoring account for the season in the return against a more fired-up Huddersfield for whom Jimmy Glazzard scored twice – the first a rocket, the second a side-foot flick – and Vic Metcalfe added a third, as Brentford went down 3-1. Lawton, unlucky with a header against an upright, did succeed in driving one in from a corner with eight minutes remaining. Then against Blackburn Rovers at Griffin Park, Billy Sperrin put the Bees one up in 20 minutes, before a sparkling Lawton finish – one of his surprises went in – but Eddie Crossan scored two to equalise. It was left to a Monk penalty on 80 minutes to seal Brentford's points.

At Sheffield United, Leslie Smith was absent due to a wrenched shoulder received while playing with his son in the garden! Terry Ledgerton took his place and scored Brentford's second goal after Derek Hawksworth's half-field run and goal from 15 yards had opened for the Blades. Goodwin had scored Brentford's first goal but, with the better-balanced team, United won when Jimmy Hagan scored his first of the season on 76 minutes. Three times they had hit the bar, too.

Back in Nottingham, Lawton renewed acquaintance with Forest centre-half Gager at the city Ground. The *Football Post* reporter commented on Tommy being 'a leaner figure than of yore'. But Forest hit first through Wally Ardron on 17 minutes. Lawton was active, went close before half-time and, in the second half, had a header and a shot saved. It took Forest until the 82nd minute to make it 2-0 through Collindridge, and a minute from time Ardron added a third.

Sheffield United, in pouring rain at Griffin Park, twice had shots cleared off the line by Monk. But Brentford came nearest to a goal on 65 minutes when Lawton chased a high ball and, in a tussle with goalkeeper Ted Burgin, it ran loose to Goodwin, who fired in from 30 yards. It was disallowed as Lawton was allegedly offside, so the match ended goalless.

Lawton's ex-Evertonians were next at Brentford. Harry Potts popped in the first goal for them on 15 minutes but Tommy made it 1-1 five minutes later. After a solo run he crashed a shot straight at the goalkeeper before burying the rebound. On 30 minutes he centred from the right wing for Tony Harper to put the Bees ahead. It stayed that way until Everton rallied to score three times in the last 25 minutes, with two from John Willie Parker and another from Potts, leaving the visitors 4-2 winners.

On 23 September, Tommy married Gaye Rose, formerly Gladys, quietly at Caxton Hall in London. Jackie Sewell was his best man. The couple spent two days on holiday in the country.

Then an interesting situation at Gigg Lane arose four days later. Bury were seeking a first home win, while Brentford searched for an initial away-day success. Bury were the better outfit but there were no goals until Plant burst into life on 62 minutes. He scored his second 20 minutes later, then was brought down for George Griffiths to convert the penalty for 3-0 to the Shakers.

The travelling victory was delayed a week until, at Doncaster Rovers, a couple of Lawton-inspired moves produced goals. On 37 minutes, Goodwin took his pass and hit a post, enabling Monk to finish. Tommy again found Goodwin on 80 minutes for the 2-0 win. But Southampton's visit to Brentford on 11 October seemed to be destined for a boring goalless draw until the last ten minutes. In four of those minutes, the Bees buzzed in three goals. Full-back Ken Horne decided to raid and Lawton headed home his cross. Tommy then hit the woodwork with another aerial effort, leaving Monk to make it two from the rebound. Smith hit the third goal after Ledgerton's good work.

On Tommy's first return to Notts County, Brentford finished a well-beaten 4-0. Lawton, up against Leuty, was held in check and had only one chance, but his header was cleared off the line by Southwell. Jimmy Jackson on eight minutes, then an own goal from Frank Latimer, put the Magpies 2-0 up after 18 minutes, and further goals from McPherson plus a second from Jackson completed the scoring.

There was an unusual start to Leicester City's visit on 25 October, the ball hitting the corner flag and allowing Ledgerton to smartly shuffle it on for Lawton to give Goodwin a goal in the first minute. Despite limping with a knee injury, Tommy beat two players and hit Brentford's second goal on 34 minutes. Jimmy Baldwin unsighted Alf Jefferies with City's goal from 30 yards and Mal Griffiths made it 2-2 in the second half. Lawton provided Dare with a goal and scored the fourth Brentford effort himself for 4-2. Seamus D'Arcy, signed in the deal that took Ron Greenwood to Chelsea, made an impressive debut for Brentford.

Lawton missed the floodlit friendly, won 4-2 at Worcester City, as well as defeat at West Ham and a draw at Fulham, where he sat on the trainer's bench. His jarred knee injury was taking time to heal. He returned at Rotherham on 15 November. The match was a triumph for Jack Grainger who scored a hat-trick for United in their 4-1 victory. Walter Rickett scored Rotherham's other counter with a Monk penalty the only Brentford offering.

Plymouth Argyle also took the points at Griffin Park, on 22 November. Maurice Tadman surprised Jefferies in the sixth minute for the first goal and a George Dews header on 26 minutes made it 2-0. Lawton found little scope but did elude Jack Chisholm on 52 minutes to head in Goodwin's centre.

Then there was a tough trip to Yorkshire to face Leeds United at Elland Road that became a personal triumph for John Charles. The former Wales international centre-half, now centre-forward, scored a hat-trick for Leeds, topping his achievement with the third and winning goal three minutes from the end when he dribbled 40 yards, beat three defenders, enticed the goalkeeper and side-stepped him before flicking the ball into the net. He had scored 11 goals in the last seven games and his last ten beat Charlie Keetley's 1929/30 record for Leeds. Dare and Ledgerton scored for Brentford and Lawton had adopted a wide-ranging foraging role that on another day would have taken a point. However, Brentford went down 3-2 and were now fourth from bottom of the league table.

There was no respite in the Midlands at Birmingham City, amid a mixture of mist, snow and sleet, plus going a goal down on 22 minutes to Peter Murphy. Tommy Lawton made it 1-1 on the half hour before Murphy scored a second City goal on 50 minutes and Cyril Trigg made it 3-1 with a quarter of an hour left. It was the Bees' fourth reverse on the trot and they had taken only one point from the last dozen available, slipping two further places in the league standings.

Tommy Lawton was ill and missed the goalless draw at Sincil Bank against Lincoln City, with the much-travelled Verdi Godwin orchestrating the Brentford attack in his stead. Incredibly, the holiday fixtures reversed Brentford's fortunes and produced six goals at Barnsley's expense. At Griffin Park on Christmas Day, Lawton was in sparkling form, twice bringing out the best in Harry Hough. On 34 minutes Tommy found Sperrin, who scored, then he fed Dare for a second helping two minutes after the break. Lawton added two goals of his own – a header and a strong shot – in the 4-0 win. On Boxing

Day at Oakwell the Bees led through an own goal after six minutes, by Matt McNeil, after a Lawton-animated attack had caused confusion. Tommy made the other Brentford goal for Ledgerton.

Then on 1 January 1953 it was announced that Tommy Lawton would become team manager of Brentford. But on the subject of playing, he told *The People*'s reporter: 'I'm good for another three or four seasons.' His first dual role experience was at Hull City where he had an early chance but delayed his shot too long. But on 11 minutes Ledgerton's centre was turned in neatly by D'Arcy for what was to be the only goal of the match. Hull tried to press home much of their midfield possession but without success. This match came a week before the FA Cup and the return of John Charles, leading Leeds United, at Griffin Park.

The mighty J. C. headed in from a corner on four minutes but there was to be no escalation. Wally Bragg glued himself to his tailing task. Within two minutes, Lawton and Dare, playing as twin centre-forwards at times, made the equaliser for Ledgerton. Already up for a pulsating cup tie, the temperature reached fever pitch on 25 minutes. Lawton, lying deep, feinted to go right, drifted left and, from 20 yards, cannoned a left-foot drive that rose to perfection into the goal. It was good enough to win any cup tie – and did.

In sharp contrast, Brentford were out of form at Ewood Park against Blackburn Rovers, who would have had an easier ride had chances led to more goals. Frank Chadwick got one in the first half – actually his only ever one – Eddie Quigley number two in the second half and Bill Eckersley converted a last-kick penalty for 3-0. Willie Kelly treated Lawton with shirt-tailed adherence.

Nottingham Forest were next at Griffin Park and, despite successfully drawing Forest centre-half Gager away from the centre of defence and opening up the game, Lawton's colleagues failed to take advantage of the strategy. In fact, it was a Lawton centre from the right from which Ledgerton put the Bees one up on 20 minutes. However, Gager did make Brentford pay when he headed the equaliser from a corner in 76 minutes for 1-1.

There was more Midlands opposition the following week, in the FA Cup at Villa Park on 31 January, and Brentford fought a rearguard action with the strong wind helping to ruin the standard of play. The nearest Tommy Lawton came to scoring was hitting the side netting from ten yards when it should have been on target. Maybe there were no goals but there was plenty of excitement and a replay to come on the Wednesday.

Brentford began well in the replay, with Lawton conducting operations, and he took the responsibility of the first goal on 35 minutes, heading in. Villa smartly responded two minutes before half-time through Davy Walsh and, seven minutes after the resumption, Tommy Thompson made it 2-1 for Villa. Brentford redoubled their efforts and Villa's defence were hanging on from that moment but they held out to go through to the next round.

It was not an afternoon to remember for a quiet Tommy Lawton at Everton on 7 February. Brentford had a debutant left-winger Micky Bull, 20, who looked promising. However, the Toffees' Dave Hickson ran the Brentford defence ragged and he had scored two goals within the first 13 minutes. Tommy Eglington scored their third on 34 minutes and Ted Buckle scored ten minutes later. In the second half, Hickson completed his hat-trick in the 5-0 win. Most of the Merseyside newspapers commented on Lawton facing a difficult task with his team.

Lawton, realising the need for change against Bury, brought in another youngster, Jimmy Bloomfield, 18, at inside-right. Tommy had two near misses before Sperrin scored to give the Bees the lead on the half hour. Stuart Imlach, on 49 minutes, levelled with a deflected goal and a few minutes later Plant, with a low header, made it 2-1 to Bury. With the Griffin Park crowd restless, it was left to debut boy Bloomfield to force a draw with a shot from distance.

With the country still in shock over the amputation of Derek Dooley's right leg above the knee, there was another home game for Brentford and points were still a requirement for safety. Doncaster Rovers at least provided Tommy Lawton with the easiest goal of his career. In the 38th minute, the Rovers goalkeeper Freddie Kingshott twice dropped a back pass, the second error leaving the ball behind him. Tommy trundled it over the line. But they all count, and Brentford won 1-0.

Such an easy ride might not have been possible at The Dell against Southampton on 28 February, though, with the Saints even more desperate for points than Brentford. However, nothing went right for Southampton. On 15 minutes they lost skipper, ex-Notts player Alec Simpson, with a broken leg and shortly after Bill Etherington put a Latimer shot into his own goal. Missed opportunities proved costly, too, and, when Lawton gave Dare the opening for a second Brentford goal with 78 minutes on the clock, it left the Saints beached on the south coast.

Entertaining his former club Notts County was Lawton's next assignment, with that five-goal drubbing against his old Everton mates still on his mind. A present at least arrived on nine minutes, when Leuty handled and Monk hit the penalty in. A minute later Harper made it 2-0. With Lawton deep-lying and spraying passes to all points, the Magpies were flapping, but to little purpose. On 65 minutes Dare scored the Bees' third goal, then on 84 minutes Lawton lifted the ball over the goalkeeper's head for number four and, with seconds left, Harper made it a nap hand after all!

At Filbert Street against Leicester City, it was another bright start for Brentford with Lawton and Dare giving Frank Morrad a goal on 15 minutes and three minutes later Bloomfield feeding Latimer for a second. Arthur Rowley snatched a City goal on 34 minutes but Latimer contrived his second after half-time. Rowley converted a penalty with four minutes to go for Leicester, but the 3-2 win brought two more points for the Bees.

It was West Ham who were given the runaround at Griffin Park. So what! They won 4-1. In addition to a failure to take decent chances, Brentford struck the bar and post. Ernie Gregory in the Hammers goal made flying saves and survived a shoulder to shoulder from Lawton. Tommy Moroney scored for West Ham on 30 minutes, then came the odd event ten minutes later that Joe Hulme of *The People* hardly believed. Harry Hooper's corner kick scraped the bar and went in off a post with the players motionless! Latimer had scored one for the Bees but both Moroney and Hooper had second helpings in the amazing Hammers win.

If that had been an unfair result, events at Craven Cottage on 28 March by no means inflated the margin between Fulham and Brentford. The *West London Observer* headlined: 'Brentford defence torn to shreds.' After a bombardment from the kick-off, Fulham took a 15th-minute lead through Bobby Robson, and Arthur Stevens headed a second eight minutes later. Lawton forced saves from Ian Black with a drive and a header but there was more trouble for Brentford after the interval. Bedford

Jezzard scored twice, the second from a penalty, and Robson completed another 5-0 trouncing.

From the holiday programme, the Bees scraped two points from a possible six, courtesy of two home draws. On Good Friday, Swansea, for whom the younger Charles – Mel of that ilk – was outstanding at centre-half until limping in the last ten minutes, earned a goalless draw. Chances were limited all round. On the Saturday, at home to Rotherham and with Lawton absent, 'rested', Ronnie Burke gave the visitors a 15th-minute lead but Bloomfield earned the point for Brentford seven minutes into the second half.

On Easter Monday at Vetch Field – Lawton-less once more – a useful Ledgerton goal after two minutes gave Brentford the lead but they were trailing 3-1 by the break from a scintillating hat-trick from Ivor Allchurch. With just a Verdi Godwin goal in the second half, Brentford lost by the odd goal in five. But Tommy was back at Home Park against Plymouth Argyle for the next match but the only goal came from Neil Dougall for the Greens two minutes before half-time. Then more Charles trouble loomed, with Leeds United due at Griffin Park on 18 April.

With just two points from their last six games, Second Division football for Brentford in 1953/54 was beginning to look unlikely. But thanks to a defensive error, Ledgerton scored against Leeds in the first minute and Coote headed a second on 17 minutes. In stepped John Charles on 35 minutes and Bob Forrest four minutes before half-time to make it all square. Lawton splendidly headed a Monk free kick home on 70 minutes but J. C. levelled nine minutes from time for 3-3. Lawton injured a thigh muscle in the second half.

Life was becoming difficult for Tommy Lawton, who had gone from centre-forward to player-tactician, player-manager and now team manager, though always playing. It was beginning to tell on him. But the publicity still surrounded him and the club with the release of *The Great Game*, a film starring James Hayter as a crooked football manager, with Tommy (cameo role) and other Brentford players in it, too, as many scenes were filmed at Griffin Park. Diana Dors provided the sex interest.

Without Lawton, three points from the last three games of the season prevented Brentford from being relegated. A draw at home with Luton, then a win away there, plus a narrow 2-1 defeat at Birmingham, ended a disappointing season for the club and its hard-pressed manager. The Bees finished 17th.

So much for Brentford's youth policy as, in July 1953, Frank Broome (38) and Ian McPherson (33) were signed from Notts County. The new season began with the two newcomers respectively at outside-left and inside-right. Lawton (33) led the line. In the trial match the Stripes beat the Whites 7-0. The *West London Observer* was impressed. 'There is plenty of talent,' it reported. Broome scored twice, McPherson and Lawton one each.

The first league match of 1953/54 brought a reasonable result at Stoke City, 1-1. Broome scored on 25 minutes, with Harry Oscroft scoring a late leveller for the Potteries side. However, Brentford were then ripped apart in eight minutes at Derby County on the following Saturday, with the damage inflicted between the 21st and the 29th minutes. Tommy Powell scored Derby's first goal, Jack Lee scored three minutes later, then he repeated the effort for 3-0. Brentford showed touches and, in the 74th minute, Lawton headed in, but Lee hit the last goal two minutes from time for 4-1. David Williams, reporting in the *Daily Herald*, considered Brentford to have been the most one-man team he had seen, Lawton being the one man!

Tommy's shrewd pass to Ledgerton for a two-minute strike was the only concrete event for the Bees against Blackburn Rovers in their next match. For Rovers, Tommy Briggs hit a treble and Eddie Quigley the other in their 4-1 win. Eckersley even fired a penalty over the bar, or it could have been worse.

Lawton had pulled a leg muscle, so he brought Dare in at centre-forward against Fulham at Griffin Park. A minute before half-time the Bees had a penalty. Jimmy Hill, ex-Brentford, now a Cottager, signalled to goalkeeper Ian Black that Monk always shot to the right. It was so obvious. Monk shot to the left and scored. Goodwin added a second goal with Charlie Mitten also getting a spot kick away in Brentford's 2-1 win. Lawton decided to keep Dare in at Blackburn and he scored twice in a useful draw at Ewood Park, with John Campbell and Quigley notching for Rovers.

The next two home games, against Bristol Rovers and leaders Doncaster Rovers, were crucial. Geoff Bradford sank Brentford in the first with a hat-trick on a day that Tommy brought back McPherson and Broome. Then, the day before the Doncaster game, Tommy announced his resignation as team manager but said that he would continue playing. 'It is affecting my football,' he said. Lawton left the veterans out and put himself at inside-left with Dare centre-forward. Lawton did crack one in from 20 yards but Peter Doherty inspired Rovers, as Brentford went down 4-1 at home.

At Lincoln City on 12 September Tommy swapped places with Dare. Harper scored three minutes from the end but City had already netted twice in three second-half minutes, initially through Andy Graver on 53 minutes, then Ernie Whittle. The return with Doncaster at Belle Vue was unlikely to be a picnic, with Brentford sitting second from bottom in the table, which was still led by their next opponents.

Maurice Robinson opened the scoring for Rovers on 31 minutes, Bert Tindill added a second five minutes later and Eddie McMorran made it 3-0 ten minutes from time. Lawton had tried hard to inspire his team, but to no avail. The next day he signed for Arsenal!

It was subsequently revealed by Joe Hulme in *The People* that Brentford chairman F. A. Davis had told Tommy he was better than this and, on the player asking where he should go next, the answer was 'Arsenal'. Lawton was delighted. However, Davis's approach to Tom Whittaker was initially turned down until the Arsenal manager telephoned Mrs Lawton. Then it happened. A substantial fee involved some £10,000 with Jimmy Robertson moving in the other direction.

Lawton went straight into the Arsenal first team at Highbury against Manchester City. The Gunners had won the First Division championship the previous season but were now sitting second from bottom without a home win to their name! Some 65,869 packed the ground. Tommy's old Everton mate Joe Mercer was also at Highbury but injured at the time. Maurice Smith in *The People* reported that 'Lawton was satisfactory, Arsenal shocking'. Doug Lishman scored twice for the Gunners, Johnny Hart and Billy Spurdle replying for City in the 2-2 draw.

On 23 September, the Ruislip-based Lawton family – Tommy, wife Gladys, and seven-year-old stepdaughter Carol – celebrated their first anniversary. Meanwhile, an ankle injury kept Lawton sidelined, missing wins over Cardiff City and Preston, as well as a floodlit friendly against Preston, just before the league match, too! Other such fixtures against QPR and Anderlecht were also missed.

Tommy returned to action at White Hart Lane against Spurs. Soon in evidence, he allowed the ball to run over his head for Jimmy Logie to score on eight minutes. Arthur Milton, Alec Forbes from a penalty, and Logie again, made it an amazing 4-1 success – the Gunners' fifth match unbeaten in a row. On the following Monday, Tommy figured in the Charity Shield match against Blackpool, the first under lights at Highbury. Mist turned to fog but a Matthews-inspired move and a ballet-like twist by Mortensen led to Blackpool scoring first. But with Cliff Holton operating as an emergency winger, the big lad contrived to cause problems. Near half-time Holton found the right pass for Lawton to latch on to and equalise. On 64 minutes the pair contrived another goal that Lishman finished off. Holton fashioned a third, again put in by Lishman.

It was familiar opposition for Lawton, with Burnley at Highbury on the Saturday, and, despite a sixth-minute lead through Alec Forbes, Arsenal finished well-beaten, 5-2. The nearest to a Tommy goal was in attempting to charge the goalkeeper in possession – a side-step sent Tommy into the net without the ball!

Apart from playing in the first floodlit friendly match staged by Rangers at Ibrox on 8 December in a 2-1 win, Lawton did not play another first-team match until 2 January, against Aston Villa. Then he deputised at inside-right for the injured Logie. The game lasted only 23 minutes in fog, by which time Holton, Lawton and Holton in that order had scored in a four-minute spell!

Tommy was inside-right again in the league match with Sunderland at Highbury on 23 January. The match was hijacked by Len Shackleton, the variety act of football tricks. Ted Purdon scored for Sunderland after just ten seconds, the first of a personal hat-trick, and Arsenal did level on six minutes through Holton, but that was it. The Shack act took over in the 4-1 win.

Tommy was deputising at centre-forward for Holton at Manchester City on 6 February, and only the brilliant goalkeeping of ex-German para Bert Trautmann prevented Arsenal from winning and Lawton from scoring at least twice, with a shot and a header in the goalless draw. Lawton was in action again the following week at Highbury against Cardiff City. The Welsh team had not scored in four games but took just ten minutes to rectify that courtesy of Trevor Ford, deflected by Len Wills. But a shrewd pass by Lawton led to Lishman equalising on 18 minutes in the 1-1 draw.

On 23 March, a floodlit friendly at Hull had Tommy in good form and flashing in a goal on 27 minutes in a 3-1 win. But he was on the losing side, 3-1, at Bristol City a week later and there was no more first-team duty for Lawton until 6 April when he again played inside-right, in the rearranged Villa game. Peter McParland gave Villa a first-half lead but, on 62 minutes, Lawton scored his first Arsenal league goal. He glided in a centre by Arthur Milton, cleverly heading in from an acute angle. Then Wills hit the bar from the penalty spot, leaving the result at 1-1.

Against Liverpool at Highbury, the match was marred by an injury to Joe Mercer, who fractured his right shin bone. Otherwise, it was an outstanding match for Lawton, in a deep-lying role supplying openings for his other forwards. Derek Tapscott scored twice and Don Roper once, and it should have been more than 3-0. Then it was same ground, same scoreline, same marksmen against Portsmouth – rubber-stamped in fact.

Then came a treat for FA Cup Final eve, with England of old meeting Young England at Highbury, 43,554 in attendance.

The Golden Oldies lined up as follows: Bartram; Mozley, Smith, Johnston, Leuty, Cockburn, Matthews, Mannion, Lawton, Shackleton, Langton. Shack reprised his standout show for Sunderland by contriving a perfect pass for Mannion to score on 14 minutes and in the second half a high cross for Lawton to direct it with the headed aplomb of yesteryear. In between, Derek Hines had scored for Young England, beaten 2-1.

Lawton then played part of the friendly against Grasshoppers in Zurich on 5 May before Holton took over. Arsenal won 3-2, then lost 3-1 to Young Boys in Berne without Tommy.

CHAPTER EIGHTEEN

The Start of the End Game

IN THE Arsenal trial match in August 1954, the centre-forward choice was between the orthodox dashing style of Cliff Holton or Tommy Lawton playing a deep-lying Nandor Hidegkuti style, bearing in mind the aftermath of England's 7-1 drubbing by Hungary only three months previously. Holton got the nod in the first two league games. Lawton had a run-out in the Combination Cup side against his old mates from Brentford and, in a high-scoring 7-4 win, he hit a hat-trick.

Four days later, on 28 August, he was brought into the first team against West Bromwich Albion at The Hawthorns. He went close to scoring once but Albion won 3-1. Three days later at Highbury, against his old club Everton, Tommy showed more of his former self in a 2-0 win, according to the *Liverpool Echo* reporter.

He kept his place for the next three matches. First came a 2-0 victory against Spurs at Highbury, then Tommy caused Bert Trautmann some discomfort in Arsenal's 2-1 loss at Manchester City when he struck a powerful drive that caught the German goalkeeper in the throat. But Lawton pulled a muscle in training after the 4-0 success against Sheffield United on 11 September.

In that one at Highbury, his handled header had led to an early penalty, but he had also shot wide from a reasonable chance.

Back for the Preston game at Deepdale on 18 September, Lawton produced two strong headed efforts, one saved, the other hitting the upright, but Walter Pilkington in the *Lancashire Evening Post* commented that his 'powers had faded with the passing of time'. Even so, the arrival at Highbury of his former club Burnley produced Lawton's first goals of the season, two in fact, and he also made the others in a convincing 4-0 win.

In a see-saw of a 3-3 draw at Leicester City, Tommy had crashed in his first goal on 33 minutes and with ten minutes left he torpedoed himself into the ball to level the scoring. There was time for a penalty but Don Roper hit the bar. The goalkeeper stopped his rebound and, in the melee that followed, the referee disallowed the effort. Lawton was then in the Arsenal team that became the first English side to play a match in Russia, against Moscow Dynamo.

This match came the day before Tommy's 35th birthday. While there, he bought a doll for his stepdaughter Carol. Arsenal were outclassed, suffering a 5-0 defeat. Lawton admitted: 'They were a good side and very fit. But our boys had missed two nights' sleep and that had its effect. Of course it's no excuse. The goals were not clear cut but they were alright. Dynamo played the usual Continental style with speed and movement.'

Arsenal manager, Tom Whittaker, reckoned 'they played together as a team more than anyone I have seen'. Lawton had also played against Moscow Dynamo in 1945 when they came to England.

Tommy had been answering football questions in the weekly *Junior Express* magazine, which gave away prizes and autographed footballs. *Soccer the Lawton Way* was also published around the same time. But as a celebrity guest on *What's My Line?*, smuggled into the BBC, he failed to beat the panel.

At Sheffield Wednesday on 9 October, goals from Jimmy Bloomfield and Don Roper secured a 2-1 win for the Gunners, but Lawton was used more as an extra midfield player. He had just one shot at goal. His next senior outing was also abroad, on 20 October in the 18th clash against old rivals Racing Club in Paris. Jimmy Bloomfield scored after 21 minutes and six minutes later Lawton headed in after a free kick. Racing Club reduced the score in the second half, but Alec Forbes converted a penalty for 3-1.

Three days later at Aston Villa, Lawton barely had a sniff of the ball, being well policed by another old-timer in Con Martin, the Irish international. Villa won 2-1. Tommy's next call was against Bolton Wanderers at Burnden Park, where he forced an early save in what proved to be a 2-2 draw.

With indifferent results, Arsenal next called up Lawton for the Christmas Day clash at Highbury against Chelsea. This followed a run-out with the Combination team against Brighton & Hove Albion on 18 December, Tommy scoring twice in a 5-1 win. In the first half against Chelsea the Gunners only had one shot at goal and it was Lawton's in the 33rd minute and it was enough to secure the points!

Two days later at Stamford Bridge, Arsenal escaped with a 1-1 draw, but Roy Bentley hit a penalty straight at Jack Kelsey – their fifth such miss in the season. On New Year's Day came another Arsenal draw, this time involving four goals with West Bromwich Albion at Highbury. Lawton was now often referred to as the 'veteran centre-forward'.

Would the FA Cup revive memories? Arsenal were drawn at Highbury to face Cardiff City, and Maurice Smith of *The*

People recalled the sole defining moment of it, three minutes from time. 'Tommy Lawton so often the hero in the past, so far removed from the Lawton that used to be, fastened on to a 40 yard lob from [Peter] Goring. He held off [Stan] Montgomery's challenge to crash the ball with his right foot in the best old Lawton style.'

Tommy was clearly on a roll. The following week in the First Division at Tottenham Hotspur's White Hart Lane and, again restricted to one real chance, he did it again. With Cliff Holton unexpectedly given the left-wing berth, his cross was too high for Harry Clarke, the Spurs centre-half, to gain sufficient purchase. It fell to Doug Lishman, who found Tommy. A quick pivot and crisp finish won the game, the third solo accomplishment from four in a row by the 'old stager'.

There was only one goal in the FA Cup match at Wolves, but it was not an Arsenal player behind it. Roy Swinbourne was the scorer at Molineux in the 60th minute, heading in from a corner. But Lawton could claim the better effort on 33 minutes, when he soared high over the Wolves defenders with a brilliant effort that was nullified by an equally superb save by Bert Williams at the expense of a corner. The *Birmingham Daily Post* considered that veterans Lawton and Walley Barnes had been Arsenal's best players.

At home to a Preston North End lacking its talisman Tom Finney, Arsenal were in control and the 'old campaigner' Lawton, using his wise head to save his legs, was influential, if not among the scorers – Derek Tapscott and Roper. Then came a renewal for Lawton at his first professional club Burnley on 12 February, but a 3-0 defeat at the end of it soured the occasion for him. Tommy was overshadowed by the performance of Bill Holden. The latest Turf Moor favourite No.9 incredibly had a similar Bolton background to Lawton's and was once on Everton's books!

Without Lawton, Arsenal began a run of ten matches without defeat, dropping only two points on the way. However, after playing in a floodlit friendly against Rangers at Highbury and scoring in a 3-3 draw with an apparently harmless header that Bobby Brown in goal failed to grasp, Tommy was included in the league side at Sunderland on 19 March. Bloomfield, playing on the left wing, was the scorer of the only goal as Arsenal's recovery continued. However, it did so without Lawton in the team, although he was in for another floodlit friendly in Edinburgh against Hibernian, playing in a deeper role, with Tapscott spearheading the attack. After being two goals down, Arsenal levelled through Lishman and Bloomfield.

On FA Cup Final eve at Highbury, Young England (under-23) took on Old England (over-30) and the parlous position of English football was underlined when the veterans won 5-0. Stanley Matthews started the semi-rout with a rare goal, and in the second half Lawton scored two in a row. The first came from an oblique angle, the second a slightly easier effort. Then he was brought down and Bobby Langton converted the spot kick. Mortensen added a fifth with a header. Swift, in goal, pulled a muscle and Kelsey had to take over.

It was then tour time for Arsenal and they shared ten goals with Grasshoppers. Lawton was included against Young Boys in Berne, Arsenal winning 3-0. Forbes on five minutes and Lawton six minutes into the second half with a header settled them, and full-back Len Wills scored a third on 70 minutes. In Germany, 1860 Munich proved trickier, but a brace from Tapscott, playing in his forward role with Lawton deeper again, won it 2-1 for the Gunners.

Tommy started 1955/56 as first-team leader at Highbury. He scored all three goals in the opening league game against Cardiff City in the 3-1 win. He volleyed the first after five minutes, picked his spot from eight yards on 33 minutes and completed his treble at the age of 36 after 52 minutes, in the slick manner of a decade earlier. He also grabbed the Arsenal goal in the 1-1 draw with Chelsea, also at home, after a half clearance. This was followed by one of his team's two goals in the 2-2 draw at Manchester City, when described by the *Daily Mirror* as 'still a master footballer'. His fourth scoring effort on the trot was away to Bolton Wanderers but Arsenal lost 4-1, where the other Bolton product of note, Nat Lofthouse, scored a hat-trick.

Was this the 'last hurrah' for the Lancashire lad who had preceded Lofthouse? Certainly, that was the end of Lawton's First Division scoring, as the next matches produced a goalless draw in the City return, followed by a trio of 3-1 defeats against Tottenham Hotspur, Portsmouth and Sunderland. He did play in the friendly against Rangers at Ibrox on 21 November, a 2-0 defeat.

Meanwhile, Kettering Town had made an unimpressive start to 1955/56, and it was not until Guy Fawkes Day that a spark was lit in celebration of a first win of the season, 5-1 against Llanelli after being behind at one stage. Early in December, two new directors were appointed, and two others left in January. On the 26th of that month it was announced 'amid great excitement', according to the *Kettering Town Handbook*, that Tommy Lawton, still a registered Arsenal player, was to become the Poppies' player-manager. He was actually signed on television! Publicity was to follow him during the rollercoaster of his twilight career. Signed on 1 February, he cost a nominal sum of £1,000 in the transfer. He had played his last game for Arsenal reserves on Boxing Day 1955 against Brentford.

He made his Kettering debut on 11 February against Yeovil on a snowy pitch and Kettering lost 2-1. They were whacked 5-1 by Bedford, too, but Tommy's Highbury connections resulted in the loan signing of goalkeeper Jim Standen until the end of the season. Results improved to the extent that only one defeat was suffered in 14 games and tenth place was the finishing position in the Southern League.

At the end of the season, a benefit for two Poppies was arranged. An All-Star XI, including some Arsenal players, met Leicester City and 6,500 watched the entertaining 3-3 draw. In the summer months, Lawton signed several players from Football League clubs, including Jack Wheeler (Bolton Wanderers), Norman Plummer (Leicester City) and Amos Moss (Aston Villa), who was made captain. Tommy stepped up the training in the pre-season and the Poppies were fit and ready for the 1956/57 season. The reserves beat the first team 6-1 in the trial match! The club entered the stiffs in the Central Alliance and an A team for the United Counties League.

After only drawing 1-1 at Merthyr in the opening Southern League game, the team settled down and did not lose until 17 November – 2-1 at Lovell's Athletic. Two weeks earlier, reaching first place, they stayed there. But the disappointments had been in cup competitions – knocked out by Spalding in the FA Cup, Bedford in the Southern League Cup and beaten by Peterborough United in the Maunsell Cup Final, 4-2, with Lawton and Moss scoring for the Poppies.

Bedford were the only league winners at Rockingham Road. That was on 16 February, 2-1, during the team's worst patch. The match had attracted 8,717. Other defeats were only by the odd goal. Tommy paced himself, a wise move at the age of 37, playing in half of the first-team fixtures and scoring 17 goals in his 26 outings. His high spot was reached on 13 October when he scored four goals in the 6-4 win over Chelmsford City, three of them from his famous headers. In his 16 months at the club he scored 20 goals in 34 appearances. The Southern League average attendance at Rockingham Road during this time was 3,834.

However, there had been controversy when in March he announced that he was to leave at the end of the season. At the club's celebration dinner in May he announced he had become manager of Notts County. It turned out to be a most unhappy 1957/58 campaign for his former club and relegation followed. After playing for Notts in a testimonial game against a Select XI on 29 April in which he scored once in a 6-1 win, then a second such benefit against Kettering, getting one in a 4-0 success, two days later Tommy Lawton was sacked. He toyed with playing again but in the end retired in July 1958.

CHAPTER NINETEEN

Judgement of Peers

HOW DID Lawton's contemporaries regard him? Manchester City goalkeeper Frank Swift became friendly with him during the war years when they were frequently in the same Army Representative XI as well as wartime internationals. The pair, jokers together on tour, also partnered each other in 'pool' table games! When questioned as to how he rated Tommy in comparison with other centre-forwards, Swift went into some detail when deciding two players virtually tied for first place – Hughie Gallacher and Tommy Lawton.

In *Football from the Goalmouth*, a 1948 publication, Swift referred to Lawton as 'big, fast moving, equally dangerous with head or foot but beautifully balanced and a brilliant ball player'. He added: 'The most difficult shot to save was the one aimed just inside the far post, the bane of any goalkeeper. Tommy always looked for such an opportunity.' With this accolade, one wondered who could top such a glowing testimonial. A year later, in *Stanley Matthews' Football Album*, Swift referred to Lawton as 'the most deadly of them all!'

While the onlooker is usually given the acknowledgement of seeing more of the game, it is often personal preference rather than selection on merit alone. When looking for a critic who had also played football at a decent level himself, it was invariably Ivan Sharpe who was chosen. He was certainly an 'establishment' figure inasmuch as he had the right background. To elucidate the point, in 1958 he was presented with a silver salver on behalf of the Football League clubs as a token of their appreciation of his 50 years' association with the league as a player and a journalist. Though always an amateur, he had played and mixed with professionals during his career. He also won England amateur international caps and was in the 1912 Olympic team.

He considered Lawton to be of similar construction to his Everton predecessor Dean in terms of shooting and heading, though with the latter's ability just a shade behind him but more efficient in approach play. However, he still placed Gallacher as his No.1 centre-forward, although the diminutive Scot was no Dean at heading.

Despite this, Sharpe commented on a match between the two Nottingham clubs – County and Forest. Lawton positioned himself on the far junction of the penalty area lines. From a corner he ran diagonally into the six-yard area and with superb timing headed a splendid goal. 'One could never see a better,' was Sharpe's comment.

Another in a similar role as a footballer-turned-journalist was Charlie Buchan, six caps for England and a lengthy career accompanying it. For him Lawton was: 'The greatest centre-forward of his time. His headwork moulded on the pattern of Dean and his clever footwork.' England captain Eddie Hapgood called Lawton 'as big as a house and full of confidence'. He recalled the 15 April 1939 international against Scotland at Hampden Park. With three minutes remaining, Matthews swerved past

Cummings to crack the ball into the middle. 'Big Tom Lawton was there and his head flashed the ball into the top corner of the net.' It was the winning goal. Tommy admitted being grateful for the opportunity for redemption after an earlier miss.

Stoke City and England centre-half Neil Franklin called Tommy 'the best centre-forward I have played against. He has ball control, speed and a deadly shot in either foot. In the air he is outstanding mainly because he times his jump to perfection and then heads downwards.'

In Franklin's first game for England against Scotland, Stan Mortensen in his *International Soccer Book* described the rigidity of the third back game – 'a terror to the stopper centre-half' – and the comparatively easy way it was to unravel such – 'Tommy Lawton gave all those who want to learn a lesson in how to get the best of the stopper centre-half. The second portion of the match was on its way and the score was 2-2. Lawton got the ball and instead of trying to make a way down the middle he veered over to the left wing. Scotland's centre-half did his shadowing job, of course, faithfully following the England centre-forward. I ran into the centre-forward position, the ball was put across by Lawton and I banged it home to register the winning goal.'

West Ham United pivot, 'Big Jim' Barrett, remembered his first meeting with Tommy Lawton playing for Burnley on 14 November 1936 at Upton Park. 'Boy, did he give me some trouble,' he remembered. 'He scored two typical Lawton goals and by the end of the match I had made up my mind that I had been playing against a future international. Everton had sent a scout to watch him that day, too.'

Walley Barnes, the Arsenal and Wales full-back, faced him, too. 'England opened the scoring with a typical effort,' he recalled. 'Gathering a loose pass Lawton slipped past Bob

Davies and myself with a clever swerve and side-step and fired in a shot from 20 yards that gave Cyril Sidlow no chance.'

Subsequently, the Welshman mentioned in his 1953 *Captain of Wales* book, Lawton being as much of a problem head on. 'He rounded Billy Hughes at top speed, collided with me and was himself laid out. I think Tommy still holds this against me, but I want to tell him here and now that the last thing I intended to do was to come into collision with his mighty frame. The truth is I just couldn't get out of his way in time!'

Another who skippered Wales was Ronnie Burgess of Tottenham Hotspur. No bones about his comment: 'The greatest centre-forward of modern times.' He also placed Lawton in his best international forward line that had none of his countrymen in it!

Tommy was also ever ready to give advice – even to Scottish players! Hugh Taylor in his *Great Masters of Scottish Football* told the story, although the circumstances were understandable as they were playing together. It was in the Great Britain v Rest of Europe match in 1947 at Hampden Park. The GB team was 2-1 ahead in the 34th minute. Billy Steel was in possession but his other four forwards were covered. Steel kept going and no opponent appeared to intervene. Goalkeeper Darui screamed, 'Regardez Steel,' but it made no impact. Twenty yards from goal Lawton shouted, 'Hit it.' Steel almost burst the ball in scoring.

Tom Finney said: 'Tommy Lawton was powerful, snap-shooting accurate with his head and an ideal middle man for Matthews' crosses.' The Preston plumber also put him in the Raich Carter, TL and Wilf Mannion inside men, as the 'terrible trio'.

As for Billy Wright, long-time England captain, he focused on 'a flick of that remarkable head'. He also added: 'He must have taken tremendous hammerings but never once did I see Tommy lose his temper or his poise. Never can I recall him deliberately fouling an opponent.' For Jackie Milburn, who replaced Tommy in the England team, it was simply 'the great Tommy Lawton'. In similar vein, in *Sport Weekly Magazine*, it was 'Tommy the Great!' In the same journal in September 1948, Alex Lee reported that Lawton was 'working miracles with Notts County'.

A Century of English International Football 1872–1972 by Morley Farror and Douglas Lamming listed him as: 'A young prodigy who handsomely realised his early promise to become a great centre-forward, brilliant on the ground, absolutely supreme in the air and a constant threat to defences throughout a longish career.'

Occasionally the seemingly off-the-cuff remark merely served to enhance Lawton's reputation. When Alf Ramsey was at Tottenham Hotspur there were discussions about varying corner kicks. The England full-back said: 'It was generally agreed that unless one possessed a player of Tommy Lawton's quality in attack, corner kicks with top class teams covering so well in defence, were nothing more than a sheer waste of time.'

An even more subtle accolade came from *Soccer – Do It This Way* by D. F. Rowe, schoolmaster at the Royal Naval College, Dartmouth and former Cambridge University Blue, a basic guide to what to do with a football, but an 'establishment' publication with a foreword by Stanley Rous. Frame-by-frame photographic illustrations in it filmed by John Barlee FRPS show all facets of kicking and heading a ball plus coaching fundamentals. However, there were also action pictures of leading players taken by newspapers. Among them were two of Lawton, one with him shooting in a Chelsea shirt during a pre-match kick-in, simply captioned 'THE MASTER'. The other was from an England v Ireland international with Lawton in mid-air perfectly poised and turning his head to direct a downward header, thwarting a challenging defender.

Of course, playing alongside the legendary Bill (Dixie) Dean at Everton as part of his learning curve at Goodison Park, one expected a more critical appraisal. In Nick Walsh's book, simply entitled *Dixie Dean*, there was little left for doubt as the Goodison legend referred to Lawton as 'blessed with much talent'. Walsh made mention of the situation, saying that the youngster was helped by Dean's generous nature, which was devoid of the usual petty jealousies that often govern the relationships of stars and their understudies. Tommy's heading technique was certainly improved by watching the maestro at first hand.

Scarcely had Lawton landed at Goodison Park than the comparisons with Dean were well in place. One player with a more clinically expert eye to the likeness was Herbert 'Duke' Hamilton, the Chesterfield full-back who had previously been with Preston North End and Everton. The 9 January 1937 edition of *Topical Times* picked up the point that the 'Duke' knew the angles and values of a centre-forward – after playing against Tommy in the previous September.

Alec E. Whitcher, Brighton & Hove Albion director and author of a trilogy of books in the last years of the conflict and immediate post-war period, said of Lawton: 'One of our country's greatest discoveries.' Alex James, Arsenal's Scotland international pocket-sized purveyor of passes said: 'Lawton was the lightest mover of any big man who played football.'

Grimsby Town and England goalkeeper George Tweedy suffered at first hand, so to speak. 'They were two of the most scorching things I have ever seen pass by my window. One from the left foot, the other from the right,' he admitted. Another suffering custodian was Jim Twomey of Leeds United. He commented: 'The first goal from Lawton's boot nearly wrenched my fingers from their sockets. I simply saw a flash as the ball left his foot. I saw where it was going, tipped it with my fingers – that was all!'

Former Rotherham United player and manager Reg Freeman was equally supportive. 'Isn't Lawton just wonderful? I didn't think we should live to see the day when the common talk of Dean the Second would come to fact and life. Yet "Dixie" had most of his success through his head. This fellow has two trusty feet and can head cleverly, too.' Huddersfield Town boss and former England international Clem Stephenson said simply: 'Why, man, this boy Lawton is a smasher.'

The more panoramic views were expressed in plucking items from the game's history through the Terence Delaney compilation *The Footballer's Fireside Book* of 1961. In one whole chapter devoted to Lawton entitled 'Faith in Genius', John Arlott provided the words in a chapter entitled 'Concerning Soccer'. One paragraph referring to a specific match said it all: 'On possibly ten occasions during the match – which Notts County won 3-1 – Lawton without appearing to exert himself, played in such a way as no other centre-forward in England, indeed in Britain or, for all I know, in the world, could have excelled: let us be accurate, not one of them could have equalled it.'

In Stanley Matthews's autobiography *The Way It Was* he described at length the England centre-forward with whom he had played. 'Tommy possessed a rocket of a shot and, like all great players, could hit the ball equally well with either foot. He was lethal in the air and, most surprisingly for a centre-forward of the time, had all the ball skill and creative prowess of the most mercurial of inside-forwards. Tommy was a goal-getter, a towering athlete with a seemingly elastic neck that enabled him to rise that inch or so above defenders, which he did often to devastating effect.'

Even the golden oldies had an opinion as 19th-century England international forward Denny Hodgetts of Aston Villa contributed. 'The boy at 18 – the complete and right centre-forward type: strong, willing, good header and very capable of leadership of a line as well as a good shot with either foot with the left his better one.'

At the end of 1938/39 and Everton's First Division success, 'Fuse', who had championed Tommy through the *Topical Times*, commented as follows in the 13 May 1939 edition: 'Lawton took on a great task and fulfilled the prophecy made in these notes before he left Burnley.

'He has graced the game by his expert shooting and heading, by his personal effort, by his demeanour, he has questioned no referee and he has questioned no rival pivot. He has taken all and given nothing but the best and fairest in return.'

Joe Mercer, who played with him at Everton and later at Arsenal as well as many times in England colours and other representative matches, referred to Tommy in *The Great Ones* as 'the greatest technical centre-forward of all time'.

Stan Cullis of Wolves and England included Lawton in the Probables selection of his 'finest players of my time'. Tiger Khomich, who faced Tommy for the Moscow Dynamo team in 1945, referred to him in his Russian book *Nineteen to Nine*: 'Woe-be the goalkeeper who plays against Lawton and fails to keep his wits about him, even for a moment.'

Bob Paisley's reckoning came out as follows: 'Modern defenders look at old films of Lawton and think they would have stopped him scoring. No way. Tommy had a gift that comes along once in a century. He could head a ball at any angle or any speed he wanted to. Unstoppable in the air and no slouch on his feet either. He'd be scoring 30 or more goals a season if he played today.' This was from *The People* newspaper, 21 April 1985.

Surely the finest accolade goes to an unnamed writer but reproduced in *World Soccer from A to Z*: 'His outstanding attribute was when the ball was in the air ... but he had many. He could shoot with both feet, irrespective of angle or distance. He could keep the ball close, he could spray passes wingers dream about, he could travel fast, on turf or mud or ice. And he composed himself like a gentleman, never given to petty retaliation, rarely showing outrage with the referee.'

The same writer commented: 'Over and above all that, though, was the extra something, the almost mystical aura that went with him, Lawton had star quality; a hackneyed phrase, but how else to describe him?'

As to character, 'Stork' in the *Liverpool Echo* in December 1938 wrote: 'Lawton is one of the nicest young fellows of my acquaintance. Not the slightest sign of "edge" about him.'

CHAPTER TWENTY

After the Boots are Finally Cleaned

THE LAST time I saw Tommy Lawton was at a testimonial game for him at Griffin Park organised by Brentford Football Club on 20 May 1985. I was wearing my *Sunday Telegraph* hat. A Brentford team played Frank McLintock's All-Star XI. The year before, Tommy had started to write a column for the *Nottingham Evening Post*. At the match he was accompanied by his second wife Gaye. It was the first time I had seen him since his playing days; the passing years and the problems he had endured were evident. But even at 65 there was still the hint of the same broad-faced smile from the days when he was the No.1 centre-forward in England.

After being Notts County manager, he was four years landlord of the Magna Charta public house in Lowdham. He sold insurance, was caretaker manager of Kettering, opened a sports shop with a friend, then worked for a betting company; variously part-time Wolves scout, Kettering manager then director; even back to Notts County as coach and scout for two years until 1970. Then there was a gradual downward spiral of unemployment and begging old friends for money. An ITV interview by Eamonn Andrews led to a directorship in a furniture business that went bust. But he still wrote cheques on them and was sentenced to three years' probation, the financial costs attached somewhat relieved by Everton after Joe Mercer revealed Tommy's situation, the club organising a testimonial match. Autobiographical *When the Cheering Stopped: The Rise, the Fall* was published. But further financial misdemeanours caused by continuing debt and failure to pay bills led to community service.

None of the foregoing detracted from what Tommy Lawton represented as a player. He had natural ability in controlling and manipulating a football from any angle with his body, feet and head. He also possessed the visual awareness of what was required in bringing other players into play. Strongly built at six foot and despite flat fleet that required arch supports, he was quick and well balanced. His timing in the air was such that he appeared to hover in anticipation of receiving the ball and his subtle deflections were as successful as his full-blooded efforts.

Corrective measures as a schoolboy to improve his weaker left foot eventually led to this being the slightly stronger one. His driven shots varied from force to finesse. He could nonchalantly dribble past opponents with subtle side-stepping feints, swerve and accelerate. He was a master at drawing opposing players to him, then feeding better-placed colleagues. In his day he was the leader in his field both from a positional sense and among his contemporaries, while always being aware of his talent's worth.

His daughter Amanda, by his first marriage, did not come back into his life until her own problems. He raised stepdaughter Carol Anne as his own and had a son, Tommy Junior, from his second marriage. He died from pneumonia on 6 November 1996 in Nottingham, aged 77, his ashes donated to the National Football Museum, and he was inducted into the English Football Hall of Fame in 2003, then the Notts County Hall of Fame in 2014.

Tommy Lawton – Stats It!

Football League appearances (goals in brackets)
Burnley 1935/36, 1936/37 – 25 (16).
Everton 1936/37, 1937/38, 1938/39, 1939/40 – 90 (69)*.
Chelsea 1946/47, 1947/48 – 42 (30).
Notts Co 1947/48, 1948/49, 1949/50, 1950/51, 1951/52 – 151 (90).
Brentford 1951/52, 1952/53, 1953/54 – 50 (17).
Arsenal 1953/54, 1954/55, 1955/56 – 35 (13).
* includes aborted 1939/40 league programme.

FA Cup (goals in brackets)
Everton 1936/37, 1937/38, 1938/39 – 8 (5).
Chelsea 1945/46, 1946/47 – 11 (5).
Notts Co 1947/48, 1948/49, 1949/50, 1950/51, 1951/52 – 15 (13).
Brentford 1952/53 – 3 (2).
Arsenal 1954/55 – 2 (1).
Kettering T 1956/57 – 1 (1).

FA Charity Shield:
Arsenal 1953/54 – 1 (1).

Jubilee Fund:
Everton 1938/39, 1939/40 – 2 (2).

Glasgow Empire Exhibition:
Everton 1937/38 – 3 (2).

Festival of Britain:
Notts County 1950/51 – 1.
Everton friendly 1936/37 – 2 (1), 1937/38 – 1.

Wartime Regional League for Everton 1939/40 to 1945/46 – 101 (134).

League War Cup for Everton not included in Regional League – 10 (14).

Everton Wartime friendly and cup ties not included in Regional League – 15 (16).

Chelsea League South 1945/46 – 20 (19).

Chelsea friendly 1945/46 1 (1), 1946/47 1.

Guest appearances:

Aldershot 46 (67); Burnley 1 (1); Charlton Athletic 2; Chester 1 (5); Leicester City 3 (5); Millwall 1; Morton 5 (9); Notts Co 1; Tranmere Rovers 2 (3).

England internationals: 1938/39, 1946/47, 1947/48, 1948/49 – 23 (22).

England v Young England: 1953/54, 1954/55 – 2 (3).

Great Britain: 1946/47 – 1 (2).

Football League XI: 1938/39, 1946/47 – 3 (6).

England Wartime and Victory Internationals: 23 (25)+.

Wartime Representative Matches: APTC 1 (1); Army 31 (45); Cardiff City Guest XI 1; Combined Services 3 (3); Eastern Command 1; England XI 1 (1); FA XI 3 (5); FA Services XI 6 (7); Football League XI 3 (4); Joe Mercer's XI 1; Mayor of Lewes' XI 1 (1); United Services 1 (2); Western Command 15 (19).

Creswell Colliery Disaster Fund: Notts County 1950/51: 1 (1).

Notts County friendly matches: 1947/48, 1950/51, 1951/52 – 5.

Arsenal friendly matches: 1953/54, 1954/55, 1955/56 – 11 (4).

Total appearances 790, total number of goals 693.

NB * includes three matches and four goals in aborted 1939/40 Football League programme.

+ Goals include own goal by Tommy Jones from a Tommy Lawton header for England v Wales 18 November 1939.

The foregoing includes all first-team fixtures in which it was known Tommy Lawton played.

Abandoned matches not included. Additionally as in *Players Match by Match, Volume 1 Tommy Lawton by Tony Brown and Keith Warsop*, with Kettering Town 34 Southern League and cup appearances 20 goals.

Bibliography

A Century of English International Football 1872-1972, Morley Farror & Douglas Lamming, Robert Hale & Co, 1972.

Aldershot Football Club Official Programme.

A E Botting.

Alec E Whitcher.

Alex James.

Alex Lee.

Alf Ramsey.

Belfast News Letter.

Billy Steel.

Billy Wright.

Birmingham Daily Gazette.

Birmingham Daily Post.

Bob Paisley.

Burnley Express.

Captain of Wales, Walley Barnes, Stanley Paul, London, 1953.

Charlie Buchan.

Chester Observer.

Clem Stephenson.

Daily Dispatch.

Daily Herald.

Daily Mail.

Denny Hodgetts.

Dixie Dean, Nick Walsh, Macdonald and Jane's Ltd, London, 1977.

Edinburgh Evening News.

Eddie Hapgood.

Empire News.

F W Carruthers ("Arbiter").

Football From The Goalmouth, Frank Swift, Sporting Handbooks Ltd, London, 1948.

Football Is My Business, Tommy Lawton, Sporting Handbooks Ltd, London, 1946.

Football Post (Nottingham).

Football With A Smile; Joe Mercer OBE, Gary James, ACL & Polar Publishing, Leicester, 1993.

"Fuse" in Topical Times.

George Green.

George Tweedy.

Great Masters of Scottish Football, Hugh Taylor, Sportsman's Book Club, 1968.

Herbert "Duke" Hamilton.

Ivan Sharpe.

Jackie Milburn.

Jim Barrett.

Jim Twomey.

John Arlott.
Junior Express.
Kettering Town Football Club Handbook.
Lancashire Evening Post.
Liverpool Daily Post.
Liverpool Echo.
Liverpool Evening Express.
L V Manning.
Middlesex Chronicle.
Neil Franklin.
Nineteen to Nine, Tiger Khomich, Russia, 1953.
Nottingham Evening Post.
Nottingham Journal.
People, The.
Picture Post.
Portsmouth Evening News.
Reg Freeman.
Rochdale Observer.
Ronnie Burgess.
Scotsman, The.
Soccer ... Do It This Way, D F Rowe, Butler and Tanner Ltd, London, 1949.
Soccer the Lawton way, Tommy Lawton, Nicholas Kaye Ltd, London, 1954.
Sporting Star.
Sports Argus.
Sport Weekly Magazine.
Star Green 'Un.
Stanley Matthews' Football Album, Marks & Spencer Ltd, 1949.
Stanley Mortensen's International Soccer Book, L T A Robinson Ltd, Brixton, 1949.
"Stork" in Liverpool Echo.
Sunday Express.
Sunday Mirror.
Sunday Telegraph.
Sunderland Echo.
The Football Association Year Book, various editions, William Heinemann Ltd, London.
The Football League 1935-36, W M Johnston, Edson (Printers) Ltd, London.
The Footballer's Fireside Book, Terence Delaney, William Heinemann Ltd, London, 1961.
The Great Ones, Joe Mercer, Oldbourne, 1964.
The Way It Was, Stanley Matthews, Headline, 2000.
The World's All Sports Who's Who for 1950, Wex Press, Hove, Sussex.
Tom Finney.
Tommy Lawton's All Star Football Book, Sampson Low, Marston & Co Ltd, 1950.
Topical Times.
Twenty Years of Soccer, Tommy Lawton, Heirloom Library, Jarrold & Sons, Norwich, 1955.
World Soccer From A to Z, Pan Books Ltd, 1973.
West London Observer.
Western Morning News.
Yorkshire Post.
and The British Newspaper Archive.